The ARMOR-CAP Playbook

Resilient Strategies for Institutional Investors

The ARMOR-CAP Playbook

Resilient Strategies for Institutional Investors

Frank J. Fabozzi

Johns Hopkins University, USA

World Scientific

NEW JERSEY • LONDON • SINGAPORE • BEIJING • SHANGHAI • HONG KONG • TAIPEI • CHENNAI • TOKYO

Published by

World Scientific Publishing Europe Ltd.
57 Shelton Street, Covent Garden, London WC2H 9HE
Head office: 5 Toh Tuck Link, Singapore 596224
USA office: 27 Warren Street, Suite 401-402, Hackensack, NJ 07601

Library of Congress Control Number: 2025054180

British Library Cataloguing-in-Publication Data
A catalogue record for this book is available from the British Library.

THE ARMOR-CAP PLAYBOOK
Resilient Strategies for Institutional Investors

ISBN 978-1-80061-868-8 (hardcover)
ISBN 978-1-80061-869-5 (ebook for institutions)
ISBN 978-1-80061-870-1 (ebook for individuals)

For any available supplementary material, please visit
https://www.worldscientific.com/worldscibooks/10.1142/Q0550#t=suppl

Desk Editors: Aanand Jayaraman/Cian Sacker Ooi

Typeset by Stallion Press
Email: enquiries@stallionpress.com

To the cadets of West Point, your willingness to lead and protect inspired me to imagine a more resilient approach to capital stewardship.

Preface

Modern capital markets face a paradox. Financial models have become increasingly sophisticated, yet investors remain vulnerable to disruptions that these models were never designed to detect, such as legal breakdowns, geopolitical realignments, vendor chokepoints, and operational discontinuities. The problem is not a lack of intelligence but a failure to recognize where financial resilience ends and structural fragility begins.

This book introduces ARMOR-CAP (Allocation for Resilient Markets and Operational Readiness-Capital Allocation Protection) a practical framework designed to bridge that gap. ARMOR-CAP does not replace traditional risk models. Instead, it asks a complementary and often neglected question: Can capital remain functional when the system breaks down? ARMOR-CAP offers a lens to identify latent fragilities in legal enforceability, jurisdictional compatibility, and operational continuity, dimensions often excluded from quantitative risk analysis yet decisive in real-world stress events.

The origins of this framework are both professional and personal. As a professor, author, and for 37 years a board member of several BlackRock fund complexes, I have seen firsthand how strong performance can obscure underlying exposures and how governance structures sometimes fail to respond when warning signals lack immediacy or context. I have also drawn inspiration from institutions that prize resilience over convenience, most notably the U.S. Military Academy at West Point. ARMOR-CAP adapts that ethos of readiness and accountability for financial institutions tasked with allocating capital in a fractured world.

The book arrives at a moment of reckoning in environmental, social, and governance (ESG) investing. For all its momentum, ESG has struggled to define what "governance" truly means and has often relied on indirect proxies for resilience. ARMOR-CAP offers a sharper, more structural complement to ESG frameworks that do not conflate disclosure with readiness or scorecard checkboxes with operational survivability. It avoids the performative traps of greenwashing and governance theater by linking diagnostics to predefined escalation pathways and fiduciary accountability. Where ESG asks, "Is this company sustainable?", ARMOR-CAP adds, "Is this company investable under duress?"

This is not a manifesto. It is a practical guide. The chapters walk the reader through the ARMOR-CAP framework's logic, design, deployment, and governance implications. The material is presented for practitioners—chief investment officers, investment committee members, oversight professionals, issuer board members, and regulators—who need to make decisions under uncertainty using more than volatility models and narratives.

The book begins by arguing why a new form of structural diagnostics is needed and then builds, step by step, toward implementation. I move from foundational concepts to detailed diagnostic tools, showing how fragility scoring reshapes portfolio construction and governance behavior. Along the way, readers will encounter stylized dashboards, internal memos, escalation minutes, and committee debates that simulate the operational realities of deploying ARMOR-CAP within an institutional setting.

In the early chapters, I trace the evolution of structural fragility and explain why capital allocators need a framework beyond financial modeling. I then introduce the three pillars of ARMOR-CAP—sovereign compatibility, supply chain resilience, and operational continuity—and show how each becomes a measurable input. Later in the book, I offer detailed tools for scoring and interpreting fragility exposures, converting abstract diagnostics into specific reallocation decisions or escalation pathways. The final chapters examine governance mechanics and provide implementation examples through stylized, fictionalized mini-cases (i.e., working group transcripts, risk memos, and resilience dashboards) that simulate how institutions make decisions when facing ambiguous but mounting threats.

Each chapter builds toward a central aim: to empower institutions to act, not just analyze. If I succeed, it will leave readers with a framework and a mindset: Fragility is not a footnote to volatility but is a first-order determinant of whether capital survives. The principles outlined in this book also align with the national security objectives articulated by the

U.S. Department of War, particularly the emphasis on continuity, operational readiness, and system-level resilience in the face of asymmetric and non-financial threats.

The remainder of this book is structured as a practical progression. A chapter-by-chapter overview follows, showing how the ARMOR-CAP framework is developed, applied, and institutionalized.

I begin by challenging the limits of traditional financial risk metrics. While these tools remain essential, they often overlook the deeper vulnerabilities that surface during structural breakdowns. In the first chapter, I introduce the idea of structural fragility and argue that legal enforceability, operational continuity, and sovereign compatibility must be treated as core investment concerns, not peripheral considerations.

Next, I define where fragility resides and how it quietly accumulates. In Chapter 2, I walk through historical and stylized examples showing how infrastructural, jurisdictional, and informational risks can escalate rapidly, often with little warning. I offer a taxonomy for diagnosing these risk vectors and show how fragility emerges long before it's captured by market volatility.

With the problem mapped, I turn to the solution in Chapter 3, where I introduce the three foundational pillars of ARMOR-CAP: sovereign compatibility, supply chain resilience, and operational continuity. Each pillar functions as a diagnostic lens for uncovering structural weaknesses and forms the core architecture of a practical framework for capital allocation under stress.

Once the pillars are in place, in Chapter 4 I shift from concept to application. I show how to generate, normalize, and interpret fragility scores using visual tools such as benchmarking heat maps to reveal concentration, outliers, and structural weak points. Throughout the chapter, I emphasize the balance between signal clarity and model restraint, ensuring that scoring adds insight, not noise.

I then show how to embed these scores into portfolio construction. In Chapter 5, I walk through examples where fragility scores reshape optimization constraints, trigger governance reviews, and prompt early reallocations. Here, I draw a sharp distinction between financial resilience and operational viability, which are often confused but must be treated separately.

From there, I explore how these diagnostics can be institutionalized. In Chapter 6, I demonstrate how to design escalation pathways, integrate fragility criteria into investment policy statements, and build decision protocols that ensure follow-through. I focus on real-world governance, where dashboards alone are insufficient and institutional muscle memory must be trained to act on early signals.

Recognizing that institutions vary widely, I tailor ARMOR-CAP for different investor types in Chapter 7. I provide practical implementation pathways for pensions, sovereign wealth funds, endowments, insurers, and family offices. To structure this guidance, I draw on five strategic imperatives: automating escalation, embedding fragility scoring into mandates, evaluating governance maturity, designing dashboards for action, and aligning fiduciary duty with structural resilience. These principles offer a flexible yet disciplined blueprint for embedding resilience into diverse investment mandates. Rather than prescribing a one-size-fits-all solution, I emphasize modular adaptation, allowing institutions to calibrate the framework to their oversight capacity, political context, and operational maturity.

To make these ideas more tangible, in Chapter 8, I present a set of extended, stylized, fictionalized scenarios, complete with internal memos, investment-committee debates, boardroom discussions, and escalation deliberations that illustrate how ARMOR-CAP might actually be used. These hypothetical cases do not describe real institutions but model how the framework functions and how human behavior shapes adoption through resistance, override, or partial implementation.

In the last chapter, I turn to the most challenging step: interpretation. Here, I demonstrate how to interpret fragility scores in context—how to track their movement over time, benchmark them across sleeves and peers, and identify divergence within and across portfolios. I explain how institutions can read trajectories, cross-domain interactions, and compound fragility patterns, and how visualization tools, such as spider charts, heat maps, band overlays, and scorecards, translate diagnostic complexity into governance-ready insights. Throughout the chapter, I use entirely fictionalized scenarios to illustrate how institutions might convert these diagnostics into strategic action whether through targeted mitigation, escalation, recalibration, or adjustments to governance protocols. Interpretation, as I emphasize, is where scores become decisions.

Each chapter builds toward one goal: equipping institutional investors to respond to volatility and fragility. I don't ask readers to abandon traditional models. I ask them to complement those models with a new readiness mindset that prepares capital to function even if the system doesn't.

Four appendices serve as reference tools for institutional users to support practical implementation. Appendix A provides a glossary of key terms and governance concepts used throughout the ARMOR-CAP framework. Appendix B outlines important methodological notes and data considerations, providing guidance on source credibility, updating protocols, and data validation. Appendix C defines each diagnostic domain and presents the scoring rubric for evaluating fragility across portfolios. Appendix D lays out the methodological foundations of ARMOR-CAP, distinguishing it from conventional risk models and grounding its design in resilience-based logic. These appendices equip practitioners with the vocabulary, data architecture, scoring logic, and methodological clarity needed to operationalize ARMOR-CAP across diverse institutional contexts.

About the Author

Frank J. Fabozzi is a professor of practice of finance in the Carey Business School at Johns Hopkins University in Baltimore, Maryland, USA. He is the editor of *The Journal of Portfolio Management* and co-editor of *The Journal of Financial Data Science*. Frank has served on the boards of directors for BlackRock Fixed Income Funds, BlackRock Equity-Liquidity Funds, BlackRock BCIA Funds, Guardian Mutual Funds, and Guardian Annuity Funds. He has taught at the Massachusetts Institute of Technology (MIT), Yale, Princeton, EDHEC Business School, New York University, Rutgers University, and Carnegie Mellon University. He is the recipient of the CFA Institute's 2007 C. Stewart Sheppard Award and the 2015 James R. Vertin Award. In 2002, Frank was inducted into the Fixed Income Society's Hall of Fame. He holds a doctorate in economics from the Graduate Center of the City University of New York and an Honorary Doctorate of Humane Letters from Nova Southeastern University. He earned the designations of Chartered Financial Analyst (CFA) and Certified Public Accountant (CPA).

Acknowledgments

I am deeply grateful to Major Caleb Stenholm, formerly a faculty member at the United States Military Academy at West Point and now with the U.S. Department of War. During his tenure at West Point, Major Stenholm taught the academy's investment course and generously invited me to lecture to the cadets. That opportunity—engaging with future leaders who must think strategically under uncertainty—helped shape and sharpen the ideas that would eventually become the foundation of this book. His support was instrumental in the genesis of ARMOR-CAP.

I am grateful to John M. B. O'Connor ("JOC"), chairman and CEO of J. H. Whitney Investment Management, LLC, and Whitney Strategic Services, LLC, developer of the Geopolitical Risk Rating (GRR). JOC's insights into the intersection of capital markets and geopolitical strategy were invaluable, and his encouragement motivated me to pursue this work further.

Earlier work on ARMOR-CAP was shared with Jennifer Bender, managing director at State Street Global Advisors, and Mark Kritzman, CEO of Windham Capital Management, LLC, and a senior lecturer in finance at MIT Sloan School of Management. I am grateful for their encouragement and support, which helped reinforce the value of expanding this work into a comprehensive framework.

Contents

Chapter 1

The Protection Imperative: From Fragility to Strategic Readiness

Strategic Priorities of This Chapter

This opening chapter introduces the intellectual urgency and practical rationale for a new diagnostic framework in asset allocation: ARMOR-CAP—Allocation for Resilient Markets and Operational Readiness-Capital Allocation Protection. It challenges the sufficiency of existing environmental, social, and governance (ESG) and portfolio theory constructs by exposing their inability to account for operational, legal, and geopolitical fragility in a fractured global environment. Drawing on recent crises—from pandemics to cyberattacks to state-led economic coercion—it redefines resilience as not merely a virtue but a precondition for capital continuity.

The chapter unfolds across five interlocking themes:

- **A — Assess the architectural limitations of ESG frameworks.** While ESG scores capture policies and intentions, they often miss infrastructure, supply chain, and jurisdictional dependencies that determine whether firms can remain operational under crisis conditions.
- **R — Recognize the reversal of globalization and its impact on portfolio assumptions.** Pandemics, wars, and techno-nationalism have exposed the systemic fragility embedded in seamless cross-border flows that were once assumed to be permanent.

- **M — Map the blind spots in traditional investment models.** Classic risk frameworks optimize for volatility, not viability. ARMOR-CAP surfaces fragilities overlooked by mean-variance models, factor regressions, and ESG overlays.
- **O — Orient the reader toward a resilience-first investment lens.** Optimization is no longer enough. Structural exposure, operational continuity, and jurisdictional risk must be treated as core inputs in portfolio design.
- **R — Reveal the academic foundations and multidisciplinary lineage of ARMOR-CAP.** From supply chain theory and digital sovereignty to behavioral finance and military planning, this chapter shows how resilience diagnostics are grounded in empirical insights and strategic necessity.

1.1 The Promise of ESG and the Limits of Its Architecture

Environmental, social, and governance (ESG) investing reshaped global capital markets over the past two decades. What began as a niche ethical stance evolved into a multitrillion-dollar movement that penetrated every tier of the investment value chain, from boutique managers to the world's largest sovereign wealth funds. ESG-themed funds proliferated, regulators mandated sustainability disclosures, and corporate boards scrambled to align with evolving norms. For many allocators, ESG has evolved beyond a moral framework; it has become a shorthand for managing long-term reputational, regulatory, and systemic risk.

The underlying idea was elegant: Companies that are responsible stewards of the ESG practices will also be more stable and profitable over time. This conviction was bolstered by some questionable empirical studies suggesting that high ESG-rated companies enjoy lower capital costs, improved stakeholder alignment, and reduced idiosyncratic risk. In theory, ESG provided a framework that helped bridge values-based investing and financial prudence.

However, in practice, ESG has increasingly demonstrated its architectural limitations. At its core, ESG was designed to measure intentions (i.e., policies, disclosures, and commitments), not the operational realities that underlie corporate resilience. A company could score highly by publishing a sustainability report, announcing net-zero targets, or achieving gender diversity on its board while still relying on single-source suppliers in geopolitically volatile regions or hosting critical cloud operations in jurisdictions with aggressive surveillance regimes. Such vulnerabilities don't show up in most ESG scores. Yet, they can bring a company to its knees overnight.

The problem isn't that ESG is irrelevant; it's that ESG is incomplete. Its architecture presumes a world where markets function, supply chains flow, and political borders don't interfere with digital infrastructure or physical logistics. That world is gone. The modern global environment is defined not by consensus but by the contestation of norms, networks, and nodes of control.

This is where ARMOR-CAP—*Allocation for Resilient Markets and Operational Readiness-Capital Allocation Protection*—enters the conversation. ESG was the right tool for a more stable past. However, in today's fractured and fragile landscape, investors require a framework that measures corporate virtue and assesses corporate viability.

ARMOR-CAP is not a replacement for ESG. It is a critical overlay. ESG captures what a company stands for. ARMOR-CAP evaluates whether it can withstand shocks when they occur. ESG measures risk posture; ARMOR-CAP measures risk exposure. Where ESG assesses internal commitments, ARMOR-CAP interrogates external entanglements (i.e., supply chains, data jurisdictions, infrastructure dependencies, and political alignments).

The next evolution in responsible investing isn't about rebranding ESG. It's about complementing it with a resilience lens that sees the world as it is, not as we wish it to be.

1.2 When Globalization Turned Inside Out

For much of the post–Cold War era, the global economy operated under a near-universal presumption: Globalization was not simply an economic trend; instead, it was a stabilizing force. The free flow of capital, information, labor, and goods across borders was seen as a self-reinforcing engine of efficiency and peace. Trade liberalization and capital account openness became synonymous with progress. Western financial institutions, multinational corporations, and policymakers aligned on the shared assumption that greater integration meant greater resilience. The very structure of portfolio construction, supply chain design, and technology deployment reflected that belief.

Investors rode this wave with confidence. Manufacturing can be outsourced with little consideration for geography. Cloud infrastructure can be spread across continents without fear of national firewalls or data traps. Currency convertibility, cross-listings, and international initial public offerings (IPOs) were signs of global cohesion. Diversification strategies were built on the idea that risk in one region could be offset by opportunity in another because correlation would always be imperfect and idiosyncratic shocks would always be localized.

However, the architecture of globalization was optimized for speed and cost rather than resilience. Supply chains were fine-tuned to minimize inventories, not to withstand disruptions. Infrastructure was designed to be lean, not layered. Firms were rewarded for reducing redundancy, not for stress-tested survivability. And investors, too, came to believe that political borders and regulatory jurisdictions were background noise (i.e., distant concerns for operational teams), not core considerations for capital allocators.

That illusion began to unravel slowly, then all at once.

The COVID-19 pandemic was the first major rupture in this consensus. What began as a public health crisis quickly cascaded into a global economic breakdown. Entire industrial ecosystems ground to a halt, not because of demand shocks, but because supply chains seized up. Hospitals were unable to access personal protective equipment. Automakers lacked semiconductors. Construction projects stalled due to a lack of basic inputs. The just-in-time manufacturing gospel suddenly read like a suicide note for operational stability. Geographic diversification became a source of entrapment rather than insulation. Firms that thought they had spread risk across continents discovered they had merely spread dependencies.

Then came the second wave of dislocation: geopolitics. The Russian invasion of Ukraine in 2022 was not simply a humanitarian catastrophe; it was a financial and infrastructural shockwave. Energy flows were weaponized. Payment systems were fractured. Transportation corridors were seized or destroyed. What had once been seen as uncorrelated asset classes suddenly moved together, as exposure to a single node, whether a pipeline, port, or currency, revealed itself as a common mode of failure. Sanctions rendered entire sectors and jurisdictions uninvestable overnight, with little warning and limited recourse.

Simultaneously, U.S.–China tensions exposed a deeper shift: the fragmentation of the technological and financial order. The post–Bretton Woods belief in a unified, rules-based economic system gave way to a world of selective decoupling. Export controls on semiconductors, bans on outbound investment, restrictions on critical minerals, and mandatory data localization laws reshaped the terrain on which companies operate. Legal asymmetry (i.e., where different jurisdictions impose conflicting rules on the same data or product) became a defining feature of international business.

This was no longer simply a matter of "headline risk." Cyberattacks emerged as full-spectrum threats to national infrastructure and corporate continuity. Incidents such as the NotPetya malware attack and the Colonial Pipeline shutdown demonstrated that digital incursions could do what natural disasters and recessions could not: halt entire economies. These attacks did not simply disrupt operations. Rather, they obliterated operational readiness and exposed the brittleness of systems previously assumed to be secure.

What these crises have in common is that they were not merely disruptions but revelations. Each one tore back the curtain on a fundamental fragility built into the modern global system: that the continuity of capital flows and operational activity depends on a series of unspoken, untested assumptions about access, legality, and control. Investors had been building models based on the idea that infrastructure works, contracts are enforceable, and geopolitical neutrality is a default setting. But none of these assumptions are safe anymore.

Yet, capital allocation models, both in academia and in practice, remain stubbornly anchored in a framework that treats these risks as tail events rather than base conditions. Portfolio strategies still assume liquidity, legal certainty, and global market access. Risk models still focus on volatility and correlation. Asset allocation remains focused on optimizing under a smooth surface rather than surviving under fractured ground.

The reversal of globalization is not a theoretical concern. It is a reality that now defines the baseline for investment strategy. Allocators who continue to model risk through the lens of yesterday's integrated world will find themselves exposed not only to market losses but also to functional breakdowns. The question is no longer whether geopolitical shocks will affect portfolios but whether portfolios are built to withstand the consequences when foundational systems fail.

This new landscape demands a fundamental shift in evaluating risk and allocating capital. The notion that geographic diversification is inherently safe or global infrastructure is inherently neutral is no longer tenable. The future of investment strategy lies not in maximizing exposure to global efficiency but in designing around global fragility. That shift begins by confronting the uncomfortable truth: Globalization, as we know it, has turned inside out.

1.3 The Blind Spots in Traditional Portfolio Construction

For decades, institutional portfolio construction has been based on the foundation of modern portfolio theory (MPT), which views risk as something measurable, diversifiable, and ultimately manageable. Investors are taught that while individual securities carry unique risks, those risks can be smoothed through diversification across asset classes, regions, and sectors. This thinking is encoded in mean-variance optimization, the Capital Asset Pricing Model (CAPM), and later extensions such as multi-factor models. The underlying presumption is that risk is both probabilistic and exogenous. It originates from outside the system, can be measured by historical volatility, and can be mitigated by diversifying exposure.

However, that framework has critical blind spots that have become increasingly dangerous in an era of structural instability. Traditional models assume that markets are always open, contracts are always enforceable, and financial instruments can always be settled and processed without interruption. In other words, the system is assumed to function. Even in extreme downside scenarios, these models rarely question the continuity of legal, technological, and infrastructural access. They model performance risk but ignore existential risk.

Take volatility, for example. It remains the cornerstone of most institutional risk models. But volatility is merely a measure of price fluctuations in functioning markets. It tells you nothing about the risk that the market might not function. A company with a low beta and stable cash flows can still be halted if its key data centers are seized under national security laws, a critical supplier is sanctioned, or its primary port of entry becomes inaccessible due to conflict or a climate-driven disaster. Traditional models lack language for these events because they treat them as tail risks. Increasingly, they are anything but.

This disconnect between what is modeled and what is materially at risk can be visualized by comparing the standard risk measures in use today with the structural exposures they fail to capture. Table 1.1 highlights this fragility gap.

Another blind spot lies in the uncritical embrace of benchmark-relative investing. Passive indexing strategies, factor tilts, and tracking-error constraints all assume that broad market exposure is inherently diversified and therefore inherently safer. Yet, the underlying composition of major benchmarks is rarely examined for structural fragility. A passive equity index may include dozens of companies with concentrated exposure to single jurisdictions, vulnerable supply chains, or politically contested infrastructure. Exposure is treated as diversified because it is quantitatively spread across names and sectors. But if those names rely uniformly on a small set of infrastructure chokepoints, legal regimes, or digital networks, the diversification is superficial, as illustrated in Table 1.2.

Moreover, diversification across countries, a core tenet of global asset allocation, no longer provides the same level of risk reduction as it once did. During the 1990s and early 2000s, geographic diversification appeared to lower correlations and buffer against country-specific shocks.

Table 1.1. The fragility gap in traditional portfolio models.

Traditional Model Measures	Structural Fragility Overlooked
Historical volatility	Infrastructure dependency
Beta and correlation	Cloud/data jurisdiction risks
Sectoral/geographic exposure	Supply chain chokepoints
ESG scores (policy-level)	Operational continuity threats

Note: This table contrasts the core variables used in traditional portfolio construction with the structural risks they routinely overlook. While standard models emphasize quantifiable, price-based metrics such as volatility, beta, and historical correlations—tools that presume functioning markets and enforceable contracts—they often miss critical sources of fragility that affect operational viability. The left column lists conventional measures used in asset allocation, risk modeling, and portfolio optimization. The right column presents examples of real-world dependencies (such as data infrastructure, geopolitical entanglements, and supply chain vulnerabilities) that can disrupt business continuity but remain unmodeled. The purpose of the table is to demonstrate that portfolios optimized for risk-adjusted returns may remain blind to systemic fragilities that can cause abrupt loss of access, asset impairment, or legal incapacitation, risks that are increasingly material in today's volatile geopolitical and environmental landscape.

Table 1.2. Diversification illusion under structural fragility.

Portfolio Holdings	Sector	Region	Critical Shared Dependency
TechCorp A	Technology	U.S.	Cloud services (AWS – U.S. jurisdiction)
AutoGlobal B	Automotive	Germany	Semiconductor supply (Taiwan)
FinServe C	Financials	Japan	SWIFT payments (U.S./EU sanctions exposure)
RetailAsia D	Consumer Discr.	Southeast Asia	Payment processing (U.S. tech firm)
PharmaHealth E	Healthcare	France	API sourcing (India/China supply)

Note: This table illustrates how a portfolio diversified by traditional metrics (e.g., sector, region, and issuer count) can be structurally fragile. Each holding in the table represents a distinct sector and geography. Yet, all share critical dependencies that are neither disclosed in standard risk reports nor captured in most asset allocation frameworks. These dependencies include concentrated reliance on specific cloud providers, payment systems, manufacturing inputs, or geopolitical corridors. While conventional portfolio theory would treat these exposures as uncorrelated, real-world stress events (e.g., sanctions, cyberattacks, or geopolitical disruptions) can simultaneously impair multiple companies that rely on the same underlying systems. The table exposes how diversification by form may mask convergence in function, leading to hidden correlations and systemic vulnerability across seemingly independent assets.

However, this logic is being tested by the rise of sovereign interventions such as export controls, data localization mandates, and foreign asset seizures. These actions, once relatively rare, are increasingly being used as routine policy tools (Bradford, 2020; Farrell & Newman, 2019). As a result, portfolios diversified across jurisdictions may now face correlated legal and political risks, particularly when those countries are connected through global supply chains or share geopolitical tensions.

Finally, traditional risk models often overlook infrastructure dependencies, such as reliance on cloud computing. Cloud services are frequently treated as operational background rather than as potential strategic vulnerabilities. Yet, as Matsakis (2021) and Chander and Lê (2015) have shown, jurisdictional control over data and cloud infrastructure introduces new political and legal risk layers. If a firm depends on cloud services in a country that enacts export controls or surveillance mandates, its operational continuity may be compromised. For investors, this means that portfolios heavily exposed to such firms may carry risks not captured by conventional diversification strategies or volatility estimates.

These overlooked structural dependencies can rapidly escalate from technical disruptions to firm-wide instability and ultimately portfolio losses. Figure 1.1 outlines how this risk propagation unfolds in practice.

Trigger	→	Disruption	→	Firm Impact	→	Portfolio Effect
Data law conflict	→	Cloud access revoked	→	Service outage, fines	→	Revenue hit, stock drop
Supply chokepoint	→	Input unavailable	→	Production halt	→	Earnings cut, downgrade
Export ban	→	Vendor blocked	→	Ops suspended	→	Sharp valuation decline
Cyberattack	→	Systems offline	→	Data loss, recovery cost	→	Sector-wide contagion

Figure 1.1. Structural risk propagation framework.

Note: This figure illustrates the sequence by which hidden operational dependencies, such as legal, technological, or supply chain vulnerabilities, can trigger cascading effects that move from an initial external shock to widespread portfolio losses. The framework is organized into four stages:

- *Trigger*: An external event or policy change, such as a new data law, export restriction, or cyberattack, initiates the risk.
- *Disruption*: The trigger causes a direct interruption to a firm's operations, such as revoked access to cloud services, blocked suppliers, or unavailable inputs.
- *Firm impact*: The disruption leads to significant consequences for the affected company, including service outages, regulatory fines, halted production, or increased recovery costs.
- *Portfolio effect*: These firm-level impacts aggregate and manifest at the portfolio level, resulting in revenue declines, stock price drops, credit downgrades, or even sector-wide contagion.

By mapping these stages, the figure demonstrates how seemingly isolated operational dependencies can escalate through a chain reaction, ultimately undermining both firm stability and portfolio performance.

In sum, traditional portfolio construction frameworks are optimized for a world that no longer exists. They were built for probabilistic uncertainty, not systemic fragility. They can handle fluctuations but not fractures. What is missing from these models is the capacity to assess *structural exposure* (i.e., the embedded dependencies on legal systems, data sovereignty, logistical continuity, and geopolitical alignment that now define the risk landscape).

As capital allocators confront this new reality, they need tools that go beyond standard deviation and correlation matrices. They need diagnostics that interrogate *where* and *how* portfolios are exposed to fragility, not just how volatile they have been in the past. ARMOR–CAP is designed to fill that gap, not by discarding the tools of financial theory but by grounding them in the real-world systems upon which financial outcomes now depend.

1.4 A New Paradigm: From Optimization to Resilience

For decades, portfolio construction has centered on a singular objective: optimization. Whether the goal was to maximize expected return for a given level of risk, minimize tracking error to a benchmark, or improve a portfolio's Sharpe ratio, the entire machinery of asset management has been built around the idea that markets are inherently stable, liquid, and knowable. Risk was defined as price volatility, and resilience was assumed, never explicitly measured.

That assumption is no longer defensible.

We live in an era where the structural continuity of markets, institutions, and infrastructures can no longer be taken for granted. The COVID-19 pandemic exposed global supply chains as brittle rather than diversified, revealing vulnerabilities in critical sectors such as medical supplies (Gereffi, 2020). The Russia–Ukraine conflict and broader geopolitical tensions have demonstrated how states can weaponize commodities and financial networks, turning interdependence into a tool of coercion (Farrell & Newman, 2019). The U.S.–China competition has contributed to the fragmentation of the global technological stack, challenging the very notion of cross-border operability (Farrell & Newman, 2019). Meanwhile, cyberattacks have rendered digital dependencies—from payments to logistics to communications—into systemic fault lines (Matsakis, 2021). In such a world, optimizing under the assumption of continuity is not merely incomplete; it is reckless.

This is the motivation behind ARMOR-CAP. It is not a model or a scorecard. It is a diagnostic lens designed to help investors assess whether companies and portfolios can function through structural shocks, those not yet priced into models but are no longer rare.

ARMOR−CAP begins with a new question: Can this entity continue operating if the world does not behave as expected? That is a very different inquiry from "Is this company well-governed?" or "Is this asset class historically low beta?" Traditional models optimize for price risk; ARMOR-CAP interrogates operational viability.

The framework is built on three mutually reinforcing pillars:

Pillar 1: Sovereign Compatibility: This dimension assesses whether a firm's core dependencies (i.e., its data centers, intellectual property, contracts, and financial infrastructure) are located in jurisdictions that offer legal stability, rule-of-law protections, and geopolitical alignment. A tech company hosting sensitive data on servers located in a state subject to extraterritorial surveillance laws, or a manufacturer whose key inputs pass through contested maritime zones, may appear financially sound but be operationally fragile.

Pillar 2: Supply Chain Resilience: The second pillar assesses the redundancy, flexibility, and geographic dispersion of critical inputs, key features that underpin resilience in global value chains. Firms that rely on single-source suppliers or have supply chains concentrated in specific regions face a heightened risk of disruption, particularly during systemic shocks such as the COVID-19 pandemic. Gereffi (2020) highlights how the structure and geographic distribution of production, as well as technological complexity, can constrain both firms and states in their responses to crises. Traditional financial models often fail to account for these systemic vulnerabilities, as recent supply chain disruptions have demonstrated.

Pillar 3: Operational Continuity: Ultimately, ARMOR-CAP assesses whether the firm can maintain its baseline functionality in the event of infrastructure failures, cyberattacks, regulatory disruptions, or geopolitical shocks. This includes business continuity plans, crisis-tested redundancies, and failover protocols. It's not merely a matter of insurance; it's a matter of architecture. A resilient firm does more than survive volatility; it is structurally equipped to remain open when the world closes.

Together, these pillars allow investors to evaluate resilience as a practical input into capital allocation, rather than a metaphor. Critically, ARMOR-CAP does not compete with existing frameworks such as ESG or enterprise risk management (ERM). Rather, it complements them. ESG focuses on what a company *stands for*; ARMOR-CAP assesses whether it can continue to stand. ERM maps internal controls; ARMOR-CAP maps *external vulnerabilities*. Where portfolio theory assumes a functioning system, ARMOR–CAP challenges that very assumption.

This comparison is summarized in Table 1.3, which highlights how ARMOR-CAP complements and expands traditional investment lenses by emphasizing structural resilience.

This is not to reject optimization but to reframe it. In a world of compounding shocks, the most efficient portfolio is the one that is still standing when others are not. ARMOR-CAP does not replace risk-adjusted return metrics; it sharpens them by anchoring them in operational reality. The future of asset management will not be determined solely by what portfolios earn in up markets but by what they survive in discontinuous ones.

Table 1.3. Comparing investment lenses: traditional vs. ARMOR-CAP.

Traditional Investment Lens	**ARMOR-CAP Diagnostic Lens**
Price volatility (standard deviation)	Operational continuity under shock conditions
Beta, Sharpe ratio, and alpha	Infrastructure dependency and failover readiness
Corporate governance structure	Jurisdictional alignment and data sovereignty risk
Diversification by asset class/region	Concentration of real-world exposure points
ESG policies and public commitments	Embedded resilience in supply chains and systems

Note: This table contrasts conventional investment analysis with the ARMOR-CAP approach by highlighting how each lens captures risk and resilience. While traditional frameworks emphasize statistical measures, governance structures, and broad diversification, ARMOR-CAP focuses on real-world operational vulnerabilities that may go undetected in financial models. It introduces diagnostics such as infrastructure failover readiness, jurisdictional risks, and supply chain resilience, factors critical to sustaining enterprise value under stress. Rather than replacing traditional metrics, ARMOR-CAP complements them by embedding structural resilience into capital allocation decisions.

1.5 The Intellectual Roots of ARMOR-CAP

ARMOR-CAP may be a novel framework, but its foundation is built on well-established insights from diverse academic and practitioner literatures. It does not reject or replace financial theory but extends it by asking a different question: What assumptions must hold in the real world for capital to remain safe and productive?

One of the most influential intellectual threads underpinning ARMOR-CAP is the literature on *weaponized interdependence*. Scholars such as Farrell and Newman (2019) have shown how states can exploit global networks of trade, finance, and information as instruments of coercive power. This challenges the neoliberal presumption that economic interdependence inherently fosters mutual security. Instead, it highlights how concentrated control points, such as the SWIFT financial messaging system, semiconductor supply chains, or dominant cloud infrastructures, can be leveraged as tools of geopolitical influence. These insights directly inform ARMOR-CAP's focus on mapping geopolitical entanglements, legal asymmetries, and infrastructure dependencies as material factors in investment risk and resilience.

Supply chain theory is a crucial foundation for understanding systemic risk in global production systems. Researchers, such as

Sheffi (2007), have cautioned that relentless efficiency drives can make supply chains vulnerable to cascading failures, a concern dramatically confirmed by the COVID-19 crisis. Studies such as that by Gereffi (2020) highlighted how dependencies on single-source suppliers, opaque multi-tiered networks, and geographic clustering exacerbated disruptions, leading to widespread operational breakdowns. For investors, this underscores that financial statements alone may conceal fragile supply chain structures and pose significant tail risks during periods of stress. The ARMOR-CAP framework addresses this by explicitly evaluating supply chain redundancy and adaptability as part of its portfolio diagnostics.

Another vital input comes from the domain of digital sovereignty and infrastructure governance. As companies migrate to cloud platforms, store critical data abroad, or rely on transnational software dependencies, they are increasingly exposed to jurisdictional constraints beyond their control. Chander and Lê (2015) introduced the concept of data nationalism, analyzing how countries assert legal control over data storage, processing, and flows based on sovereignty claims. This trend suggests that cloud service providers and their clients may become entangled in geopolitical disputes, potentially subjecting a firm's IT backbone to unpredictable intervention (Aaronson, 2024; Daskal, 2016). In a world where cloud access is a business continuity condition, these risks are not peripheral but core to operational viability.

Behavioral finance also plays an important role in motivating the ARMOR-CAP framework. Despite repeated episodes of low-probability, high-impact events, such as financial crises, cyberattacks, and geopolitical shocks, investors continue to underweight these risks in portfolio construction. Kahneman and Tversky's (1979) work on prospect theory and decision-making under uncertainty helps to explain why. Human decision-makers systematically misestimate the likelihood and consequences of rare events, particularly when those events involve non-financial triggers or indirect propagation channels. ARMOR-CAP operates as a corrective lens, counterbalancing the cognitive and institutional biases that cause capital to cluster in fragile configurations.

These insights are not isolated. Together, they form the intellectual architecture of ARMOR-CAP. Table 1.4 summarizes the key academic and practical traditions that inform the framework's core dimensions.

Table 1.4. Intellectual foundations of the ARMOR-CAP framework.

Disciplinary	Field Key Insight	Relevance to ARMOR-CAP
Geopolitical finance	Global networks can be weaponized (Farrell & Newman, 2019)	Sovereign compatibility and legal asymmetry risks
Supply chain theory	Efficiency often trades off with fragility (Sheffi, 2007; Gereffi, 2020)	Supply chain resilience and input redundancy
Infrastructure governance	Data jurisdiction affects continuity (Chander & Lê, 2015; Matsakis, 2021)	Operational risk through cloud and digital dependencies
Behavioral finance	Rare events are systematically underweighted (Kahneman & Tversky, 1979)	Corrective overlay to mitigate blind spots

Note: This table maps the interdisciplinary research traditions that inform the design and logic of the ARMOR-CAP framework. Each field offers a distinctive lens for identifying structural vulnerabilities that conventional financial models may not capture. From a geopolitical finance perspective, the framework adopts the insight that global interdependence can be strategically exploited, compelling investors to evaluate sovereign compatibility and legal asymmetries as real capital risks. Supply chain theory provides insight into how efficiency-driven production systems can introduce fragility, underscoring ARMOR-CAP's emphasis on redundancy, flexibility, and multi-tiered visibility in input sourcing. Infrastructure governance and digital sovereignty highlight the jurisdictional risks associated with cloud platforms, data localization laws, and cross-border tech dependencies, making operational continuity a core component of investment analysis. Finally, behavioral finance explains why investors often fail to account for rare but catastrophic events, cognitive blind spots that ARMOR-CAP seeks to correct through its resilience-oriented overlays. The table presents these foundational domains, aligning each with the specific ARMOR-CAP diagnostic dimension it supports.

1.6 Strategic Discipline and the ARMOR-CAP Mindset

The case for ARMOR-CAP is not simply theoretical or empirical; it is deeply operational. Its logic mirrors a broader shift already underway among sophisticated asset managers: a shift toward strategic discipline, inspired partly by the planning frameworks, command structures, and resilience doctrines of modern military operations.

Whether on battlefields or in markets, in high-risk environments, success hinges less on idealized planning and more on resilient execution. This lesson unites ARMOR–CAP with military-informed thinking, as detailed in "Strategic Discipline: How Asset Management Mirrors Military Operations" (Fabozzi & Stenholm, 2025). At the core of both frameworks lies a sobering truth: Resilience is not a moral virtue or a back-office function but a precondition for performance.

Military doctrine provides a comprehensive framework for understanding resilience in practice. The Observe, Orient, Decide, Act (OODA) loop, initially developed by Air Force Colonel John Boyd, has been embraced by institutions such as JPMorgan Chase to frame rapid decision-making in fluid, high-stakes environments. CEO Jamie Dimon has openly adopted this model to navigate shifting regulatory, geopolitical, and technological terrain. The same mindset underpins ARMOR-CAP's emphasis on recognizing disruptive trends early, repositioning dynamically, and executing with discipline when systemic assumptions collapse.

Meanwhile, Bridgewater Associates employs a different yet complementary approach: radical transparency and open-mindedness. Both principles, like battlefield debriefs and chain-of-command clarity, are designed to eliminate ego, surface blind spots, and reinforce shared situational awareness. They echo the idea that structural fragility is rarely due to insufficient intelligence; more often, it stems from institutional failure to address known vulnerabilities. ARMOR-CAP functions as an institutional OODA loop, turning intelligence about supply chain dependencies, jurisdictional risk, and operational bottlenecks into actionable diagnostic insights.

Just as military planners assess terrain, enemy capability, and logistical chokepoints before launching a mission, ARMOR-CAP guides allocators to examine where capital is exposed to contested jurisdictions, vulnerable infrastructure, and single-point failures. A commander cannot afford to deploy troops through narrow passes or overextended supply lines during combat. In finance, the same caution must apply to portfolios entangled in networks that are efficient in peacetime but brittle under pressure.

This convergence of financial and military doctrines leads to a shared conclusion: Discipline must precede optimization. A resilient unit or portfolio is not the one with the most aggressive plan or highest theoretical return; it is the one that can remain functional under stress. Whether facing a cyberattack, a sovereign seizure, a liquidity crisis, or a contested shipping route, operational readiness becomes the foundation for long-term outperformance.

Moreover, the military concept of *Commander's Intent*—a clear articulation of mission objectives, constraints, and desired end state—resembles the *Investment Policy Statement* in institutional asset management. Both documents serve the same function: to anchor strategy in purpose, guide decision-making under uncertainty, and provide continuity when plans fail or conditions change. ARMOR-CAP strengthens that continuity by introducing diagnostic foresight into what could disrupt execution at the operational level.

In both war rooms and investment committees, fragility often stems not from bad strategies but from a mismatch between strategic ambition and operational capability. This is why military planners emphasize logistical capacity, redundancy, and morale, in addition to tactics. In finance, the equivalent ensures that infrastructure, data systems, counterparties, and even internal culture are aligned with the reality of disruption, not just the fantasy of performance under blue skies.

ARMOR-CAP does not attempt to anticipate the next crisis. It prepares the allocator for a world where the crisis is already embedded in the market's architecture. The similarities with military doctrine are not figurative; they reflect underlying structural principles. The environment in which capital is deployed has fundamentally changed. Today, capital must be allocated and managed under persistent uncertainty, rather than assuming stability as the default.

As the following chapters explore how to implement ARMOR-CAP in practice, the link to strategic discipline remains foundational. Resilient portfolios are not merely engineered; they are commanded.

1.7 A Roadmap for the Reader

This book is not a manifesto. It is a diagnostic manual for a world where financial stability can no longer be decoupled from operational viability. The chapters ahead are designed to move systematically from problem identification to practical applications, offering institutional investors, corporate boards, policymakers, and fiduciaries a structured approach to resilience-informed capital allocation.

In Chapter 2, I begin with a deeper dive into what might be called the "infrastructure inversion" of global finance: the reversal of assumptions that once underpinned globalization, liquidity, and diversification. Using case examples from technology, manufacturing, and finance, I illustrate how systemic fragility has become the new baseline. Where past investment frameworks relied on global integration to mitigate volatility, I now observe how integration can accelerate the spread of contagion. These illustrations are not academic hypotheticals. They are drawn from real-world events such as the semiconductor supply crisis, sovereign cyberattacks, and state-driven capital controls.

Chapter 3 introduces the core components of the ARMOR-CAP framework. I unpack the three foundational pillars—sovereign compatibility, supply chain resilience, and operational continuity—and connect them to practical governance mechanisms, from board-level oversight to compliance mapping. Each component is illustrated with stylized scenarios demonstrating how firms and investors could apply these principles to conduct more robust due diligence. Readers familiar with ERM will recognize some parallels. Still, ARMOR-CAP extends beyond internal controls to assess the external vulnerabilities and exposures that most ERM frameworks overlook.

In Chapter 4, the discussion contrasts ARMOR-CAP with ESG and ERM frameworks, not to displace them but to clarify their boundaries and complementarities. ESG evaluates intent and governance; ERM measures internal procedural risks. ARMOR-CAP evaluates survivability in a structurally unstable environment. In this chapter, I argue that these frameworks are not substitutes but instead layers, each essential yet incomplete. Their proper alignment can create a multidimensional view of organizational robustness.

Chapter 5 reframes fiduciary duty for the 21st century. I argue that legal and ethical obligations extend beyond traditional financial prudence, including scenario-aware allocation and proactive management of systemic risks. In a world where geopolitical and infrastructural shocks are increasingly common, fiduciaries who fail to consider structural exposure risks may fall short of evolving best practices and regulatory expectations. Drawing on legal scholarship and regulatory precedents, the chapter explores how foresight and risk awareness can be embedded into investment policy statements, board charters, and stewardship principles. Additionally, insights from behavioral economics, particularly Kahneman and Tversky's (1979) work on prospect theory, highlight how cognitive biases and risk perception can influence fiduciary decision-making, underscoring the need for frameworks that account for rational analysis and behavioral realities.

The second half of the book moves from principles to implementation. Chapter 6 provides a detailed blueprint for institutional investors, from asset owners to managers, on integrating ARMOR-CAP into their allocation processes. It includes checklists, screening tools, and stress-test structures tailored for multi-asset portfolios.

In Chapter 7, I adapt the framework for corporate applications, focusing on boardroom governance, risk committees, and operational audits. I outline how chief investment officers, chief risk officers, and general counsels could collaborate to elevate operational readiness from a compliance concern to a strategic advantage.

In Chapter 8, I present deep-dive fictional case studies across critical sectors: energy, finance, technology, pharmaceuticals, and logistics. Each case illustrates a different mode of structural fragility (including jurisdictional conflict, cyberattack, bottleneck dependency, or regulatory asymmetry) and evaluates how an ARMOR-CAP diagnostic might have flagged the exposure in advance. These examples are entirely fictional and are designed to show how the proposed framework could be applied in practice. ARMOR-CAP is not currently used by any institution; rather, these examples serve as stylized illustrations of how its tools, scoring logic, and governance responses might function in a real-world context.

Chapter 9 turns to regulation, where I examine how global frameworks, such as the EU's Digital Services Act and the SEC's evolving climate and cyber disclosure rules, converge with ARMOR-CAP's principles, often unintentionally. I argue that regulatory harmonization around structural transparency is both necessary and inevitable, and exploring the ARMOR-CAP framework proactively could help future-proof institutions ahead of compliance mandates.

In addition to the nine chapters, the book includes four appendices that provide essential reference materials for readers and practitioners. Appendix A offers a glossary of ARMOR-CAP terms and governance concepts to ensure clarity and consistency; Appendix B details the framework's methodological underpinnings and data assumptions; Appendix C defines each fragility domain with illustrative scoring rubrics; and Appendix D explains the conceptual and interdisciplinary foundations of ARMOR-CAP, including its design rationale, escalation bands, and prototype constraints. These appendices are entirely fictionalized and intended to support deeper engagement with the framework, encouraging future testing and institutional dialogue.

In these chapters and appendices, I offer a roadmap for resilience-informed investing. They challenge traditional assumptions while proposing a practical, testable alternative that integrates structural fragility into capital allocation. The goal is not to dictate a single path but to open a conversation on how boards, senior managers, and fiduciaries might evolve in an era of heightened systemic uncertainty.

1.8 Summary and Transition

As we close this opening chapter, the purpose and urgency of a resilience-focused investment lens can be distilled into five core ideas, each reflected in the very name of the framework:

- **A**ssumptions must be challenged.
  Capital allocation models that assume continuous access to markets, infrastructure, and legal systems are increasingly detached from reality. The conditions that allowed traditional optimization to work are no longer globally reliable.
- **R**esilience is not abstract.
  It is a measurable and diagnosable attribute that depends on tangible structures: where data are stored, how supply chains are built, and which jurisdictions control critical flows of goods, services, and information.
- **M**arket models remain incomplete.
  Risk tools that rely on volatility, beta, or ESG disclosures cannot detect fragilities rooted in operational dependencies or geopolitical chokepoints. These omissions are not minor; they are systemic.
- **O**perational continuity is now strategic.
  The ability to remain functional through disruption, whether from cyberattacks, sanctions, or supply shortages, is no longer just a management issue. It is a financial survival issue.
- **R**eframes risk as readiness.
  ARMOR-CAP is not about predicting crises; it is about equipping portfolios and institutions to withstand them. In a world of uncertainty, the edge goes to those who build for disruption, not simply for performance.

The following chapter shifts from strategic framing to operational diagnosis. It applies the ARMOR-CAP framework across real-world examples to identify how hidden fragilities (legal, digital, and infrastructural) are embedded within today's portfolios. In doing so, Chapter 2 begins to surface the structural exposures investors must now recognize, map, and address.

Chapter 2

Unseen Fault Lines: Mapping Systemic Fragility in Capital Markets

Strategic Priorities of This Chapter

Chapter 1 introduced ARMOR-CAP as a response to a world where capital allocation is increasingly exposed to infrastructural chokepoints, jurisdictional constraints, and systemic operational risks. That chapter outlined the intellectual case for a resilience-first investment lens and described the foundational pillars of the framework. This chapter moves from theory to diagnosis, applying ARMOR-CAP to uncover how systemic fragility manifests in real portfolios.

Here, ARMOR-CAP is not introduced but activated and used as a diagnostic lens to surface the hidden conditions under which portfolios become structurally vulnerable. The focus shifts from broad critiques of environmental, social, and governance (ESG), optimization, and globalization to mapping the specific mechanisms through which financial fragility is embedded in modern capital systems. From semiconductors to legal asymmetries, from cloud platforms to payment rails, this chapter demonstrates how fragility permeates infrastructure, not just markets, and how investors can begin to identify and track it.

While Chapter 1 framed the philosophical and strategic necessity of ARMOR-CAP, this chapter illustrates how to use it: to disaggregate types of systemic risk, to expose shared transmission pathways, and to challenge the baseline assumptions that still underlie most portfolio design.

The chapter unfolds across five diagnostic themes; each theme is aligned with a pillar of the ARMOR-CAP framework:

- **A — Assess structural fragility as the dominant risk vector.** Traditional risk models emphasize market volatility, but the more consequential threat now lies in systemic exposure to chokepoints, contested jurisdictions, and digital dependencies. Resilience begins not by modeling prices but by interrogating the scaffolding that makes price discovery possible. When infrastructure, legal continuity, or supply lines fail, even the most optimized portfolios can disintegrate.
- **R — Reveal hidden dependencies across critical systems.** From semiconductors and logistics to data flows and legal regimes, today's portfolios are embedded in complex networks that can fail in nonlinear, unpredictable ways. ARMOR-CAP helps surface these hidden dependencies, whether in cloud service reliance, international settlement systems, or vendor concentration, so that investors can identify structural risks before they become financial losses.
- **M — Map operational blind spots in conventional portfolio design.** Benchmark-relative and passive strategies often obscure real fragility by treating exposure as diversified simply because it is distributed across sectors or regions. But structural dependencies, such as multiple holdings relying on a single infrastructure node or jurisdiction, can render superficial diversification ineffective. Mapping these blind spots is critical to preventing unpriced risk from accumulating.
- **O — Orient readers to fragility as an unpriced beta.** Infrastructure risk silently propagates across institutions, not as idiosyncratic volatility but as a latent and contagious form of systemic risk. ARMOR-CAP reframes these unmodeled exposures as structural betas (i.e., factors that do not appear in regressions but determine outcomes under stress). Recognizing these propagation channels is essential to rethinking portfolio resilience.
- **R — Reframe fiduciary responsibility in the age of infrastructural contestation.** In a world of data localization laws, cyber conflict, and extraterritorial regulation, prudent allocation must now account for the resilience of the systems upon which capital depends. Fiduciaries can no longer assume that legal enforcement, technological continuity, or cross-border access will persist uninterrupted. ARMOR-CAP equips decision-makers with the language and tools to integrate these concerns into investment policy and governance.

2.1 The Myth of Structural Continuity

For much of modern financial history, markets have been modeled as systems that operate within a continuous infrastructure (i.e., stable legal systems, open payment rails, seamless logistics, and uninterrupted digital connectivity). These assumptions became so deeply embedded in portfolio construction, asset pricing, and capital budgeting that they were rarely examined. Continuity was the baseline. Disruption was the outlier.

The longstanding assumption that financial systems operate on a neutral, reliable, and apolitical foundation is becoming increasingly difficult to defend. In truth, the channels that move capital, data, goods, and services are anything but neutral. They are increasingly subject to interference. From supply chains and cloud services to cross-border payments and regulatory frameworks, the systems supporting global finance are contested, uneven, and increasingly fragile.

Traditional finance does not ignore disruptions. Instead, it simply misclassifies them. Crises are modeled as exogenous shocks, representing tail risks outside the system. However, this framing overlooks a deeper point: The system is fragile, with many of its critical components under strain from geopolitical and technological factors. When the foundation is unstable, disruption is no longer an aberration. It becomes the base case.

The 2020–2022 global semiconductor shortage is a prime example. It was not caused by a financial shock or mispricing of risk. It resulted from an industrial system built on just-in-time manufacturing, geographic concentration, and geopolitical miscalculations. A factory fire in Japan, pandemic-induced plant shutdowns, and surging demand for consumer electronics paralyzed global auto production. For asset managers, the result was billions in lost earnings, unexpected inventory write-downs, and valuation corrections that were invisible to any model based on trailing beta or forward earnings guidance.

Similarly, the Russian invasion of Ukraine in 2022 transformed previously investable sectors, such as Eastern European utilities and global energy logistics, into operational minefields. Supply chains were severed, commodity prices spiked, and foreign-owned assets were expropriated or frozen. What had been considered geopolitical "noise" became investment "materiality." Payment platforms were shut down, transportation corridors were blockaded, and cross-border equity exposures were rendered illiquid. These were not merely market risks; they were system risks.

The fragility of digital infrastructure has become impossible to ignore. Increasing reliance on cloud computing, artificial intelligence (AI) model hosting, and third-party data services has concentrated risk among a handful of firms, many domiciled in a single jurisdiction. As Matsakis (2021) notes, cloud platforms such as Amazon Web Services, Microsoft Azure, and Google Cloud form the invisible backbone of the digital economy. However, these platforms can also act as chokepoints, vulnerable to national security directives, data localization mandates, or cyberattacks. When a company's core systems are hosted in jurisdictions that may impose export restrictions, surveillance requirements, or even outright disconnection, operational continuity depends on service contracts and political alignment.

Long taken for granted, the stability of legal frameworks underpinning global commerce is also under strain. The assumption that property rights, contract enforcement, and cross-border recourse mechanisms are universally stable is no longer valid. In recent years, governments have increasingly used financial sanctions, asset freezes, and foreign ownership restrictions as punitive measures and standard policy levers. What was once exceptional, such as freezing central bank reserves or forced divestitures, has become normalized. As explained in the previous chapter, Farrell & Newman (2019) describe this shift as "weaponized interdependence," where the very openness of global systems becomes a channel for coercive influence. In this world, firms and investors must now evaluate not only what they own but also where and through whom they own it.

These examples underscore a central truth: Structural continuity is not a given. It is a contingent condition that depends on political alignment, technical redundancy, legal reciprocity, and jurisdictional compatibility. And yet, most financial models still treat the infrastructure of global capitalism as a black box. They measure what is priced but ignore what is *preconditional*. The result is a profound mispricing of systemic fragility.

Table 2.1 illustrates how traditional financial frameworks embed structural assumptions (i.e., legal, digital, and operational) that no longer reflect the fragmented and contested realities capital must now navigate. The table lists five levels at which financial systems rely on implicit structural assumptions (i.e., assumptions that have historically enabled seamless global capital flows but are increasingly vulnerable in today's geopolitical and technological environment). Each row contrasts an

Table 2.1. The fragile foundation of modern finance.

Level	Assumed Continuity	Structural Risk Ignored
Capital allocation & pricing	Markets are open and liquid	Sanctions, capital controls, illiquidity under stress
Portfolio construction	Diversification reduces exposure	Hidden concentration in shared infrastructure or jurisdictions
Financial infrastructure	Cross-border clearing, custody, SWIFT	Interruption of payment rails, asset freezes
Digital infrastructure	Cloud, data access, internet uptime	Data sovereignty, cyberattack, export control risk
Legal and sovereign assumptions	Contract enforcement, ownership rights	Nationalization, forced divestiture, jurisdictional asymmetry

Note: This table identifies five foundational layers of global finance: capital allocation, portfolio construction, financial infrastructure, digital systems, and legal assumptions, each of which embeds implicit beliefs about continuity. It contrasts these assumptions with emerging structural risks that reveal how fragile and contested these systems have become. ARMOR-CAP surfaces these hidden fault lines to reframe resilience as a primary design input rather than an afterthought.

assumed condition of continuity with a category of structural risk that traditional financial models often overlook.

At the top level of the table, capital allocation and pricing assume open and liquid markets; however, events such as sanctions, capital controls, and liquidity shortages during crises expose the fragility of this assumption. Portfolio construction rests on diversification principles that appear robust on the surface but can conceal hidden concentrations, such as multiple holdings relying on the same cloud provider or subject to a critical legal regime.

Moving down the table, financial infrastructure assumes uninterrupted cross-border clearing and custodial operations, typically routed through systems like SWIFT. However, these can be disrupted through geopolitical targeting or operational blockades. Digital infrastructure is assumed to be always on and globally accessible, yet it faces threats from cyberattacks, data localization laws, and export restrictions.

Finally, legal and sovereign assumptions, such as reliable contract enforcement and stable property rights, can be undermined by forced divestitures, nationalizations, or legal asymmetries across jurisdictions. ARMOR-CAP directly addresses this overlooked dimension by making such structural preconditions visible and actionable within the investment process.

ARMOR-CAP challenges this mindset by foregrounding operational viability as a first-order investment criterion. It argues that resilience is not a hedge. It is an input. Capital should not merely be deployed for optimal returns under normal conditions but for survivability under discontinuous conditions. That shift requires abandoning the myth of structural continuity and embracing the messy, fragmented architecture of the real world.

The remainder of this chapter unpacks how this myth persists within modern portfolio management, how it distorts risk allocation, and why a resilience-based diagnostic is not optional—it is overdue.

Unless otherwise cited, the examples and illustrations in this chapter are fictionalized or stylized. They are constructed to reflect common fragility patterns observed in institutional portfolios and global financial systems. No specific company, investment, or event is intended to be identified or represented.

2.2 Types of Systemic Fragility

Systemic fragility does not take on a single form. It is not merely a function of volatility or confined to specific asset classes or geographies. Rather, fragility arises from deep structural exposures (i.e., dependencies on infrastructures, jurisdictions, or flows vulnerable to disruption), often beyond the firm's control and outside conventional risk metrics. To meaningfully diagnose and manage these vulnerabilities, we must disaggregate systemic fragility into its operational components. This section identifies three recurring forms of fragility: infrastructural, jurisdictional, and informational.

2.2.1 *Infrastructural fragility*

Infrastructural fragility occurs when the physical or digital systems supporting commerce, finance, and logistics become chokepoints vulnerable to external disruption or internal failures. In traditional finance, these systems are abstracted as "pipes" that reliably carry trades, payments, and data. However, when those pipes clog, break, or are rerouted by political actors, the smooth functioning of capital markets is disrupted.

A striking example is the global overreliance on semiconductor fabrication centered in Taiwan. As of 2023, over 90% of advanced chips are produced by a single firm (Taiwan Semiconductor Manufacturing

Company, TSMC) located in a politically contested region at the heart of the U.S.–China strategic rivalry. If that facility were damaged, embargoed, or blockaded, the global impact would ripple through the automotive, defense, telecommunications, and cloud computing sectors. Portfolio managers holding otherwise "unrelated" assets across these industries would experience correlated drawdowns, not because of market contagion but because of shared infrastructural dependence.

The same logic applies to digital infrastructure. Firms increasingly rely on several cloud service providers (Amazon Web Services, Microsoft Azure, and Google Cloud) to host their critical operations. These providers, while technically robust, are subject to jurisdictional influence. National security directives, surveillance mandates, or export control policies can disrupt service delivery, block user access, or force data relocation. In such cases, the operational core of a firm and, by extension, the financial viability of its securities, rests on the infrastructure it owns or manages.

Infrastructural fragility is dangerous not because it is invisible, but because it is assumed away—analysts model price behavior, not server outages; investment committees debate business models, not maritime chokepoints. And yet, it is these very systems that increasingly determine whether capital can be deployed, protected, and recovered.

2.2.2 *Jurisdictional fragility*

Jurisdictional fragility refers to the legal, regulatory, and geopolitical risks associated with a company's location, operation, and holding assets or interactions with counterparties. These risks are not always obvious. The most significant jurisdictional exposures often arise when legal systems are presumed to be equivalent, regulatory actions are considered apolitical, and foreign enforcement risk is dismissed as implausible.

Recent history offers a corrective. In 2022, following the Russian invasion of Ukraine, numerous Western firms with operations in Russia, including energy majors, retailers, and manufacturers, were forced to write down assets, abandon facilities, or transfer ownership under duress. Foreign investors in Russian equities saw their holdings frozen or delisted. Even central banks were not immune: Over $300 billion in Russian foreign reserves held in Western financial institutions were immobilized through coordinated sanctions.

But jurisdictional fragility is not limited to sanctioned regimes. It also manifests in more subtle forms, such as capital controls, export bans, data localization laws, and discriminatory tax enforcement. Companies that rely on cross-border licensing agreements, technology transfer, or data sharing may find themselves in violation of new national security statutes, with no warning or appeal.

The globalization of the past three decades lulled many investors into believing in the convergence of legal norms. But we now live in a world of legal divergence, where sovereignty is reasserted and extraterritorial jurisdiction is expanding. In this environment, a portfolio's risk is not solely a function of company fundamentals but also of the legal systems that define ownership, access, and compliance. ARMOR-CAP treats jurisdiction as a critical variable, not a footnote.

2.2.3 *Informational fragility*

Informational fragility arises when companies, investors, or entire markets operate on incomplete, distorted, or systematically delayed information. Unlike misinformation, which is deliberate, informational fragility stems from structural opacity, a breakdown in the ability to observe and respond to critical signals in real time.

In traditional financial theory, market prices are presumed to incorporate all available information. But what happens when the data are constrained, gated, or deliberately withheld? This is not a theoretical concern. In many sectors, especially those reliant on subcontracted supply chains, offshore data processing, or politically sensitive geographies, reporting lags, selective disclosure, and strategic silence are the norm.

The COVID-19 pandemic vividly exposed this. Companies that claimed operational resilience often had little real-time visibility into their Tier 2 or Tier 3 suppliers; in fact, a McKinsey & Company survey found that only 2% of companies had visibility beyond their second-tier suppliers during the crisis (Alicke, Barriball, & Trautwein, 2021). According to the same survey, asset managers conducting ESG analysis on factory conditions or environmental compliance often relied on self-reported data, industry averages, or opaque third-party ratings, contributing to significant informational deficits. As a result, investors and companies frequently discovered critical risks such as labor shutdowns, input scarcities, or regulatory liabilities only after these issues had already impaired their returns.

In today's digital economy, information can become more fragile because so much of it flows through just a few major platforms. When a handful of companies or algorithms decide what investors see and when, the old idea of fair and open price discovery begins to fall apart. Capital ends up chasing signals that may not reflect what's happening on the ground. ARMOR-CAP pushes back against this by stressing the importance of checking where information comes from and having backup sources. If you are relying on data that you cannot double-check, or are delayed by design, you cannot manage risk effectively. Real resilience starts with the ability to see clearly.

2.2.4 *Interlocking fragilities and their compounding effects*

These three forms of systemic fragility—infrastructural, jurisdictional, and informational—are not merely abstract categories. They are observable, diagnosable, and, most importantly, compounding. When a company's data are hosted in a vulnerable jurisdiction, transmitted through contested infrastructure, and modeled with opaque inputs, their fragility is not additive. It is exponential. ARMOR-CAP offers a structured methodology for identifying these failure points before they metastasize into unrecoverable losses.

Table 2.2 outlines the three core dimensions of systemic fragility identified in the ARMOR-CAP framework: infrastructural, jurisdictional, and informational. Each dimension is defined, illustrated with a concrete example, and tied to the potential financial consequences of ignoring its associated risks.

Crucially, while each form of fragility can independently disrupt operations or portfolio performance, their interaction is nonlinear. When all three align, such as a company relying on unverifiable ESG data hosted on foreign infrastructure under regulatory pressure, the risks do not add up; they amplify. ARMOR-CAP confronts this dynamic by mapping, measuring, and mitigating interlocking fragilities at the portfolio level.

2.3 Fragility Hiding in Plain Sight

One of the most dangerous aspects of systemic fragility is that it often doesn't appear risky until it suddenly causes major disruption. The financial industry has become remarkably adept at identifying traditional exposures, including creditworthiness, liquidity, duration, and volatility.

Table 2.2. Three forms of systemic fragility.

Fragility Type	Definition	Example	Financial Impact
Infrastructural	Dependence on physical or digital systems vulnerable to disruption	Semiconductor concentration in Taiwan; cloud dependence on AWS	Cross-sector supply chain failures; operational shutdowns
Jurisdictional	Exposure to unstable or adversarial legal and regulatory environments	Sanctions freezing Russian assets; U.S. export controls affecting tech firms	Asset seizure; forced divestiture; trading restrictions
Informational	Reliance on opaque, delayed, or unverified data for decision-making	ESG self-reporting; limited visibility into offshore supply tiers	Mispricing of risk; delayed response to emerging threats

Note: ARMOR-CAP classifies systemic fragility into three mutually reinforcing domains: infrastructural, jurisdictional, and informational. Each can independently threaten operational continuity, and in combination, they create compounding risk exposures that traditional models fail to detect.

But the structural threats described in the previous section (i.e., those rooted in infrastructure, jurisdiction, and information) rarely present themselves as red flags in standard investment reports. They masquerade as ordinary operations, routine inputs, or well-functioning platforms. Fragility is normalized through familiarity.

This illusion is reinforced by the very tools designed to measure risk. Financial models rely on historical data to project future volatility, correlation matrices to simulate diversification benefits, and market prices to infer investor sentiment. Yet, none of these tools account for structural dependencies that lie beneath the surface. When risk is embedded in non-price-based systems, such as logistics, legal regimes, or cloud architectures, it remains invisible to models that only track what is priced.

Take, for example, the global transition to cloud computing. This migration was celebrated for years as a cost-efficient, scalable, and secure alternative to legacy systems. Investment analysts praised companies that moved aggressively to the cloud, assigning higher valuation multiples for their "digital transformation." What these reports rarely noted, however, was that many of these same companies had become operationally dependent on a small number of vendors (primarily based in a single legal jurisdiction). A dispute involving that jurisdiction, a sanction directive, or a cyberattack could trigger a business failure not modeled in any cash flow forecast.

Similarly, many portfolios appear geographically diversified because they span global equities, credit, and alternatives. But beneath that apparent dispersion lie deeply entangled supply chains, shared data dependencies, and overlapping regulatory exposures. A food manufacturer in France, a consumer electronics firm in South Korea, and a logistics company in the U.S. might all depend on the same chipmaker in Taiwan or the same container port in Singapore. When these critical dependence points fail, losses ripple across assets that seem unrelated on the surface. The weakness isn't rooted in portfolio allocations but in the underlying structure.

Another example is the treatment of geopolitical risk. Asset managers frequently categorize it as a top-down, macro input that affects regional exposure, currency volatility, or commodity prices. However, geopolitical fragility is often embedded at the firm level in the way it stores data, how it moves money, or with whom it transacts. A technology firm serving global clients may be forced to halt operations in certain jurisdictions due to new data localization laws or sanctions. A financial institution may be unable to clear payments or enforce contracts in regions subject to extraterritorial claims. These operational disruptions manifest as earnings shocks, credit events, or liquidity freezes.

Perhaps most troubling is the failure of standard ESG frameworks to detect structural fragility. ESG analyses often focus on policies and disclosures, including what companies state about their carbon targets, labor practices, or board diversity. However, ESG scores rarely capture whether a firm's operations depend on a data center in a politically unstable jurisdiction or a critical supplier with no second source. In this sense, ESG can create a false sense of security, suggesting resilience where only reputation has been managed.

The persistence of unrecognized fragility is not merely a technical problem. It represents a governance failure. It reflects the gap between what is measurable and what is material. Boards, risk committees, and investment professionals have become accustomed to equating "trackable" with "manageable." But fragility is often neither. It is embedded, relational, and nonlinear. It accumulates quietly until it doesn't.

Table 2.3 explores a critical blind spot in mainstream financial analysis: the reliance on surface-level portfolio metrics that suggest robustness while overlooking deeper structural fragilities. Each row in the table

Table 2.3. Structural fragility hidden beneath portfolio-level metrics.

Surface-Level Metric	What It Suggests	What It Misses
Geographic diversification	Reduced exposure to country-specific shocks	Shared supply chains, infrastructure, or data vendors across regions
ESG rating	Strong governance and sustainability profile	No visibility into operational dependencies, infrastructure, or jurisdictional risk
Low portfolio beta	Stability relative to the market	Exposure to non-market shocks (e.g., cloud service failure, sanctions)
Strong earnings forecast	Positive expected growth	Blind to regulatory disruption, legal conflict, or cyber-induced operational loss
Cash flow models	Predictable performance under normal ops	Assumes uninterrupted access to legal, logistical, and data infrastructures

Note: This table shows how common portfolio metrics can overlook deeper structural risks. By focusing on what is measurable rather than what is foundational, these indicators may give a false sense of security, ignoring dependencies on infrastructure, jurisdiction, or data integrity that are critical to sustaining value.

highlights a commonly used metric (geographic diversification, ESG ratings, beta, earnings forecasts, and cash flow models) and contrasts its intended signaling function with what it tends to ignore. For example, geographic diversification is often assumed to reduce risk through regional spread. Still, it can mask shared exposures when companies across different countries rely on the same cloud provider, shipping lanes, or legal frameworks. Similarly, a high ESG score may signal strong governance or sustainability credentials, yet offer no insight into whether a company's operations are vulnerable to infrastructure failures or jurisdictional disputes. Even traditionally conservative metrics, such as low beta or strong projected earnings, are built on implicit assumptions of stability that may not hold in practice.

The table clarifies that many widely trusted indicators embed assumptions of operational continuity without testing them. ARMOR-CAP is designed to make those assumptions visible, measurable, and challenging. They shift the focus from surface metrics to the foundational conditions that make financial performance possible in the first place.

ARMOR-CAP exists to surface this blind spot. Its purpose is not to predict every failure but to identify conditions under which failure is more likely and consequential. It turns attention to what enables financial strategies to function in the first place: legal access, logistical continuity, data integrity, and jurisdictional alignment. These are not edge cases. They are the scaffolding of value creation.

As the following section explains, portfolios built without awareness of this scaffolding are not diversified; they are vulnerable to exposure. The risk lies not in the returns. It is assumed that returns are always extractable.

2.4 When Optimization Obscures Exposure

Optimization is the holy grail of modern portfolio theory. From mean-variance efficiency to Sharpe maximization and factor-based construction, asset management has long been built on the idea that capital can be optimally deployed across risk and return dimensions with enough data and mathematical rigor. This framework has delivered real benefits: reduced costs, greater transparency, and more disciplined diversification. But it has also created a dangerous blind spot. In optimizing portfolios based on what can be measured, investors have come to ignore what must be assumed.

Optimization treats markets as continuous, liquid, and probabilistically stable. It assumes that returns are drawn from a distribution that can be modeled, that volatility can be estimated, and that correlations, though unstable, are not discontinuous. Within this framework, the architecture of capital allocation is agnostic to infrastructure, jurisdiction, or operational context. It doesn't matter where a company's servers are hosted, how its products are transported, or which country adjudicates its contracts. Optimization abstracts those variables away.

This abstraction becomes especially problematic in environments where foundational assumptions no longer hold. A portfolio constructed to minimize volatility across regions may inadvertently concentrate investments in digital infrastructure housed within a single geopolitical bloc. A factor-neutral strategy may load on companies that appear uncorrelated but share exposure to the same maritime chokepoint, regulatory body, or embedded technology provider. These exposures are invisible to the optimizer, not because they are immaterial but because they are unmodeled.

The problem is not that optimization is flawed. It's that the inputs are incomplete. Most optimization engines assume that the instruments are tradable, the legal protections are enforceable, and the firms' operational capacities are stable. These are heroic assumptions in a world of contested sovereignty, weaponized interdependence, and infrastructure strain. A model suggesting a 30-basis-point improvement in risk-adjusted return is meaningless if the underlying securities become non-fungible during a regime shift, cyber event, or legal freeze.

Moreover, as portfolios are increasingly constructed using systematic methods such as quantitative screens, passive exposures, or algorithmic rebalancing, the detachment from real-world conditions deepens. Allocators may have perfect exposure to style, sector, or region but zero awareness of whether those securities are functionally viable under stress. Optimization may reduce measured volatility while increasing actual fragility.

This is not a theoretical concern. In March 2020, as markets collapsed under pandemic panic, many portfolios optimized for low tracking error or minimum variance underperformed precisely because they lacked operational resilience. Their holdings, although theoretically uncorrelated, faced simultaneous operational breakdowns. Factories shut down, supply chains froze, and legal jurisdictions imposed contradictory regulations. Models failed not because the math was wrong but because the environment had changed in ways the math didn't see.

A similar pattern emerged with the freezing of Russian securities following the invasion of Ukraine. Many global portfolios had optimized exposure to emerging markets through benchmark-relative strategies. They held Russian equities, sovereign debt, and quasi-sovereign corporate debt. They did so not because of discretionary conviction but because that's what the optimizer said to do. When those assets became legally inaccessible, the models had no mechanism for adjustment. The optimization embedded exposure but offered no exit.

ARMOR-CAP accepts optimization but reframes it. It argues that optimization should not begin with historical return data but with operational viability. Suppose a company cannot function under plausible stress scenarios. In that case, its core infrastructure is jurisdictionally vulnerable, or its legal rights are subject to arbitrary reinterpretation. Regardless of the return forecast, it cannot be treated as equivalent to a company without those exposures.

This shift is not anti-quantitative. It is post-quantitative. It insists that the world has changed faster than our models and that real resilience requires reinserting context into calculations. Optimization should not obscure exposure. It should be preceded by a diagnostic that filters out structurally fragile assets before entering the efficient frontier.

Table 2.4 compares traditional portfolio optimization assumptions to the real-world fragility diagnostics emphasized by ARMOR-CAP. The left column lists commonly accepted premises embedded in optimization routines, such as continuous asset traceability, comprehensive risk capture through volatility measures, and the reliability of historical correlations. These assumptions are often taken for granted in quantitative finance, forming the backbone of allocation decisions.

The middle column identifies what these assumptions typically overlook. For example, continuous tradability overlooks the possibility that assets can be frozen, delisted, or restricted due to sanctions, regulatory actions, or market closures. Similarly, reliance on historical correlations

Table 2.4. What optimization models assume vs. what ARMOR-CAP demands.

Traditional Optimization Assumption	What's Overlooked	ARMOR-CAP Diagnostic Priority
Asset tradability is continuous	Assets can be frozen, delisted, or become inaccessible	Legal and jurisdictional accessibility
Market volatility captures all risk	Structural risk is not priced in	Operational viability and failure thresholds
Historical correlations are reliable	Correlations collapse under systemic stress	Shared dependencies and systemic propagation pathways
Infrastructure is neutral and stable	Firms may rely on contested or chokepoint infrastructures	Infrastructure mapping and redundancy
ESG scores reflect resilience	ESG may miss jurisdictional, cyber, and supply exposures	Independent resilience audit and external risk mapping

Note: This table compares the hidden assumptions underlying traditional portfolio optimization with the structural diagnostics required by ARMOR-CAP. It shifts the focus from abstract modeling to real-world constraints, making resilience, not simply return, the foundation of portfolio design.

ignores how these relationships can collapse during systemic stress, leaving supposedly diversified portfolios to be fully exposed.

The right column introduces the ARMOR-CAP perspective. Rather than rejecting optimization, ARMOR-CAP reframes it by layering structural diagnostics into the model before it is run. This involves explicitly checking jurisdictional accessibility, identifying single points of infrastructure failure, and evaluating whether inputs such as ESG scores accurately represent resilience. The goal is not to ask for more optimization algorithms, but to demand more from allocators by ensuring that what goes into the optimization reflects the real conditions that enable capital to remain safe, mobile, and productive.

ARMOR-CAP does not ask the optimizer to do more. It asks the allocator to do better.

2.5 Fragility as a Transmission Mechanism

Fragility is not merely an attribute of companies or systems. It serves as a pathway for the spread of contagion. When overlooked vulnerabilities become critical, they do not remain confined to a single security or sector. They propagate. They move laterally through shared dependencies, regulatory linkages, and confidence channels. In this way, fragility acts as a transmission mechanism, turning isolated failures into portfolio-wide events. Understanding this propagation dynamic is crucial for developing truly resilient strategies.

Traditional risk models treat shocks as localized, random, and exogenous. If a company misses consensus earnings, a bond issuer defaults, or a country imposes capital controls, the model assumes that the consequences will largely be contained to that issuer or region. Diversification, the theory goes, limits the damage. But this view assumes independence across exposures. It overlooks the extent to which seemingly unrelated assets share a reliance on the same vendors, infrastructures, legal regimes, or geopolitical alignments. In fragile, highly interdependent systems, vulnerabilities are often latent and can be exposed or amplified by operational or geopolitical stressors. Rather than remaining static, the relationships between system components can shift rapidly under duress, leading to cascading failures and systemic risk (Farrell & Newman, 2019).

Consider a portfolio holding a global basket of equities spanning logistics, energy, consumer tech, and industrials. The portfolio appears well-diversified on paper: The sectors are uncorrelated, the geographies span both developed and emerging markets, and the position sizes are risk-adjusted. Yet, if every one of those firms relies on a single critical node, such as Taiwan Semiconductor Manufacturing Company for chips, AWS for digital operations, or SWIFT for payment processing, disruption to any of these nodes (whether due to sanctions, cyberattacks, or geopolitical blockades) could trigger cascading value destruction across the portfolio. This risk does not arise from traditional financial contagion but from structural propagation through global operational dependencies (Matsakis, 2021).

Fragility is also transmitted through legal and regulatory asymmetries. A shift in data localization rules in one country can compel multinationals to alter their IT architecture globally. A new export control measure in the U.S. can trigger retaliatory sanctions, leading to the deplatforming of service providers and compliance uncertainty for all counterparties. For asset managers, this creates a situation where a single regulatory action, not modeled as a risk, can trigger a portfolio-wide mark-to-market event (Chander & Lê, 2015).

Cyberinfrastructure represents another potent transmission channel. Because so many firms across sectors and regions now depend on shared cloud services and network security protocols, a breach in one platform can simultaneously impair dozens of unrelated holdings. The 2021 attack on Kaseya's software update infrastructure, for example, disrupted operations at companies that had no direct business with the vendor, demonstrating how a single cyber incident can propagate through architectural dependencies rather than direct firm-to-firm connections.

There is also reputational propagation, particularly within ESG-focused portfolios. When fragility is exposed in one company, it can force a reevaluation of others with similar structures. If a high-profile company is penalized for data governance failures or sourcing from a fragile jurisdiction, investors often re-rate comparable firms, even if no scandal has yet emerged. The result is a feedback loop where fragility in one node triggers price compression in related assets, not because the fundamentals have changed but because confidence has evaporated.

This transmission mechanism is not a flaw of diversification. Instead, it is a flaw in what we assume diversification protects against. The conventional model cannot distinguish between financially distinct yet structurally entangled assets. ARMOR-CAP corrects this by mapping propagation pathways in advance. It highlights when multiple holdings share exposure to the same infrastructure, legal environment, or operational assumptions. It flags when an unpriced risk in one asset can plausibly trigger write-downs in others.

In a world of interconnected fragilities, portfolios do not break gradually. They fracture suddenly and simultaneously. By treating fragility as a transmission mechanism, ARMOR-CAP reframes resilience not as the absence of shocks but as the ability to contain their spread.

Table 2.5 illustrates how fragility in institutional portfolios is not simply about asset price co-movements or market correlations. Instead, it shows how seemingly diversified holdings may be interconnected through hidden transmission pathways, including supply chains, digital infrastructure, legal frameworks, and geopolitical alignments. Each row identifies a trigger node, such as a semiconductor factory shutdown or a SWIFT system disconnection, and traces how that node can initiate cascading disruptions across a wide range of portfolio exposures.

For example, a factory outage at TSMC, a critical semiconductor supplier, can trigger a global chip shortage, impacting companies across various sectors, including automobiles, defense, and healthcare. Similarly, disconnection from SWIFT disrupts banks and reverberates across cross-border e-commerce and logistics firms that depend on payment continuity. ARMOR-CAP responds to these challenges by treating fragility as a

Table 2.5. Fragility as a transmission mechanism.

Trigger Node	Transmission Pathway	Affected Portfolio Assets
TSMC factory outage	Global chip shortage	Auto, tech, defense, industrials
SWIFT disconnection	Payment system blocked	Banks, cross-border e-commerce, logistics
AWS export ban or failure	Cloud infrastructure halted	SaaS, retail, fintech, healthcare IT
Cyberattack on supply chain	Software update chain corrupted (e.g., Kaseya incident)	Firms using compromised IT infrastructure
Data localization law	Forced segmentation of cloud/ data operations	Global multinationals, tech platforms, outsourcing providers
Reputational spillover	ESG breach in one firm triggers markdown of similar firms	Thematically aligned ESG holdings across regions/sectors

Note: This table demonstrates how shared operational or legal dependencies can amplify fragility across asset classes, invalidating assumptions of safety through diversification.

transmission mechanism, not just a stress scenario. Rather than focusing narrowly on financial metrics, the framework proactively maps operational, legal, and reputational entanglements to identify where risks could propagate and contaminate unrelated holdings.

The final row underscores that fragility can also be reputational: An ESG failure in one firm can trigger markdowns across thematic ESG funds globally—an illustration of narrative contagion rather than balance sheet risk. In each case, ARMOR-CAP reframes resilience as the ability to isolate, contain, and absorb shocks rather than merely predicting or preventing them.

2.6 From Hidden Exposure to Actionable Diagnostics

Recognizing fragility is only the first step. What makes ARMOR-CAP distinct is that it transforms conceptual insights into diagnostic tools, frameworks that can be used by institutional investors, risk managers, and corporate boards to evaluate exposure before it becomes a loss. Suppose traditional financial models are blind to operational dependencies, legal asymmetries, and infrastructure chokepoints. In that case, a new diagnostic logic is required, one that begins not with returns but with the conditions that enable returns to exist in the first place.

The premise of ARMOR-CAP is deceptively simple: Resilience must be treated as a primary constraint in portfolio construction rather than a secondary consideration applied after the fact. Before capital is deployed, optimization models are run, and undesired exposures are hedged, a portfolio or business line must pass a basic viability check under conditions of discontinuity. Can the entity function if a jurisdiction cuts off access? If a supplier is sanctioned? If a cloud provider is disrupted? Are legal protections voided by an executive order or a geopolitical conflict?

This diagnostic stance reframes the question of risk. It no longer only asks, "How much might I lose if the market moves?" It asks, "What breaks if the infrastructure beneath this investment stops working?" That second question is not rhetorical. It is operational. And ARMOR-CAP structures it into a repeatable process.

The diagnostic approach begins with mapping dependency surfaces, identifying where firms, portfolios, or institutions rely on third-party infrastructure, legal systems, or cross-border permissions. These dependencies are often non-obvious and nonlinear. For example, a U.S.-domiciled firm with local customers might rely on a foreign cloud provider subject to export controls. Or a logistics firm with domestic operations might depend on container traffic routed through contested maritime zones. The headline risk appears minimal in each case, but the embedded fragility is material.

Next, ARMOR-CAP evaluates the sovereign alignment of these dependencies. How compatible are the systems on which the firm relies with the jurisdictions in which it operates, holds assets, or serves clients? This alignment matters because access to infrastructure and legal protections is not merely a technical issue; it is geopolitical. Recent history shows how quickly access can be revoked for reasons unrelated to commercial behavior. Sovereign alignment is thus not about patriotism or politics. Instead, it is about operational continuity.

The final diagnostic step is to assess redundancy and adaptability. If a key supplier fails, is there a backup? Can systems shift jurisdictions without violating local laws if a data center is compromised? Is an escrow or unwind mechanism in place if a counterparty is sanctioned? In many cases, the answer is no, not because firms are negligent but because the risk was never considered material enough to warrant contingency planning. ARMOR-CAP changes that calculus.

The concepts of redundancy and adaptability warrant further consideration. Legal redundancy involves structuring asset rights, contractual enforcement, and capital pathways to operate across multiple jurisdictions, ensuring that operations can continue uninterrupted if one legal system becomes compromised. Digital portability requires that companies can migrate their systems across vendors or geographic regions if access is disrupted or revoked, especially when cloud services are entangled in sovereignty or export controls. Supply chain rerouting isn't merely about having alternative suppliers; it requires pre-negotiated logistics arrangements, escrow mechanisms, or legal permissions to activate alternate lanes in real time. These are not theoretical constructs. They are practical fault lines. And their presence or absence can determine whether a portfolio survives a shock or disintegrates in its wake.

By reframing fragility as a diagnosable condition rather than an unpredictable one, ARMOR-CAP returns agency to investors and operators. It creates a language for assessing resilience not as a narrative but as a measurable property. It does not require perfection; it only requires that institutions move from passive assumptions to active inquiry. Resilience is not free, but neither is fragility. The cost of preparing is almost always less than the cost of recovery.

Table 2.6. The ARMOR-CAP diagnostic sequence.

Step	Key Question	Diagnostic Focus
1. Map Dependency Surfaces	What infrastructure, legal systems, and third parties does this asset rely on?	Cloud hosting, supply chains, payment rails, legal recourse pathways
2. Assess Sovereign Alignment	Are those dependencies under the control or influence of aligned jurisdictions?	Exposure to adversarial legal regimes, export controls, extraterritorial law
3. Evaluate Redundancy and Adaptability	Can operations continue or shift if one of these nodes fails?	Backup capacity, contingency planning, legal and digital portability

Note: This table presents the core three-step diagnostic process ARMOR-CAP uses to identify critical dependencies, assess geopolitical alignment, and evaluate operational resilience.

The following chapter formalizes these diagnostics into a structured framework, detailing how ARMOR-CAP can be applied across asset classes, corporate assessments, and institutional mandates. But the transition begins here with a mental model shift. Capital can no longer be deployed solely based on valuation or volatility. It must be tested for viability first.

Table 2.6 lays out the structured diagnostic process at the heart of the ARMOR-CAP framework. This three-step sequence enables institutional allocators to transition from identifying latent vulnerabilities to assessing an asset's capacity to withstand or adapt to systemic disruptions. Rather than treating resilience as a qualitative overlay or *post hoc* consideration, this framework integrates resilience analysis into the early stages of portfolio construction and risk evaluation:

Step 1. Map Dependency Surfaces: This initial step asks what infrastructure, legal systems, and third parties this asset relies on to function. It shifts the focus from asset characteristics (e.g., volatility, Sharpe ratio) to the underlying ecosystem that supports operational continuity. Diagnostic tools at this stage map dependencies, including cloud service providers, critical suppliers, payment systems, and legal protections. By surfacing these interconnections, allocators understand the invisible scaffolding that must remain intact for asset value to be realized.

Step 2. Assess Sovereign Alignment: Once dependencies are mapped, the next question is: Are these dependencies embedded in jurisdictions aligned with the investor's legal and strategic interests? This step examines sovereign exposure, including reliance on cloud infrastructure subject to foreign export controls, operations exposed to adversarial regulatory regimes, or legal enforcement mechanisms beyond the allocator's reach. This diagnostic draws attention to extraterritorial vulnerabilities, such as U.S. sanctions, China's data localization laws, or EU privacy directives, which can alter an asset's viability overnight.

Step 3. Evaluate Redundancy and Adaptability: The final diagnostic step examines whether the asset or issuer has credible operational work-arounds during disruption. Can systems fail gracefully, reroute services, or invoke backup jurisdictions? This includes assessments of contingency plans, dual-sourcing strategies, legal portability of data and contracts, and off-grid infrastructure. This step answers the following question: If a node breaks, can the function survive?

Together, these three steps reframe risk management as a proactive inquiry into real-world functionality and not just financial performance. The ARMOR-CAP diagnostic sequence is thus a tool for anticipatory governance, helping allocators shift from risk reaction to structural foresight.

2.6.1 *From diagnosis to design*

The fragilities outlined in this chapter are not hypothetical; they already exist in institutional portfolios, embedded in operational, legal, and geo-political dependencies that traditional models overlook. Familiar metrics and smooth historical data may obscure these risks, but they can transform routine market stress into systemic disruption when activated.

As we've seen through the examples in Tables 2.4 and 2.5, even a single infrastructure failure or legal shift can ripple across sectors and jurisdictions, undermining the protective logic of diversification.

This book proposes a new design framework—ARMOR-CAP—that responds to these emerging vulnerabilities by rethinking capital allocation. ARMOR-CAP is not yet in practice, but the chapters ahead offer both the ingredients and rationale for its adoption. It treats fragility not as a statistical anomaly but as a structural feature that can be mapped, measured, and mitigated.

Chapter 3 introduces the core architecture of ARMOR-CAP. Built on three foundational pillars—sovereign compatibility, supply chain resilience, and operational continuity—the framework provides a disciplined approach to confronting hidden vulnerabilities. As we will see, building resilient portfolios requires more than diversification or hedging; it demands strategic foresight and institutional design. ARMOR-CAP is intended as that blueprint.

2.7 Summary and Transition

This chapter shows that fragility is no longer rare, hidden, or irrelevant. It is structural, transmissible, and deeply embedded in the very architecture of global capital markets. The goal of ARMOR-CAP is not to eliminate risk but to reclassify the kinds of risk that matter most. The following five core principles summarize the diagnostic worldview advanced in this chapter:

- **A**cknowledge that infrastructure is not neutral.
  Capital relies on systems such as laws, internet infrastructure, and shipping, which can break down or be exploited as tools of pressure. Ignoring these risks means investors may end up exposed without even realizing it.
- **R**ecognize that diversification can deceive.
  Superficial dispersion across sectors and geographies does not guarantee protection when shared dependencies tie holdings to the same failure points.
- **M**ap fragility before modeling return.
  Optimization without diagnostic screening embeds unpriced structural risks. Viability, not volatility, is the new starting point.
- **O**verlay resilience as a portfolio constraint.
  ARMOR-CAP inserts geopolitical, infrastructural, and jurisdictional viability into the asset selection process, not as exclusions, but as qualifying criteria.
- **R**eplace reaction with readiness.
  In fragile systems, there is no time for mid-crisis modeling. ARMOR-CAP creates a forward-looking screen that identifies what may become inaccessible when it's too late to reallocate.

Chapter 3

From Concept to Pillars: Engineering Resilient Capital with ARMOR-CAP

Strategic Priorities of This Chapter

The previous chapter examined how fragility permeates capital markets, not as price volatility but as hidden dependencies embedded in infrastructure, legal regimes, and digital systems. This chapter shifts from diagnosis to implementation. If ARMOR-CAP helps investors recognize fragility, the next step is to act on it: translating structural awareness into investment policy, governance tools, and day-to-day capital allocation practices.

The goal is not only to acknowledge fragility but also to manage around it. That requires rethinking internal governance, risk mandates, sourcing policies, and the very metrics by which success is measured. This chapter shows how ARMOR-CAP can be operationalized through formalized procedures, embedded diagnostics, and evolving institutional norms.

The discussion unfolds across five applied themes:

- **A — Align governance structures with resilience mandates.** Traditional investment committees and chief investment officer functions often focus on performance benchmarks and asset class silos. However, resilience requires cross-functional coordination among legal, operational, and investment teams. ARMOR-CAP encourages institutions to incorporate strategic fragility into their decision-making protocols and oversight structures.

- **R — Reconfigure risk models to incorporate structural exposures.** Value at risk, stress tests, and tracking error are insufficient if they ignore jurisdictional chokepoints or critical vendor reliance. This chapter examines how resilience overlays and early-warning diagnostics can be integrated into traditional models without compromising financial rigor.
- **M — Measure what was previously invisible.** Whether it's legal portability, infrastructure redundancy, or cyber backup integrity, institutions must begin quantifying qualitative dimensions. ARMOR-CAP does not replace risk analytics; it expands them to include operational continuity and sovereign alignment as measurable factors.
- **O — Operationalize resilience through codified procedures.** Resilient strategy is not *ad hoc*. This chapter outlines the process of formalizing new resilience protocols through investment policy statements, manager selection criteria, sourcing frameworks, and escalation triggers. These are not checklists but living governance artifacts.
- **R — Reinforce institutional readiness through practice and review.** Even the best frameworks degrade without testing and feedback. This chapter discusses red teaming, war gaming, and scenario-based reviews as tools to enhance preparedness. ARMOR-CAP recommends continuous adaptation as conditions evolve.

3.1 From Framework to Function

The two previous chapters established the core argument of this book: that in a world of infrastructure strain, geopolitical fracture, and digital interdependence, traditional financial models fail to capture the systemic fragilities that matter most. ARMOR-CAP—Allocation for Resilient Markets and Operational Readiness, focusing on Capital Allocation Protection—was introduced as a diagnostic framework designed to detect these unpriced exposures before they metastasize into portfolio-wide losses.

While Chapter 1 set the philosophical foundation and Chapter 2 illustrates how fragility hides in plain sight, this chapter marks a shift from problems to methods. Here, I define and operationalize the three diagnostic pillars of ARMOR-CAP (i.e., sovereign compatibility, supply chain resilience, and operational continuity), first introduced in Chapter 1. Until now, they have served as organizing concepts. In this chapter, they become actionable instruments.

Each of the three pillars is presented with a clear definition, diagnostic questions, and examples illustrating its application across various asset classes and sectors. Where conventional risk frameworks focus on price behavior, balance sheets, or environmental disclosures, the ARMOR-CAP pillars examine the underlying support systems, examining what the asset depends on to function, who controls it, and whether it remains viable under strategic stress. Taken together, these pillars form practical architecture for building portfolios that do not merely aim for return but are designed to endure rupture.

We begin with sovereign compatibility, which is the extent to which the legal, technological, and regulatory environment upon which an asset depends aligns with the investor's home or host jurisdiction. From there, we explore supply chain resilience and operational continuity, ultimately weaving these three into a unified resilience lens for capital deployment.

Unless otherwise cited, the examples and illustrations in this chapter are fictionalized or stylized. They are constructed to reflect recurring fragility patterns observed in institutional portfolios and do not refer to any specific company, entity, or event.

3.2 Sovereign Compatibility

At its core, sovereign compatibility poses a simple yet often overlooked question: Can your capital operate effectively within the legal, regulatory, and political environment it relies on? In a globalized investment landscape, portfolios routinely span dozens of jurisdictions, each with its own rules for capital flows, property rights, digital governance, and contractual enforcement. Sovereign compatibility is not about political alignment or ideological preference but about operational survivability under stress.

Historically, institutional investors assumed a baseline of convergence: Jurisdictions adhering to broadly liberal market principles would honor contracts, facilitate cross-border transactions, and provide fair dispute resolution. This assumption held for much of the post–Cold War era, supported by a thickening layer of trade agreements, capital mobility norms, and legal harmonization efforts. However, in recent years, that foundation has begun to fracture.

Sovereign compatibility became a front-page issue with the freezing of Russian sovereign assets in 2022. Following the invasion of Ukraine, over $300 billion in Russian central bank reserves held in the U.S. and EU were immobilized by coordinated sanctions. Foreign investors in Russian equities and bonds were blocked from exiting positions or collecting interest payments, not because the assets themselves failed financially but because they were operationally severed from global capital systems due to political decisions. Similar episodes have occurred previously: Argentina's selective bond default and the ensuing litigation in U.S. courts, China's retaliation against foreign audit access demands, and India's unexpected retroactive tax ruling against Vodafone. In each case, the disruption was not due to market fundamentals but to legal and regulatory interventions that altered asset accessibility and value.

But the issue extends beyond headline events. A company may appear entirely creditworthy and fundamentally sound, but it may operate in an environment where its operational rights can be curtailed without warning. For example, companies operating data centers in jurisdictions with expansive cybersecurity or national security laws (e.g., China, Russia, or India) may be compelled to comply with data localization requirements that increase operational complexity, raise costs, and sometimes conflict with the legal expectations of other jurisdictions. This is not a theoretical concern: As Chander and \(2015) document, multinationals have faced conflicting compliance demands from multiple sovereigns, forcing them to restructure business units or abandon markets altogether.

From a portfolio perspective, sovereign compatibility must be assessed both at the firm and portfolio construction levels. Firm-level questions include the following:

- Is the company's legal operating environment stable and predictable?
- Are its critical assets or contracts exposed to expropriation, retroactive regulation, or discriminatory enforcement?
- Are its dispute resolution mechanisms enforceable across borders?

Portfolio-level questions expand to include the following:

- Do multiple holdings share exposure to the same fragile legal regime or political risk?
- Are asset classes (e.g., American Depositary Receipts (ADRs), sovereign debt, dual-listed securities) subject to coordinated political action that could restrict access, transferability, or payouts?

Sovereign compatibility also interacts with the obligations of asset managers. Fiduciary duty is typically interpreted in financial terms; however, if a fund's assets are subject to unpredictable political override, can that be squared with a duty of prudence? For pension funds, insurance firms, and public investment authorities, ignoring this exposure layer is no longer a viable option.

Table 3.1 illustrates the multi-layered nature of sovereign compatibility risk and shows that exposures extend beyond a single issuer or security. Instead, compatibility with sovereign systems must be assessed at three interdependent levels—firm-level, asset-level, and portfolio-level—to capture the operational vulnerabilities that can fully propagate through portfolios.

At the firm level, the assessment centers on whether an issuer can function reliably within its jurisdiction. Even fundamentally sound companies may become uninvestable if governments impose retroactive taxes, mandate forced data localization, or engage in arbitrary legal interference. This level asks: Can the firm continue to operate in good standing under its legal and political regime? When firms are subject to unpredictable enforcement or shifting legal obligations, capital is exposed to asymmetric risk that is often invisible in credit ratings or financial statements.

The asset-level probe determines whether an investor can legally access, trade, and enforce a specific security. A sovereign bond or corporate note may be issued under local law, with provisions that do not align with the investor's legal rights. Examples include sanctioned instruments, frozen ADRs, or capital controls that prevent dividend repatriation or redemption payments. This level captures the enforceability gap between holding a claim and exercising it.

At the portfolio level, sovereign compatibility evaluates concentration risk across jurisdictions, especially when assets share dependencies on the same fragile legal or regulatory infrastructure. An investor holding multiple emerging market (EM) bonds or a suite of tech firms subject to a single regulator may face amplified systemic risk, even if each position appears independently sound. The issue is not whether each holding is legal and enforceable but whether interlinked legal, regulatory, or geopolitical dynamics could impair the portfolio in the event of a correlated shock.

Rather than serving as a *post hoc* risk screen, Table 3.1 serves as a pre-optimization diagnostic tool for investors and allocators applying the ARMOR-CAP framework. It helps to flag positions where legal enforceability or political alignment may not support capital resilience under stress. The table does not prescribe blanket exclusion of high-risk jurisdictions. Instead, it encourages investors to operationalize political and legal risk, evaluating whether an investment is grounded in enforceable rights or assumptions of continuity and cooperation.

In today's environment of weaponized interdependence, where infrastructure, capital markets, and even rule-of-law standards are used as levers of statecraft, such an assessment is no longer optional. Table 3.1 illustrates how ignoring sovereign compatibility transforms political risk into operational risk, undermining returns, access, liquidity, and governance continuity. ARMOR-CAP incorporates sovereign compatibility as a screening mechanism upstream of risk modeling. Assets or issuers that fail basic tests of legal access, regulatory predictability, or jurisdictional continuity are flagged for exclusion, reweighting, or additional due diligence. This does not mean investors should avoid all emerging markets or geopolitically active regions. But it does mean that political risk must be operationalized, not merely acknowledged in footnotes or priced as volatility.

The failure to assess sovereign compatibility is not simply a blind-spot error. It confuses price behavior with asset accessibility and governance ratings with enforceable rights. No resilience framework can afford to do that in a world of contested sovereignty and weaponized interdependence.

Table 3.1. Layers of sovereign compatibility risk.

Risk Layer	Core Question	Examples of Fragility
Firm-level	Can the firm operate freely within its legal environment?	Retroactive taxes, expropriation, local data law conflict
Asset-level	Can the asset be accessed, held, and legally enforced?	Sanctioned bonds, frozen ADRs, restricted cash repatriation
Portfolio-level	Do multiple assets share jurisdictional exposure?	Clustered EM sovereign debt, tech firms dependent on same regulator

Note: This table identifies how sovereign compatibility risk manifests across firm, asset, and portfolio levels, revealing legal, regulatory, and jurisdictional fragilities often ignored by traditional risk models. The table serves as a diagnostic tool within the ARMOR-CAP framework, guiding investors in assessing enforceability and accessing upstream information prior to allocation decisions.

3.3 Supply Chain Resilience

If sovereign compatibility addresses *where* an asset is legally and jurisdictionally located, supply chain resilience addresses *how* it operates functionally. It focuses on the physical and digital flows of goods, services, and information, enabling companies and, by extension, the portfolios that include them to generate value.

Supply chain resilience is no longer a secondary operational metric in a world increasingly shaped by logistical disruptions, geopolitical realignments, and embedded dependencies. It is a central determinant of capital durability.

Global supply chains had been optimized for cost efficiency, speed, and just-in-time production for decades. Firms outsourced upstream components, concentrated manufacturing, and minimized inventory buffers. These systems delivered extraordinary margin improvements but at the cost of structural fragility. They assumed uninterrupted access to ports, borderless movement of components, and cooperative political relationships between supplier nations. Those assumptions are now cracking.

COVID-19 exposed this fragility across global systems. Lockdowns, export bans, and capacity imbalances created shortages across semiconductors, personal protective equipment, pharmaceuticals, and shipping capacity. More recently, geopolitical tensions have reinforced the lesson. The U.S.–China technology rift has produced restrictions on chip exports, cloud infrastructure access, and critical raw material flows. Meanwhile, the Red Sea crisis and the Suez Canal blockage demonstrated how a single chokepoint can impact industries ranging from autos to retail within a matter of days. None of these were hypothetical stress tests; they were live-fire exercises in fragility.

Supply chain resilience is not limited to physical assets, such as trucks and factories; it also encompasses digital supply chains—encompassing application programming interfaces (APIs), platforms, and cloud infrastructure—that organizations rely on for data storage, transactions, and operational management. As companies increasingly adopt software-defined services, they may inadvertently introduce single points of failure, such as dependence on a logistics platform located in a politically unstable jurisdiction or reliance on vendors without redundancy. The 2020 SolarWinds incident, in which a compromised software update in a widely used IT monitoring tool enabled a major cyberattack affecting both public agencies and private firms, underscores the critical need for digital supply chain resilience.

ARMOR-CAP evaluates supply chain resilience by asking which dependencies a company cannot afford to lose and whether it has any plan in place if it does. This includes the following:

- *Sourcing concentration*: Does the company rely heavily on a single country, vendor, or transportation route?
- *Input substitutability*: Can key components or data flows be rerouted or substituted under stress?
- *Visibility across tiers*: Does the company understand the fragility, not only of its direct suppliers but also of their suppliers?

At the portfolio level, the concern multiplies. Even if no single firm represents excessive supply chain risk, a portfolio may become concentrated in similar exposures. ARMOR-CAP flags when multiple holdings depend on the same infrastructure, platform, or jurisdictional corridor. For example, a portfolio might appear geographically diverse but rely on Taiwan for semiconductors, the Red Sea for physical shipments, and AWS for digital continuity. If all three come under threat, correlations spike because exposure was not diversified in function, only in name.

Investors often assume that if a firm's stock price isn't reflecting a risk, that risk must not be material. But pricing does not always capture operational vulnerabilities. Supply chains, especially when stable, are based on valuation models. ARMOR-CAP brings them forward.

Ignoring supply chain resilience is not simply an oversight; it is a mispricing of dependency. ARMOR-CAP makes the hidden visible by interrogating what sits beneath value creation. When value depends on frictionless flow, any disruption—natural, political, or digital—becomes a shock amplifier. Resilience isn't a bonus feature; it's a precondition for continuity.

Table 3.2 outlines five major forms of supply chain exposure that are frequently overlooked in institutional portfolios. Each type of exposure reflects a different mode by which operational continuity may be compromised, not through market volatility but through real-world frictions in logistics, technology, or resource flows. These exposures are often backgrounded in traditional financial analysis because they do not always manifest as pricing signals until stress materializes. ARMOR-CAP

Table 3.2. Types of supply chain exposure in institutional portfolio.

Exposure Type	Description	Examples
Single-source dependency	Overreliance on one vendor or input with no substitute	Semiconductor supply from TSMC; single-source rare earths from China
Geographic chokepoint	Physical or geopolitical transit bottlenecks	Suez Canal, Strait of Hormuz, Red Sea shipping lanes
Tier-2 fragility	Supplier-of-a-supplier disruption, not visible to firm	Magnesium shortages in Germany due to upstream Chinese export controls
Digital platform risk	Dependence on cloud, API, or software with no fallback	AWS service outages; vendor-specific ERP systems
Systemic vendor overlap	Many portfolio firms use the same service providers or tech	Shared reliance on Microsoft Azure, Oracle, or SWIFT for transactions

Note: This table categorizes the most common types of supply chain fragility, from single-source inputs to digital dependencies, that can compromise portfolio resilience. ARMOR-CAP identifies these vulnerabilities as latent amplifiers of systemic risk.

corrects this by treating supply chain architecture as a first-order input to risk assessment.

1. Single-source dependency refers to concentrated reliance on a sole vendor, supplier, or critical input, with no available substitute. While such relationships may appear efficient under stable conditions, they can become catastrophic bottlenecks during disruption. Examples include dependence on TSMC for semiconductors or rare earth imports from China, both of which represent critical input monopolies for multiple sectors.
2. Geographic chokepoint exposures occur when physical routes, such as canals, straits, or contested borders, serve as single points of failure for global logistics. These chokepoints are vulnerable to blockages from conflict, piracy, weather events, or diplomatic breakdowns. Disruptions in the Suez Canal or Red Sea, for instance, have had far-reaching effects on global shipping and supply timelines.
3. Tier-2 fragility captures risks embedded further upstream in the supply chain, where disruptions do not directly involve a portfolio company's immediate suppliers but affect its suppliers' suppliers. These

latent exposures are more complex to map but potentially more destabilizing. An illustrative case is the magnesium shortage in Germany, caused by export controls in China and an upstream vulnerability that rippled through European manufacturing.

4. Digital platform risks arise when companies rely heavily on proprietary software, cloud infrastructure, or API-based services that lack redundancy or fallbacks. Because these platforms often centralize essential business operations (e.g., Enterprise Resource Planning (ERP) systems, transaction processing, and customer interface), any outage or breach can suspend core functionality. AWS outages or overreliance on a single vendor's ERP suite exemplify this category.
5. Systemic vendor overlap refers to the concentration of critical service providers or platforms across seemingly diverse portfolio holdings. Even when firms operate in different industries or geographies, shared reliance on vendors such as Microsoft Azure, Oracle, or SWIFT can create correlated operational risks. This overlap creates a fragility layer invisible to asset-level analysis but highly relevant at the portfolio level.

Together, these exposure types underscore the need to move beyond surface-level diversification toward a more infrastructural view of risk. ARMOR-CAP surfaces these hidden dependencies to inform capital allocation under real-world stress conditions.

3.4 Operational Continuity

The final pillar of the ARMOR-CAP framework, operational continuity, addresses a simple yet critical question: Can an entity continue to function when disrupted? While sovereign compatibility focuses on external alignment, supply chain resilience examines embedded dependencies, and operational continuity centers on internal readiness (i.e., the firm's capacity to deliver its product or service amid shock).

This pillar is intentionally agnostic to the source of disruption. The threat might be a cyberattack, a utility failure, a labor strike, a regulatory audit, a pandemic, or a sudden change in jurisdictional law. What matters is not how the disruption begins but whether the firm can maintain control over its production, fulfillment, communication, and compliance without interruption.

For many institutional investors, this dimension of risk remains invisible because it does not appear in earnings guidance or standard financial statements. However, failures in continuity often come before visible causes such as financial collapse. The ransomware attack on Colonial Pipeline in 2021 forced the company to shut down its 5,500-mile pipeline after its billing and accounting systems were compromised, causing widespread fuel shortages and market disruption across the U.S. East Coast. Maersk, the world's largest shipping company, suffered nearly $300 million in losses after its global IT infrastructure was paralyzed by the NotPetya malware in 2017. In both cases, the firms were not overleveraged or mismanaged; they were unprepared for operational paralysis.

Operational continuity is particularly fragile in digitized environments. As more business functions become cloud-hosted, API-dependent, and automated, even short service outages can cascade into days of lost productivity. A payment processor lacking a manual fallback, a legal department unable to access encrypted files, or a logistics chain unable to reroute around a single broken node creates risk not due to financial weakness but to operational inflexibility.

ARMOR-CAP treats operational continuity as a diagnostic domain. It asks the following questions:

- Does the firm maintain functional backups for critical systems and infrastructure?
- Are there regionally redundant data centers or legal entities prepared to take over operations?
- Can the firm comply with new regulatory conditions (e.g., localization laws) without breaking continuity?
- Are there escalation paths and playbooks in place for managing geopolitical, cyber, or physical disruptions?

This pillar also applies at the portfolio level. A portfolio heavily weighted in capital-light digital firms may appear low-risk from a balance sheet perspective. Still, operational continuity is a shared point of failure if all holdings depend on the same cloud service or content delivery network. Similarly, firms with operations in different countries may all be exposed to similar fragilities if they outsource compliance or payroll to the same vendor.

What distinguishes ARMOR-CAP's view is that it does not treat continuity as a static checklist. It understands that the meaning of "business as usual" changes with political alignment, environmental volatility, and regulatory adaptations. Firms that are operationally robust under one legal regime may be dysfunctional under another. Those that cannot adapt organizationally or technologically quickly pose a hidden drag on portfolio resilience.

This need for organizational adaptability echoes insights drawn from military operations. As explored in the *strategic discipline* framework (Fabozzi & Stenholm, 2025), elite military units build resilience through decentralized decision-making, stress-tested routines, and cultural alignment. The Observe, Orient, Decide, Act (OODA) loop, used widely in both combat and crisis leadership, offers a model for continuous recalibration under uncertainty. Financial institutions have quietly adopted similar thinking. As noted in Chapter 1, JPMorgan's CEO Jamie Dimon has publicly referenced OODA-based decision cycles in his shareholder letters, emphasizing the importance of speed and flexibility in volatile environments.

ARMOR-CAP treats operational continuity in the same spirit. It's not enough to install digital backups or redundancy protocols. Investors must evaluate whether the organization itself can execute rapidly, improvise under stress, and maintain continuity without perfect information. Just as military teams rehearse scenarios, conduct after-action reviews, and prioritize "commander's intent" over rigid procedures, firms aligned with ARMOR-CAP must develop institutional reflexes beyond compliance and be operationally battle-ready.

Where ESG looks for governance procedures and enterprise risk management maps internal control processes, ARMOR-CAP probes whether operations can survive a meaningful disruption outside of the system. If a firm must operate perfectly to deliver value, then the value itself is fragile. Continuity cannot be assumed; it must be proven.

Operational continuity is not merely a firm-level concern. It can propagate silently across an entire portfolio through shared systems, legal environments, or vendor dependencies. Table 3.3 outlines five critical domains where continuity can fail: digital infrastructure, regulatory adaptability, crisis planning, substitutability of key functions, and portfolio-level concentration. For each domain, ARMOR-CAP poses a core diagnostic question that reframes risk from traditional performance metrics to survivability under stress. These questions are designed not only to evaluate

Table 3.3. Operational continuity under disruption: Key questions for ARMOR-CAP assessment.

Continuity Domain	Key Diagnostic Question	Example of Fragility
Digital infrastructure	Are mission-critical systems regionally redundant and recoverable?	Firm locked out of cloud-based systems due to cyberattack
Legal & regulatory readiness	Can operations adapt if laws shift suddenly (e.g., data, IP, export)?	Operations halted due to failure to meet new localization rules
Crisis playbooks	Are there clear contingency plans for geopolitical, cyber, or physical shocks?	Firm improvises during disruption, leading to reputational damage
Functional substitutability	Can alternate systems or vendors be deployed quickly?	Payment halted due to single-vendor failure with no fallback
Portfolio concentration	Do multiple holdings share a common continuity risk?	Several holdings rely on the same third-party SaaS platform

Note: This table highlights how operational continuity risk can remain hidden until it triggers portfolio-wide consequences. What may seem manageable at the firm level can cascade when multiple holdings depend on the same fragile infrastructure, vendor, or jurisdiction. ARMOR-CAP addresses this exposure by evaluating whether companies and portfolios are structurally prepared to withstand disruption, not merely financially resilient but operationally viable. It emphasizes preparedness, flexibility, and adaptability as essential conditions for sustaining capital in environments where continuity cannot be assumed.

preparedness but also to expose structural fragilities that might remain dormant until triggered by disruption. The examples provided illustrate how even well-capitalized or diversified portfolios can become brittle when continuity dependencies are overlooked or overly centralized.

3.5 From Pillars to Practice: Activating the ARMOR-CAP Framework

The three pillars of ARMOR-CAP—sovereign compatibility, supply chain resilience, and operational continuity—offer more than just conceptual clarity. They provide a structured lens through which fragility can be identified, evaluated, and managed before it threatens capital. However, their value depends on translation into investment practices.

In the chapters ahead, the framework moves from theory to application. We will explore how ARMOR-CAP can be used to construct diagnostic screens, inform asset allocation decisions, shape due diligence processes, and align with regulatory or fiduciary requirements. The goal is not to replace existing risk tools but to complement them by addressing what they often omit: the real-world conditions that make returns possible in the first place.

Chapter 4 begins this shift by laying out the ARMOR-CAP diagnostic toolkit. It shows how institutional investors can use these pillars to filter asset classes, evaluate strategic exposures, and develop comparative scoring approaches. Just as credit risk was formalized through ratings and models, the next frontier is to formalize resilience. However, this should not be done as a story but as a system.

Capital that endures does not merely seek returns; it anticipates ruptures. And it does so with structure. Table 3.4 bridges the conceptual and the operational, showing how each diagnostic pillar of ARMOR-CAP is not an endpoint but a precursor to tangible investment actions. The framework begins as a lens to identify hidden risks—jurisdictional, infrastructural, or operational—but it culminates in a set of tools to manage them. Whether through exclusion screens, reweighting rules, stress tests, or scenario dashboards, each pillar maps directly onto a category of

Table 3.4. From diagnostic pillars to deployment toolkit.

ARMOR-CAP Pillar	Diagnostic Focus	Next-Step Application (Chapter 4)
Sovereign compatibility	Legal, jurisdictional, and regulatory exposure	Exclusion screens, reweighting rules, legal-risk overlays
Supply chain resilience	Functional and geographic input dependencies	Sector tilts, contingency scoring, diversification audits
Operational continuity	Internal readiness and fallback infrastructure	Stress-testing for continuity, system redundancy scoring
Composite fragility mapping	Cross-pillar correlations and feedback loops	Integrated risk dashboards, scenario modeling tools

Note: This table previews how the ARMOR-CAP framework moves from diagnostic insights to practical implementation. Each pillar identifies a distinct category of structural risk and connects directly to an actionable pathway, such as screening, reweighting, or stress-testing. This table sets the stage for the deployment tools introduced in Chapter 4, showing how ARMOR-CAP evolves from an analytical lens to an operational toolkit.

implementation techniques. This translation from diagnosis to deployment sets the stage for Chapter 4, where these tools are formalized and embedded into portfolio construction practices.

3.6 Interactions Between the Pillars: Diagnosing Composite Fragility

The three pillars of ARMOR-CAP—sovereign compatibility, supply chain resilience, and operational continuity—are presented separately for clarity, but they rarely operate in isolation. Fragility is often layered, and its most dangerous manifestations occur when weaknesses in one domain amplify or mask vulnerabilities in another. Diagnosing such composite fragility is critical to building truly resilient capital strategies.

Consider a logistics firm operating through a centralized platform built on U.S.-based cloud infrastructure, facilities in politically unstable regions, and contractual dependencies on international counterparties. The firm may appear operationally robust on paper: It has redundancy plans, a diversified customer base, and positive cash flow. But look more closely: Its digital layer is jurisdictionally vulnerable to export restrictions (sovereign compatibility); its warehousing relies on just-in-time replenishment from a single port (supply chain fragility); and its platform has no functional offline fallback (operational continuity risk). The firm passes traditional financial risk screening, but under ARMOR-CAP, it is flagged as having convergent fragility across all three pillars.

This kind of cross-pillar exposure is dangerous precisely because it isn't visible through conventional risk silos. A supply chain disruption may not trigger concern until it intersects with a jurisdictional chokehold or a software-based continuity failure. And once one pillar collapses, the others often follow. A cyberattack that compromises data integrity may lead to regulatory violations that activate sovereign penalties, resulting in the loss of access to infrastructure or legal protections.

ARMOR-CAP treats these interdependencies as diagnostic signals. A key objective of the framework is to help allocators and analysts screen for individual risks and identify patterns of systemic entanglement, which might be called "fragility clustering." These clusters can exist at the firm level (e.g., a tech startup that relies on a foreign cloud provider and offshore coders) or at the portfolio level (e.g., multiple holdings that depend on the same content delivery network or legal arbitration treaty).

To support this, the following chapter introduces tools for scoring and screening composite fragility. Users can assess not only whether a firm has sovereign, supply chain, or operational risks but also how tightly coupled those risks are and how quickly they might propagate under stress. The result is not just a diagnostic snapshot but an early warning system.

In financial terms, fragility compounds. But unlike financial compounding, which is positive, fragility compounding accelerates failure. ARMOR-CAP breaks the cycle by mapping individual weak spots and how they connect. That way, it's possible to spot trouble before it spreads and to steer capital toward setups that are more likely to hold up when things get tough.

Fragility rarely confines itself to a single category of risk. A disruption in one domain, whether legal, logistical, or technical, often sets off chain reactions across others. Table 3.5 captures this dynamic by mapping how risks within the three core ARMOR-CAP pillars (sovereign compatibility, supply chain resilience, and operational continuity) can reinforce or accelerate one another when left unchecked. For example, a new export control regime (sovereign risk) can block key inputs (supply chain risk), which,

Table 3.5. Composite fragility: Cross-pillar risk amplification.

Primary Fragility Source	Amplifies Risk in Sovereign Compatibility	Amplifies Risk in Supply Chain Resilience	Amplifies Risk in Operational Continuity
Sovereign compatibility	—	Export controls, data nationalism hinder flow	Legal sanctions block platform or cloud access
Supply chain resilience	Relocation causes exposure to unstable jurisdictions	Regional chokepoints introduce systemic stress	Failure of logistics impairs service operations
Operational continuity	Downtime violates foreign compliance standards	Lost functionality disrupts supply coordination	—

Note: This table illustrates how fragility in one domain—sovereign, supply chain, or operational—can trigger or intensify vulnerabilities in the others. Fragility is rarely isolated; it propagates across systems. This table emphasizes the importance of detecting these interconnections early to prevent localized disruptions from escalating into systemic crises.

in turn, can halt digital operations dependent on those inputs (operational risk). These interdependencies are often underestimated in traditional risk models because they emerge only under stress, yet they are precisely what turn isolated fragilities into systemic failures. By diagnosing these connections early, ARMOR-CAP enables capital allocators to act before vulnerabilities compound into crises.

3.7 The Illusion of Robustness: When Traditional Metrics Mask Fragility

For decades, institutional capital has relied on a familiar set of metrics to assess portfolio quality: Sharpe ratios, volatility bands, beta, tracking error, correlation matrices, and, increasingly, ESG scores. These tools serve valuable functions. They quantify relative returns, risk-adjusted performance, diversification, and alignment with stakeholder principles. But they share one critical limitation: They are backward-looking, behaviorally contingent, and structurally blind.

These metrics measure how assets behave under historical or normal market conditions. They do not measure whether those assets or the systems they rely on can continue functioning under stress. A firm with a low beta or stable earnings may depend entirely on a vulnerable digital infrastructure, an adversarial legal regime, or a fragile logistics network. But those dependencies are not priced into its volatility or Sharpe ratio. Nor are they reflected in correlation tables or ESG scores that rely on self-disclosed governance metrics rather than third-party system mappings.

This disconnect creates the illusion of robustness. Assets appear diversified because their historical price movements have not been correlated. Portfolios seem low-risk because standard deviation, a common risk metric, remains low. However, if all those assets depend on the same sovereign platform, legal framework, or delivery infrastructure, their real-world behavior may suddenly synchronize under stress. In such cases, fragility does not stem from a failure of modeling per se but from a failure in the scope of what is modeled. This is a point emphasized by Taleb (2007).

A particularly telling example arises in high-quality sovereign debt portfolios. Bonds from developed countries are often characterized by low volatility and deep secondary markets, making them cornerstones of conservative allocations. However, when geopolitical events occur (e.g., sanctions, capital controls, or defaults triggered by external governance conflicts), these bonds can become inaccessible, unpayable, or subject to legal disputes. The true risk is not merely volatility, but the fragility of legal infrastructures governing access to international liquidity and the structural vulnerabilities inherent in an unequal and sometimes unstable international order. This fragility has been highlighted in recent waves of sovereign defaults and restructurings, which have led to litigation over the validity and enforceability of bond provisions.

Similar illusions exist in ESG. Companies with high scores on transparency or emissions may still source inputs from contested regions, rely on opaque subcontractors, or store data in jurisdictions with surveillance risk. ESG frameworks are often too focused on intentions and disclosures, not on dependencies and continuity. ARMOR-CAP accepts ESG, complementing it by treating resilience as a precondition for sustainability.

Even quantitative risk systems that incorporate stress testing rarely include non-financial disruption scenarios. They model rate shocks, equity drawdowns, and inflation spikes. However, they seldom model what happens if an asset becomes operationally inaccessible due to a legal injunction, digital takedown, cyber incident, or regulatory ban. The assumption is that the market will reprice the asset. ARMOR-CAP challenges that assumption by asking: What if the market cannot access the asset to reprice it?

The illusion of robustness persists because traditional metrics are elegant, consistent, and testable. But that consistency stems from simplifying assumptions that no longer hold in a fractured, interdependent world. What investors need now is not simply more data but a new lens. ARMOR-CAP provides that lens by measuring structural conditions, not just statistical behavior.

Table 3.6 contrasts traditional risk metrics with the diagnostic tools offered by ARMOR-CAP, highlighting how the framework supplements market-based analysis with structural screening. Conventional measures such as the Sharpe ratio, beta, and tracking error are built on historical return behavior and assume continuity of legal, operational, and geopolitical systems. These metrics perform well under stable conditions but tend to obscure risks that arise only during disruption when enforceability, infrastructure, or political alignment falters. ARMOR-CAP does not replace these tools but adds a structural layer, enabling allocators to detect invisible fragility in backward-looking models. For example, a portfolio may show low tracking error but still be vulnerable to systemic failure if its holdings rely on the same

Table 3.6. Traditional metrics vs. ARMOR-CAP diagnostics.

Traditional Risk Metric	What It Measures	What It Misses	ARMOR-CAP Diagnostic
Sharpe ratio	Return per unit of volatility	Legal access, infrastructure reliability, continuity of operations	Operational continuity screening
Beta	Asset's movement relative to a benchmark	Fragile sovereign exposure, asymmetrical legal jurisdictions	Sovereign compatibility assessment
Tracking error	Active deviation from index	Shared operational dependencies across holdings	Portfolio-wide systemic fragility checks
Correlation matrix	Co-movement of asset returns	Common vendors, platforms, or regulatory corridors masked by diverse returns	Composite fragility screening
ESG rating (standard)	Disclosed environmental, social and governance scores	Supply chain opacity, resilience under stress, jurisdictional viability	Supply chain resilience + sovereign mapping

Note: This table compares traditional financial metrics with the structural diagnostics introduced by ARMOR-CAP. Conventional tools focus on return behavior under normal market conditions but overlook systemic fragilities that emerge only under stress. ARMOR-CAP complements these tools by screening for hidden infrastructure, sovereignty, and operational continuity exposures.

cloud provider, legal regime, or cross-border chokepoint. By embedding diagnostics such as sovereign compatibility assessments and composite fragility screenings, ARMOR-CAP transforms conventional risk reporting into a forward-looking, resilience-informed process.

The following chapter introduces the tools needed to apply that lens in practice.

3.8. Codifying Resilience: Where the Pillars Lead

The three diagnostic pillars of ARMOR-CAP (sovereign compatibility, supply chain resilience, and operational continuity) are not meant to sit in isolation. They form an integrated design logic that redefines what it means for capital to be "resilient." These pillars serve as lenses that convert fragility from a vague notion into a practical, structured, and testable condition. They do not replace existing portfolio tools, but they reveal what those tools systematically miss.

Traditionally, investors relied on proxies (e.g., volatility, tracking error, and Sharpe ratios) to infer how capital might behave in different environments. These metrics remain useful but insufficient. They are agnostic to whether the underlying system still functions. ARMOR-CAP does not dismiss those models; it challenges their boundaries. It asks: What if the trading venue closes? What if a supplier is embargoed? What if a legal judgment is unenforceable? These are not tail events. They are system dependencies that, when surfaced, become measurable.

By codifying these questions into a repeatable framework, ARMOR-CAP enables portfolio designers to run "viability checks" in parallel with optimization routines. The framework enables structural diagnostics to be conducted before capital is deployed, rather than reverse-engineering fragility after it has been priced in. This represents a foundational shift from reactive hedging to preemptive design.

What begins as a set of pillars will now evolve into a functional toolkit. Chapter 4 introduces the next stage of ARMOR-CAP—how to transform these diagnostics into screens, scoring systems, dashboards, and strategic overlays. This is where structure becomes action.

Table 3.7 marks the transition from ARMOR-CAP's conceptual structure to its applied functionality. Each pillar (i.e., sovereign compatibility, supply chain resilience, and operational continuity) is mapped to a diagnostic focus and linked to a corresponding deployment toolset. These tools range from jurisdictional screens and legal overlays to supply chain audits, digital continuity dashboards, and fragility heat maps. The table illustrates how the ARMOR-CAP framework evolves from a theoretical lens into a practical system for identifying, scoring, and mitigating structural vulnerabilities across a portfolio. It sets the stage for Chapter 4, which details how these tools can be integrated into investment workflows, portfolio monitoring, and strategic asset allocation.

3.9 From Framework to Function

ARMOR-CAP now has structure. Its three pillars (i.e., sovereign compatibility, supply chain resilience, and operational continuity) do more than organize diagnostics; they introduce a new lens for portfolio design rooted

Table 3.7. From pillars to deployment: The ARMOR-CAP flow.

ARMOR-CAP Pillar	Diagnostic Focus	Deployment Tool
Sovereign compatibility	Legal regimes, access rights, regulatory exposure	Jurisdictional screens, legal fallback mapping, treaty overlays
Supply chain resilience	Input dependency, chokepoints, geographic concentration	Supplier audits, logistics alternatives, critical vendor tracking
Operational continuity	Internal systems, digital platforms, fallback readiness	Stress-testing routines, continuity dashboards, portability scoring
Composite fragility view	Cross-pillar amplification, failure cascades	Multi-factor scoring, scenario modeling, fragility heat maps

Note: This table illustrates the transition from the ARMOR-CAP framework to actionable deployment tools. Each pillar links to specific diagnostics and implementation mechanisms, including screens, audits, dashboards, and scoring models. This table transforms structural insights into strategy, enabling preemptive risk identification and operational resilience.

in structural durability. But a framework alone is not enough. The next step is application.

Chapter 4 shifts from design to execution by introducing the ARMOR-CAP toolkit. This includes diagnostic screens, fragility scoring models, scenario walkthroughs, and deployment overlays across asset classes and mandates for real-world use. These tools are not theoretical. They are built to fit how capital is allocated in investment committees, model portfolios, enterprise dashboards, and cross-border strategies.

ARMOR-CAP enables a shift from narrative claims of resilience to measurable indicators, from informal judgments to structured diagnostics, and from intuition to instrumentation. In a world where fragility is increasingly systemic, the ability to screen for structural durability in advance is no longer optional. It is a necessary condition for sound capital deployment.

3.10 Summary and Transition

This chapter developed the structural foundation of ARMOR-CAP by detailing its three diagnostic pillars and revealing how they interact to surface unpriced, system-level fragility. Together, these principles shift risk analysis from reactive to preemptive and from statistically modeled to structurally grounded. The five strategic takeaways are as follows:

- **A**nalyze capital through structural exposure, not just market behavior. Traditional risk tools focus on how assets have behaved. ARMOR-CAP starts by asking what those assets depend on to function and whether those conditions will hold.
- **R**ethink diversification beyond asset classes.
  Portfolios can appear diverse but share concentrated exposure to legal regimes, logistics systems, or digital infrastructure. Real diversification must include systemic dependencies.
- **M**ap composite fragility across domains.
  Risks are not isolated. Sovereign, supply chain, and operational vulnerabilities often intersect and amplify. Diagnosing these interactions helps prevent hidden correlations from turning into a shared collapse.
- **O**vercome the illusion of robustness.
  Metrics such as Sharpe ratios and beta offer clean narratives. But they often mask deeper fragility, mainly when based on normal-period data. ARMOR-CAP surfaces what those models miss.
- **R**eplace fragmented risk silos with an integrated diagnostic lens.
  ESG, enterprise risk, and portfolio theory each offer partial views. ARMOR-CAP unifies them by treating resilience not as a specialty function but as a frontline capital criterion.

Chapter 4

From Framework to Function: The ARMOR-CAP Diagnostic Toolkit

Strategic Priorities of This Chapter

The previous chapter introduced the structural foundations of the ARMOR-CAP framework: diagnosing fragility through three core pillars: sovereign compatibility, supply chain resilience, and operational continuity. This chapter shifts from structural insights to practical instrumentation. If ARMOR-CAP can help investors recognize fragility, the next question is how such recognition might be translated into governance processes, allocation decisions, and day-to-day portfolio oversight.

The goal is not to assert adoption but to demonstrate how such a framework *could* operate. The tools introduced (screens, scoring systems, and diagnostic overlays) are proposed to complement existing risk models, filling gaps that conventional approaches often leave unexamined. These strategic priorities outline how institutional investors might build structural awareness into their investment practices.

The discussion unfolds across five applied themes:

- **A — Activate the diagnostic logic of ARMOR-CAP using scalable and repeatable tools.**
  This chapter proposes a set of pre-trade screens, scoring rubrics, and diagnostic overlays that institutions could use to surface structural fragility before it becomes financially visible.

- **R — Replace fragility blind spots with structural visibility through targeted screens.**
  Traditional risk models often miss vulnerabilities rooted in legal enforceability, supply dependencies, or operational chokepoints. ARMOR-CAP screens are designed to expose these gaps as a first filter.
- **M — Measure vulnerability using composite scoring systems that map dependencies across jurisdictions, supply chains, and operational functions.**
  Institutions could implement scoring methods that quantify exposure to fragility over time rather than solely relying on backward-looking risk metrics.
- **O — Operate across asset classes by tailoring diagnostics to portfolio type, geography, and institutional mandates.**
  ARMOR-CAP is a modular toolkit that can be adapted to various use cases, from sovereign debt portfolios to multi-asset strategies, without requiring a single unified model.
- **R — Realign existing risk oversight by integrating ARMOR-CAP diagnostics into governance and review structures.**
  As proposed, dashboards and overlays surface structural risks in formats suitable for chief investment officers (CIOs), risk committees, and boards, linking diagnostics to oversight and accountability.

4.1 Overview of the Toolkit and Its Role in Practice

Chapter 3 introduced the diagnostic pillars of ARMOR-CAP (i.e., sovereign compatibility, supply chain resilience, and operational continuity). This chapter advances from structure to function by translating those pillars into operational tools that can be embedded in pre-trade decisions, ongoing monitoring, and strategic oversight.

These tools do not replace traditional models or ESG screens. Rather, they intervene earlier by screening for structural viability before applying metrics such as volatility, Sharpe ratio, or factor exposures. This diagnostic layer assesses whether the systems supporting an investment can withstand periods of stress.

The toolkit includes qualitative and quantitative components: jurisdictional screens to flag legal asymmetries, supplier maps to reveal chokepoints, continuity dashboards to simulate stress responses, and fragility scores to benchmark and budget structural risk. These are not crisis tools; they are designed for routine deployment.

Like contingency planning in military and public health settings, ARMOR-CAP assumes disruption is normal and builds tools around survivability, not ideal conditions. It focuses on whether investments can function when legal access, infrastructure, or digital systems come under pressure.

The tools are modular and adaptable by asset class, portfolio type, or governance layer. They support gatekeeping (screens), comparison (scores), and response (dashboards and overlays). When used together, they align institutional objectives ("ends") with methods and capacity ("ways" and "means"), making resilience not merely an aspiration but a deployable strategy.

Table 4.1 outlines the key tools in the ARMOR-CAP toolkit and how they map distinct phases in the capital deployment process. Each tool corresponds to a different decision-making juncture, from pre-trade screening to ongoing monitoring. These tools are not reactive measures for emerging risks; they function as structural filters that identify vulnerabilities before they can translate into financial losses:

- *Viability screens* are applied during mandate design or pre-trade evaluations, acting as yes-or-no filters to block investments that depend on weak infrastructure, disputed platforms, or single vendors.
- The *sovereign dependency audit* is a legal and jurisdictional map identifying exposure to misaligned regulatory regimes or weak enforceability. It is deployable before and after positions are initiated, and it flags inconsistencies between jurisdictional norms and investor protections.
- The *fragility scoring rubric* converts qualitative and structural fragility indicators into numeric scores. It operates on the portfolio review cycle, allowing allocators to compare exposures across holdings and flag concentrations of unpriced structural risks.
- The *continuity dashboard* tracks dynamic stress signals from legal, digital, and supply-side systems. It provides an operational overlay for asset allocation teams and board-level stakeholders, supporting tactical shifts and resilience disclosures.

These tools transform ARMOR-CAP from a diagnostic framework into an implementable risk architecture. They offer institutions a way to align structural integrity with capital strategy at every stage of the allocation lifecycle.

Table 4.1. The role of ARMOR-CAP tools in capital deployment.

Tool Type	Function	Timing	Outcome
Viability screens	Yes/No gating logic for infrastructure exposure	Pre-trade/mandate design	Blocks exposures with fragile systemic dependencies
Sovereign dependency audit	Maps legal regime risks and access asymmetries	Pre- and post-trade	Flags alignment gaps across jurisdictions
Fragility scoring rubric	Quantifies exposure to composite structural risks	Portfolio review cycle	Generates ARMOR-CAP scores and heat maps
Continuity dashboard	Monitors real-time stress on legal, digital, and supply systems	Operational monitoring	Informs asset allocation and board-level reporting

Note: This table outlines how ARMOR-CAP tools integrate into different stages of the capital deployment process. Each tool is mapped to a specific function, from screening fragile exposures before investment to monitoring continuity risks during portfolio operations. Together, they enable institutions to identify and manage structural vulnerabilities before they lead to financial losses.

4.2 Screens as Gatekeepers of Fragility

Conventional dashboards monitor performance after capital is allocated. ARMOR-CAP screens intervene earlier, filtering out exposures that carry structural risk before they enter the portfolio. These tools are diagnostic, not predictive. They do not forecast price behavior; they flag underlying infrastructure, legal, and supply chain setups that may fail under stress. The central question they help answer is not how an asset might perform but whether it should be held at all.

These are not environmental, social, and governance (ESG) screens. They are not value filters or compliance tests. They do not assess corporate policies. They interrogate operational systems. If a company relies on one country's cloud infrastructure, another's shipping corridors, and a third's legal framework, the screen does not ask what the ESG rating says. It asks what happens if all three jurisdictions become contested or constrained.

The ARMOR-CAP framework proposes viability checks that assess legal enforceability, infrastructure access, vendor concentration, and chokepoint exposure. These screens are designed for use during mandate design or as a pre-trade overlay, filtering structural risks before capital is committed. They can also be applied retrospectively to help explain portfolio breakdowns during non-financial stress events that conventional risk models may overlook.

These screens would act as structural gatekeepers—yes-or-no filters that assess whether an asset's foundation is compatible with resilient capital deployment. The screen does not weigh tradeoffs if the legal regime is misaligned, the infrastructure is unreliable, or vendor dependency is extreme. It flags the position as structurally nonviable. Not "risky." Not "underpriced." *Nonviable*.

Structural viability screens are designed to be modular and can be tailored to different asset types or mandate structures. For example, a sovereign bond strategy might be screened for jurisdictional asymmetry, flagging situations where legal recourse depends on courts exposed to political interference or cross-border disputes. Infrastructure equity portfolios could be screened for single-node failure risk, such as dependence on a sole supplier, cloud host, or government partner. In corporate credit, screens might surface operational fragility resulting from reliance on sanctioned trade corridors, data storage subject to foreign control, or export restrictions.

These screens do not generate scores. They generate binary outcomes: A position either passes the structural viability test or it does not. This binary logic is deliberate. It reassigns the burden of proof. Risk teams must argue why a position is too dangerous within traditional workflows. Under the ARMOR-CAP proposal, the burden shifts. An asset must demonstrate its structural viability before allocating capital.

While pre-trade structural audits are not yet standard practice, there is growing interest in approaches that resemble elements of the ARMOR-CAP framework. Some development-oriented finance institutions, for instance, now conduct legal-regime simulations before allocating capital to high-friction jurisdictions (OECD, 2022). Similarly, certain infrastructure investors have begun incorporating security audits into project evaluation workflows. These developments suggest a broader shift: Resilience is increasingly seen not merely as a narrative but as a structural, testable condition that can inform capital deployment.

Table 4.2 outlines a proposed approach for assessing the structural resilience of capital positions. Each row highlights a different category of exposure that could compromise operational continuity or legal enforceability under stress. The table pairs a diagnostic question with a sample pass/fail threshold for each exposure type, providing a template for applying viability screens within an allocation workflow.

Table 4.2. ARMOR-CAP structural viability screens by risk type.

Exposure Type	Diagnostic Question	Pass/Fail Threshold Example
Legal regime	Can legal rights be enforced under stress or cross-border blockage?	Must have dual enforcement mechanism or treaty fallback
Operational infrastructure	Can core systems be migrated or reactivated in alternative environments?	Cloud redundancy or digital sovereignty strategy
Supply chain chokepoints	Can the firm source key inputs from alternative suppliers or regions?	At least one backup supply chain node in secure region
Sovereign alignment	Is the firm's operational footprint aligned with friendly jurisdictions?	<20% exposure to contested jurisdictions
Vendor concentration	Can operations continue if a key vendor fails or is sanctioned?	Plan B system documented and tested

Note: This table summarizes the ARMOR-CAP structural viability screens, each serving as a pass/fail checkpoint for key risk exposures—legal, operational, supply chain, sovereign, and vendor. These screens ensure that only investments with robust, stress-tested safeguards advance in capital allocation.

The five exposure types covered are as follows:

- *Legal regime*: This question asks whether legal rights can be enforced during periods of stress or in the face of cross-border restrictions. Passing the screen requires safeguards such as dual enforcement mechanisms or treaty-based fallback options.
- *Operational infrastructure*: This area focuses on whether core systems can be migrated or reactivated in alternative environments. A passing threshold might involve cloud redundancy or a digital sovereignty strategy.
- *Supply chain chokepoints*: Evaluates whether the firm can source critical inputs from alternative suppliers or regions in case of disruption. There should be at least one secure backup supply chain node through which to pass.
- *Sovereign alignment*: Assesses whether the firm's operational footprint aligns with politically stable, cooperative jurisdictions. A common threshold is having less than 20% exposure to high-risk or contested regions.

- *Vendor concentration*: Examines the firm's ability to maintain operations if a key vendor fails or is sanctioned. Passing requires a documented and tested contingency plan for vendor failures.

These proposed screens function collectively as gating conditions, designed to ensure that only positions with demonstrable structural resilience are considered viable for capital allocation under known stress scenarios.

4.3 Scoring and Heat Maps: Quantifying Fragility Across Holdings

Screens offer a binary safeguard: An asset either passes or fails a viability threshold. But not all structural risks are binary. Some exposures do not guarantee outright exclusion but still raise concerns. That's where ARMOR-CAP scoring comes in: as a tool for grading capital positions based on how tightly coupled their legal, operational, and supply structures are and how likely those couplings are to fail under stress.

Scoring is designed to complement traditional portfolio analytics. While conventional systems track volatility, beta, and correlation, ARMOR-CAP scoring maps the risk of functional failure, where an asset may remain priced. Still, it becomes non-operational or irrecoverable in a crisis. This is not a substitute for value-at-risk or scenario analysis. It's a structural overlay that captures fragility long before it materializes in price data.

The scoring rubric assigns exposure levels across the pillars of sovereign compatibility, supply chain resilience, and operational continuity. Each dimension is evaluated using a defined set of stressors, such as legal enforceability failures, infrastructure chokepoints, and vendor dependencies. Scores can be applied at the asset, fund, or portfolio level, depending on the scope of the analysis. Table 4.3 provides a sample rubric.

These composite pillar scores can be modularly constructed from domain-level sub-scores to increase transparency and adaptability further. Table 4.4 illustrates one possible breakdown of these submodules, which supports granular scoring and helps institutions tailor ARMOR-CAP to their asset mix.

Unlike binary screens, fragility scores enable prioritization and triage. A sovereign bond fund might pass all five structural viability screens yet

Table 4.3. Sample fragility scoring rubric across ARMOR-CAP pillars.

Pillar	Exposure Factor	Scoring Criteria	Score Range	Example Threshold
Sovereign compatibility	Legal enforceability	Can legal claims be upheld during cross-border stress or political conflict?	0–3	3 = No enforceable treaty, weak rule of law; 0 = Dual-enforcement fallback present
	Jurisdictional alignment	Alignment of legal and political systems with investor's home jurisdiction	0–3	3 = >40% of exposure in high-risk states; 0 = <5% in low-trust jurisdictions
Supply chain resilience	Geographic concentration	Dependence on specific regions or corridors for essential inputs	0–3	3 = Single-source reliance; 0 = Diversified, secure multi-node sourcing
	Substitutability of inputs	Availability of alternative suppliers or platforms under stress	0–3	3 = No tested alternatives; 0 = Verified and active substitutes
Operational continuity	Digital infrastructure dependence	Exposure to single cloud provider or unregulated tech infrastructure	0–3	3 = No redundancy or portability; 0 = Proven migration protocol
	Contingency planning	Presence of documented and tested operational fallback plans	0–3	3 = No fallback plan; 0 = Plan B tested and board-reviewed

Note: This table presents a proposed scoring rubric for ARMOR-CAP fragility assessments. Each pillar is broken down into key exposure factors, with example criteria and a scoring range that allows institutional teams to quantify structural risk across portfolios.

still register a high fragility score due to clustering in contested legal regimes or shared reliance on politically exposed payment networks. Rather than disqualifying the holding, the score signals the need for further review or the addition of hedging strategies to contain cross-pillar failure risk.

Table 4.4. Modular construction of ARMOR-CAP scores.

Domain	Submodule	Description	Example Inputs
Jurisdictional fragility	Sovereign alignment index	Degree to which the host country aligns with the investor's treaty and rule-of-law network	Bilateral investment treaties, WTO enforcement indexes
	Political and legal stability score	Composite of regime durability and legal system independence	World Bank Governance Indicators, Freedom House scores
	Sanctions and restriction monitor	Presence of sanctions or data restrictions affecting capital flows	OFAC lists, national tech barriers, IMF restrictions
Operational fragility	Vendor concentration risk	Exposure to single or dominant third-party providers	Procurement databases, GRC vendor maps
	Cross-border digital reliance	Dependency on foreign data or cloud providers subject to extraterritorial rules	Cloud service footprints, data sovereignty assessments
	Infrastructure redundancy score	Backup systems and substitutability of core ops (IT, logistics, personnel)	Cyber continuity plans, staffing redundancy, DR testing logs
Legal/ structural fragility	Step-in rights enforceability	Ability to intervene in distressed assets or contracts	Cross-border enforceability reviews, law firm risk memos
	Bankruptcy ring-fencing	Legal separability from sponsor or holding company in stress scenarios	Bankruptcy jurisdiction mapping, asset-level legal audits
	Legal treaty protection status	Degree of legal protection via multilateral or bilateral treaties	ICSID participation, arbitration clauses, MIGA status

Note: This table illustrates how ARMOR-CAP scores are built from three modular domains—jurisdictional, operational, and legal/structural—each composed of interpretable submodules. Institutions can tailor these modules and weights to their mandates, asset mixes, and fragility focus. This table is fictionalized for illustrative purposes. It reflects stylized submodules based on institutions piloting ARMOR-CAP and is not drawn from any specific scoring product.

Heat maps translate fragility scores into visual diagnostics across the portfolio. They surface structural clusters and compound vulnerabilities that might otherwise go unnoticed. A concentration of elevated scores may reveal overreliance on a single vendor ecosystem, an unstable jurisdictional corridor, or fragile digital infrastructure. The objective is not to eliminate all risk but to identify systemic fragility and improve resilience through diversification, substitution, or operational safeguards.

While ARMOR-CAP's scoring and heat mapping tools are conceptual, they are designed for practical deployment. They draw on established practices, such as supply chain audits, sovereign risk modeling, and operational continuity planning, but integrate them into a unified diagnostic lens for capital allocators. The scoring rubric is not static; it evolves in response to geopolitical realignments, legal reforms, and technological shifts. It is intended as a living diagnostic that adapts in parallel with the structures it assesses.

Figure 4.1 illustrates how these scores can be distributed across a sample portfolio, revealing fragility clusters and relative resilience zones. These diagnostic outputs are intended to inform investment teams, risk committees, governance boards, and pre-trade review panels, making structural fragility a visible and quantifiable input to capital strategy.

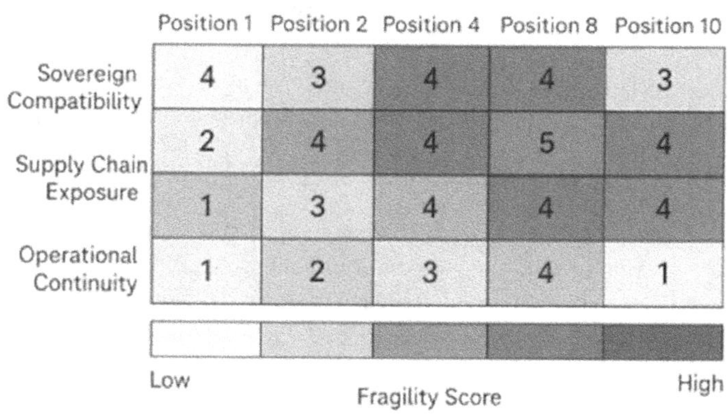

Figure 4.1. Scoring the fragility footprint: Portfolio stress diagnostics.

Note: This figure presents a diagnostic heat map that disaggregates fragility scores across individual portfolio holdings and the three core ARMOR-CAP pillars: sovereign compatibility, supply chain exposure, and operational continuity. Each cell shows a normalized fragility score, with darker shades indicating higher structural vulnerability. This visualization enables comparative triage, identifying both asset-level weaknesses and system-wide concentrations that may remain hidden within traditional financial metrics.

Rather than summarizing fragility scores in aggregate, Figure 4.1 disaggregates them across individual holdings and the three core ARMOR-CAP dimensions: sovereign compatibility, supply chain resilience, and operational continuity. The resulting diagnostic grid enables comparative analysis not only of individual assets but also of the structural pattern embedded in the portfolio.

Each cell in the grid represents a normalized fragility score for a specific holding under a particular dimension. Higher scores (in darker grayscale tones) indicate elevated structural exposure: legal regimes with weak enforceability, chokepoint-dependent supply networks, or critical digital systems without redundancy. Conversely, lighter tones denote resilience: diversified legal protections, substitutable suppliers, and tested continuity plans.

The figure serves two purposes. First, it flags specific positions for immediate review or mitigation, those that register high scores across multiple dimensions or cluster in a single risk domain. Second, it reveals system-level concentrations. A portfolio that appears diversified by geography or sector may, under ARMOR-CAP diagnostics, reveal convergence around a fragile infrastructure platform or contested legal jurisdiction.

Importantly, this scoring visualization does not prescribe action but demands attention. It equips asset managers and oversight committees with a structural lens that complements financial analytics. For example, two positions with similar volatility or Sharpe ratios may carry radically different fragility profiles, which only become visible through a diagnostic tool like this.

The practical value of such a heat map lies in triage and planning. High-score concentrations can trigger deeper due diligence, scenario overlays, or explicit resilience budgeting. They may also inform asset-level decisions, such as adding enforceability clauses, diversifying supply chains, or requiring cloud portability as a condition of continued exposure.

By translating abstract fragility metrics into a comparative visual format, Figure 4.1 makes resilience, often treated as a narrative ideal, a quantifiable capital allocation component.

This diagnostic grid displays normalized fragility scores across a sample portfolio, evaluated against the three ARMOR-CAP pillars: sovereign compatibility, supply chain resilience, and operational continuity. Each cell reflects a score from 0 (resilient) to 3 (fragile), with darker tones indicating higher exposure to structural risk. High-score clusters reveal vulnerability concentrations that may not be apparent in traditional financial metrics. The figure enables comparative triage, helping identify both asset-level weaknesses and system-wide fragility patterns.

These structural concentrations often act as amplifiers during periods of stress, consistent with macro-financial models that describe fragility as an endogenous feature of interconnected systems (Brunnermeier & Sannikov, 2014).

This scoring capability is not merely a monitoring tool but a mechanism for resilience budgeting. Just as institutions manage duration or credit exposure, they can track and control their fragility footprint. ARMOR-CAP proposes making that process measurable, repeatable, and comparable, turning what was once a narrative concern into a quantifiable dimension of portfolio design.

Table 4.5 presents a comparative fragility analysis of two hypothetical portfolios using the ARMOR-CAP scoring rubric. While both portfolios may appear diversified in conventional risk terms, such as sector allocation, geographic spread, or volatility profiles, the structural diagnostics reveal stark differences in their ability to function under stress.

Table 4.5. Comparing portfolio fragility profiles using ARMOR-CAP scores.

Fragility Subcomponent	**Portfolio A: Developed Market Equity**	**Portfolio B: EM Growth Tech**
Jurisdictional alignment	1 – Fully aligned	4 – Partially adversarial
Legal enforceability	1 – Dual treaty fallback	5 – Single regime, contested
Geographic redundancy	2 – Regional alternative in place	5 – Single-source supplier
Chokepoint exposure	2 – Multiple transport routes	5 – Dependent on key corridor
Digital portability	1 – Multi-cloud, tested	4 – Single vendor, limited exit
Continuity planning	2 – Documented and reviewed	5 – Not defined
Composite Fragility Score	**15 (Low Fragility)**	**33 (High Fragility)**

Note: The table illustrates how the ARMOR-CAP framework can surface structural fragility that conventional models typically miss. Traditional analytics emphasize volatility, correlation, and return attribution, but they rarely account for whether capital remains accessible and functional when stress affects legal systems, digital infrastructure, or supply networks. While not yet in use, ARMOR-CAP offers a way to move beyond price-based metrics and begin budgeting for resilience as a quantifiable structural property of portfolio design.

Portfolio A, a developed market equity portfolio, demonstrates high resilience across all six subcomponents. It operates within jurisdictions aligned with the investor's legal norms, has fallback mechanisms for legal enforceability, and maintains diversified infrastructure and vendor setups. Its composite fragility score of 15 reflects low systemic exposure and strong continuity planning.

In contrast, Portfolio B, focused on emerging market (EM) growth technology, exhibits elevated fragility across all dimensions. It is heavily concentrated in legally adversarial jurisdictions, dependent on single-source suppliers, reliant on a single digital infrastructure provider, and lacks defined contingency plans. The resulting composite score of 33 signals a high fragility profile, not necessarily an argument for exclusion but a warning that the portfolio is structurally brittle and may require mitigation strategies.

This table illustrates how ARMOR-CAP diagnostics make visible the operational, legal, and supply chain dependencies that traditional financial risk models overlook. By breaking down fragility into distinct subcomponents, institutional investors can isolate the drivers of structural vulnerability and respond accordingly through diversification, renegotiation of legal terms, improved contingency plans, or capital reallocation.

4.3.1 *Modular construction and customization of scores*

Beyond consolidated fragility profiles, as shown in Table 4.5, institutions may wish to adapt the scoring architecture to their specific mandates, asset types, or operational constraints. ARMOR-CAP's design supports this customization through modular score construction and domain weighting.

Institutions may further customize this structure by:

- adding modules (e.g., ESG governance alignment or cyber-redundancy),
- adjusting domain weights (e.g., increasing legal weight for private debt portfolios),
- embedding modules into preexisting frameworks (e.g., integrating with an internal operational risk scorecard).

For example, a pension plan heavily exposed to infrastructure may prioritize jurisdictional fragility, while a venture capital (VC) fund allocator may emphasize data infrastructure resilience and vendor enforceability clauses. The modular framework allows for this degree of specificity while retaining cross-institutional comparability when desired.

ARMOR-CAP thus provides both structure and flexibility—structure through domain consistency and flexibility through module weighting and tailoring. It turns fragility from a concept into a customizable diagnostic architecture.

4.4 Normalization and Score Calibration

One of the most difficult challenges in institutional fragility diagnostics is ensuring that scores are comparable across asset classes, geographies, and governance systems. A score of 78 in a private equity deal in Southeast Asia should carry a similar signal weight to a score of 78 in a sovereign bond allocation in Eastern Europe, assuming the fragility components are similarly weighted and normalized. Without comparability, fragility signals can lead to misaligned oversight, false prioritization, or tactical overcorrection.

To address this, ARMOR-CAP uses a two-step process to calibrate scores across modules and institutions:

- rescaling raw module values to standardized scores, typically on a 0–100 scale, using *z*-score transformations or quantile bins, depending on the data structure;
- normalizing across domains and asset types, applying institutional weighting schemes, and then mapping to common interpretation bands (e.g., green/yellow/red).

Table 4.6 illustrates how these two steps translate raw inputs into standardized fragility scores and governance bands, offering a transparent scoring pathway from data ingestion to oversight action.

This process ensures that ARMOR-CAP scores remain interpretable and actionable, even when institutions operate under different mandates and data regimes.

Research on score comparability, particularly in credit ratings and ESG scoring, emphasizes that users often conflate score precision with score trustworthiness (Berg, Koelbel & Rigobon, 2022). Standardization does not guarantee accuracy, but it does promote alignment in decision-making. Similarly, Bholat (2015) argue that the real value of risk metrics

Table 4.6. ARMOR-CAP score normalization and interpretation bands.

Step	Description	Output Example
1	Raw input collected (e.g., legal score of 2 on 5-point scale)	Raw score: 2/5
2	Rescale to 0–100 scale using z-score or binning	Standardized: 64.0
3	Weight modules by asset type or mandate	Weighted composite: 72.3
4	Map to fragility band thresholds	Band = Yellow (Review)
5	Assign governance flag	Requires escalation memo

Note: This table outlines how raw submodule inputs are transformed into standardized fragility scores, then aggregated and assigned to institutional interpretation bands used for governance triggers. This table is fictionalized and used solely for illustrative purposes. It reflects typical score-processing logic found in ARMOR-CAP pilot frameworks.

lies in their governance signal, not just in their statistical accuracy. That principle underpins ARMOR-CAP's approach to rescaling: fidelity to consequence over data illusion.

While institutions may ultimately adopt different fragility band thresholds, one plausible illustrative standard is as follows:

- *Green (0–60)*: No action required.
- *Yellow (61–80)*: Review or secondary validation recommended.
- *Red (81–100)*: Escalation required before approval or continued holding.

These bands echo thresholds in operational risk and credit risk models. For example, Solvency II in Europe and NAIC risk-based capital frameworks in the U.S. already map inputs to regulatory triggers, not simply risk labels.

In practice, score normalization has three benefits:

- It reduces false confidence when comparing assets in different jurisdictions.
- It allows governing bodies to track trends over time.
- It supports cross-institutional benchmarking, which can inform board discussions and fiduciary education.

In the future, standardizing the methodologies behind rescaling, not just the outputs, may be crucial for ARMOR-CAP's credibility as a scoring regime. Institutions should maintain documentation and audit trails for each transformation step and periodically backtest interpretation bands against real-world incidents or decision reviews.

4.5 Dashboards and Overlays: Institutionalizing Fragility Monitoring

While viability screens and fragility scores help gate capital deployment and prioritize risk reviews, they become even more effective when embedded into the daily operations of investment institutions. Therefore, the ARMOR-CAP framework proposes a third diagnostic toolset: dashboards and overlays. These are not enterprise software platforms but modular visual layers designed to sit atop existing systems, offering real-time visibility into the structural fragility embedded within portfolios.

Traditional dashboards track performance metrics, style exposures, and compliance indicators. They often miss structural vulnerabilities (i.e., exposure to infrastructure loss, jurisdictional freezes, or system failures that may remain invisible until stress materializes). ARMOR-CAP dashboards are designed to close this gap. They display fragility across three key dimensions: (1) current exposure to the three ARMOR-CAP pillars, (2) changes over time in fragility scores, and (3) simulated stress overlays.

A fragility dashboard is not a forecast. It is a snapshot of structural health. A supply chain heat map might indicate increasing reliance on contested shipping corridors. A digital overlay could show that most firms in a portfolio use the same sovereign-linked cloud provider. A legal stress tracker might flag eroding enforceability in certain jurisdictions. These visuals are not predictions; they are decision aids, helping governance teams ask better questions: Where is fragility accumulating? How fast is it moving? And how exposed are we?

Event overlays go further. They simulate how portfolios would behave under targeted disruptions. What if access to Hong Kong is restricted? What if SWIFT is revoked in a key market? What if the EU enforces complete data localization? These scenarios may sound remote—until they aren't. Russia's seizure of foreign assets and the pandemic's collapse of logistics both demonstrated that fragility often accumulates unnoticed until it snaps.

This emphasis on preemptive visibility aligns with emerging institutional priorities. For example, the World Economic Forum's Resilience

Table 4.7. ARMOR-CAP fragility dashboard and event overlay.

Dashboard View	Example Output	Use Case
Fragility snapshot	Pie chart of fragility sources across holdings	Governance board reporting
Pillar score timeline	Time-series plot of composite fragility over 12 months	Detecting structural drift
Scenario overlay	Shock map: If cloud provider A is lost, 23% of the portfolio is affected	Crisis planning and red-team simulation
Regional heat map	Geographic exposure to contested legal regimes	Allocation rebalancing

Note: This table demonstrates how ARMOR-CAP dashboards and overlays transform diagnostic insights into actionable, real-time tools for institutional risk management. These dashboards provide continuous visibility into structural vulnerabilities across portfolios by integrating features such as snapshots, timelines, and geographic heat maps. Rather than replacing existing systems, ARMOR-CAP overlays enhance them by surfacing hidden fragilities and supporting more informed tactical and strategic decisions.

Consortium has called for new diagnostics that surface systemic exposures beyond conventional risk metrics (World Economic Forum, 2022).

Discussions within the asset owner community suggest increasing interest in visual tools representing non-financial vulnerabilities, particularly those related to legal enforceability, digital dependency, and geopolitical chokepoints. Although ARMOR-CAP has not yet been implemented by any institution, the dashboards I propose within the framework are designed to promote operational transparency and structural risk awareness.

Table 4.7 illustrates a sample layout of an ARMOR-CAP dashboard designed to provide multidimensional visibility into portfolio resilience and operational risk. The dashboard integrates several distinct views (e.g., snapshots, timelines, overlays, and geographic heat maps), each tailored to support specific decision-making contexts:

- *Snapshots*: These offer real-time summaries of key risk indicators, such as current exposure levels, flagged vulnerabilities, and the status of critical controls. Snapshots enable the user to quickly assess their portfolio's overall health and identify areas requiring immediate attention, making them invaluable for daily tactical adjustments.
- *Timelines*: Timelines track the evolution of risk factors and mitigation actions over time. By visualizing trends such as the frequency of supply

chain disruptions or changes in legal risk exposure, users can identify emerging patterns, evaluate the effectiveness of past interventions, and inform ongoing governance discussions. This historical perspective is essential for understanding how risk posture changes in response to both internal decisions and external events.

- *Overlays*: Overlay views allow users to superimpose multiple risk dimensions (e.g., legal, operational, and geopolitical) onto a single interface. This integrated perspective helps decision-makers understand the interplay between different risk types, revealing compound vulnerabilities that may not be apparent when risks are viewed in isolation. Overlays are particularly useful during strategic rebalancing, highlighting areas where concentrated exposures could undermine overall resilience.
- *Geographic heat maps*: These visualize risk concentrations and resilience gaps across regions or jurisdictions. By mapping exposures spatially, organizations can quickly pinpoint geographic clusters of fragility, such as overreliance on a single country for critical suppliers or heightened legal risk in specific markets. Geographic heat maps support tactical responses (e.g., rerouting supply chains) and long-term strategic planning (e.g., diversifying operational footprints).

Together, these dashboard views enable organizations to seamlessly move from granular, real-time monitoring to high-level strategic analysis. The ARMOR-CAP dashboard thus serves as a dynamic tool for aligning day-to-day risk management with broader governance objectives and long-term capital allocation strategies.

Another emerging diagnostic tool worth noting is the Geostrategic Resilience Rating (GRR), developed by J. H. Whitney Data Services.[1] GRR is being piloted in some institutional screening pipelines, not as an exclusionary filter but as a forward-looking indicator of systemic resilience. Scenario studies have suggested that firms with higher GRR scores were more robust during geopolitical disruptions, outperforming peers even in negatively affected sectors. Incorporating this geostrategic resilience signal into ARMOR-CAP dashboards could strengthen their ability

[1] J.H. Whitney Data Services. (2025). *Geostrategic Resilience Rating (GRR) Methodology Overview*. Retrieved from https://www.jhwhitney.com/data-services. See also GRR scenario analysis results in *GRR_Scenario_Analysis.pdf*, March 2025.

to visualize and respond to geopolitical shocks, supporting more proactive risk oversight.

4.6 Integrating ARMOR-CAP with Existing Investment Processes

ARMOR-CAP is not meant to replace existing investment processes. It is designed to interface with them as a structural lens that enhances traditional risk tools, capital budgeting systems, and governance workflows. The framework's power lies in its adaptability: Diagnostic measures can be incorporated at various points in the investment process, including the screening phase, portfolio construction, periodic risk assessments, and board reporting. This flexibility ensures that institutions can incorporate ARMOR-CAP without overhauling their infrastructure.

The most natural integration point is within pre-trade investment committee (IC) workflows, where asset managers or CIOs present proposals that typically include return expectations, volatility metrics, and factor exposures. ARMOR-CAP adds a structural viability overlay: a pre-check that asks whether the underlying position can function under legal stress, supply chain disruption, or digital blockade conditions. It's a sanity check for system continuity, not an alternative to valuation models but a filter before they are applied.

A second integration point is risk budgeting and scenario planning. Most institutions allocate risk based on volatility, duration, or credit exposure. ARMOR-CAP adds a new lens: fragility budgeting. If a portfolio already has high exposure to a single jurisdiction, digital ecosystem, or geographic supplier network, new positions should be flagged if they compound that fragility. Risk parity models overlook this dimension, but ARMOR-CAP captures it by turning hidden correlations into strategic constraints.

Third, ARMOR-CAP diagnostics are functional across compliance, ESG, and fiduciary governance. Boards are beginning to explore how investment strategies can better reflect geopolitical risk, cybersecurity threats, and supply chain resilience. ARMOR-CAP proposes a vocabulary and toolkit that could support this effort through dashboards, scoring systems, and pre-trade audit trails. In ESG reporting, for example, a diagnostic framework like ARMOR-CAP could complement the "G" pillar by drawing attention to operational governance and continuity planning.

Finally, integration can occur in crisis playbooks and red-team exercises, where the same tools that diagnose exposure can be used to simulate failures. As banks conduct liquidity stress tests, asset managers can run structural fragility drills: What positions would we be forced to exit if a key jurisdiction were sanctioned? What assets are frozen if a legal regime collapses? How would our exposure shift if cross-border data flows were restricted?

However, red teaming should not be limited to external simulations. The diagnostic tools themselves must also be challenged. In military strategy, red teams do not merely simulate enemy attacks; they interrogate the internal assumptions of a plan. Similarly, ARMOR-CAP scoring, overlays, and screens should be subject to structured dissent: challenge rounds, adversarial reviews, or scenario probes designed to test whether the metrics surface uncomfortable truths or reinforce institutional narratives. A fragility score that never changes under pressure is not resilient; it is ceremonial. Real resilience requires exposing even the diagnostic lens to stress.

These use cases do not require full system adoption. Institutions can begin with a single overlay, such as adding fragility scores to manager reviews or integrating ARMOR-CAP dashboards into quarterly risk memos. Over time, these diagnostics can expand into strategy selection, allocation limits, and board-level mandates.

Table 4.8 maps ARMOR-CAP diagnostics onto five core institutional investment and governance stages. It shows how each proposed toolset—viability screens, fragility scores, dashboards, overlays, and scenario playbooks—can be integrated without disrupting existing processes. Rather than displacing established models, these tools are designed to augment conventional analytics by focusing on structural risks that are typically invisible to price-based or ESG-driven assessments.

ARMOR-CAP adds structural viability screens at the pre-trade review stage, flagging legal, operational, or geopolitical exposures before capital is deployed. During portfolio construction, fragility audits assess chokepoints and jurisdictional dependencies that optimization routines may miss. For risk budgeting and monitoring, dashboards offer early warning signals as portfolios drift into higher-fragility zones. At the governance level, structural reporting supports fiduciary decision-making by surfacing risks not captured in ESG ratings or compliance checklists. And during stress testing, ARMOR-CAP playbooks provide cross-border and continuity scenarios beyond traditional market shocks.

Table 4.8. Embedding ARMOR-CAP into investment and governance processes.

Process Stage	**Existing Tools**	**ARMOR-CAP Addition**
Pre-trade investment review	Expected return, factor exposure, ESG	Viability screens, fragility scores
Portfolio construction	Optimization models, diversification	Chokepoint and jurisdictional dependency audit
Risk budgeting and monitoring	Tracking error, duration, credit VaR	Fragility dashboards and drift alerts
Governance and fiduciary oversight	ESG scoring, board compliance memos	ARMOR-CAP structural reporting and scenario overlays
Red-team simulations and stress tests	Liquidity drills, market scenarios	Operational continuity and cross-border risk playbooks

Note: This table illustrates how ARMOR-CAP diagnostics can be embedded into conventional investment workflows without requiring a structural overhaul. At each stage, from pre-trade review to governance oversight, ARMOR-CAP tools complement existing models by addressing what they often miss: structural viability. The additions enhance visibility into legal, operational, and supply chain fragility, offering a forward-looking layer of risk intelligence.

The table underscores the chapter's central theme: ARMOR-CAP is not a replacement for traditional models but a complementary system designed to close critical blind spots in institutional risk oversight.

4.7 Customizing ARMOR-CAP by Mandate or Institution Type

While the ARMOR-CAP framework offers a unified diagnostic structure, its proposed implementation is not a one-size-fits-all solution. Different institutions face distinct vulnerabilities and operate under regulatory, geopolitical, and fiduciary constraints. As a result, ARMOR-CAP must be calibrated, not diluted, to fit each allocator's strategic posture and operational reality. Customization is not merely an operational feature of the framework but central to its relevance.

A sovereign wealth fund managing cross-border infrastructure projects will place greater importance on legal regime compatibility and the continuity of public-private operating agreements. In contrast, a digital-native hedge fund with high-frequency strategies may emphasize operational continuity, particularly in digital portability and cyber dependency. An endowment fund might prioritize supply chain resilience for its real asset allocations while weighing down that dimension in its liquid public equities portfolio.

Public pensions often operate with long-dated liabilities and are subject to political oversight, making sovereign alignment and jurisdictional exposure politically sensitive. Theoretically, dashboards based on the ARMOR-CAP model could help visualize regional fragility footprints and track structural drift over time. In contrast, family offices and private wealth managers may be more concerned with digital sovereignty and continuity planning, especially for asset servicing arrangements, custody, or legal access during geopolitical conflicts.

The level of granularity also varies by mandate. ARMOR-CAP diagnostics may focus on issuer-level screening and supply chain mapping for single-asset class strategies. For multi-asset portfolios or fund-of-funds platforms, the emphasis may shift to manager-level scoring, aggregate heat maps, and scenario overlays that capture correlated fragility exposure across managers who appear diversified on the surface but share legal or infrastructure dependencies.

Customization also includes how the tools are embedded. Some institutions may integrate ARMOR-CAP diagnostics into pre-trade checklists or IC memos. Others may assign fragility scores to managers, products, or sub-portfolios as part of quarterly risk reporting. A few may even align internal capital charges or performance benchmarks with structural risk scores, rewarding teams not only for returns but also for engineering resilience.

ARMOR-CAP is also adaptable to public-sector settings. A financial stability board, for example, might theoretically use its scoring system to identify systemic risk clusters. In this context, ARMOR-CAP becomes a portfolio diagnostic and a public-sector surveillance tool that flags operational fragility as a form of hidden systemic risk.

These customizations are not deviations from the framework; rather, they are the reason it remains robust across contexts. Like any strong architectural design, ARMOR-CAP's strength lies in its modularity. It provides institutions with the building blocks to identify the fragility most relevant to their structure, strategy, and mission. The following section offers practical examples of these variations in action.

4.8 Implementation Snapshots: Stylized Use Cases

The following implementation snapshots are fictionalized but institutionally plausible. They are constructed to illustrate how ARMOR-CAP tools might operate in practice across varied mandates and organizational types. While inspired by real-world governance practices, none of the examples refer to specific entities, transactions, or individuals.

Case 1. Sovereign wealth fund: Legal regime audit before infrastructure allocation

A sovereign wealth fund based in a politically neutral jurisdiction is considering a $400 million equity investment in a logistics joint venture spanning three regions: Sub-Saharan Africa, Southeast Asia, and Eastern Europe. Conventional analysis suggests geographic diversification and attractive return projections, but the fund applies ARMOR-CAP's sovereign compatibility diagnostics before committing capital.

The legal enforceability screen flags two jurisdictions where the local court system lacks a treaty-based fallback and is subject to executive override. A scenario overlay suggests a regional political crisis could prevent capital repatriation for up to 18 months. The project passes ESG filters and shows a solid internal rate of return; however, ARMOR-CAP scores it as highly fragile. The fund's IC reconsiders its position and instead structures the deal with escrow-based unwinding provisions and a dual-domicile agreement under international arbitration.

This example demonstrates that ARMOR-CAP does not kill investments; it clarifies the conditions under which they can proceed.

This fictional scenario illustrates how ARMOR-CAP diagnostics could clarify the conditions under which an investment might proceed.

Case 2. University endowment: Cloud dependency in venture portfolio

A large U.S. university endowment has committed $80 million to a series of VC funds focused on artificial intelligence and fintech. The ARMOR-CAP dashboard, introduced as part of a portfolio-level governance overlay, reveals that 78% of the companies rely on a single U.S.-based cloud vendor that is under congressional scrutiny for data governance violations and foreign affiliations. The continuity overlay simulation asks: What happens if this provider is suddenly restricted from serving firms with specific end users or data types?

The outcome suggests that more than half of the portfolio's companies would face platform migration within 60 days, an operational challenge for which they are not currently prepared. The endowment does not exit the funds but begins a program of quarterly digital resilience audits and requires future fund commitments to include disclosures on cloud dependency and contingency migration capabilities.

ARMOR-CAP serves as a hypothetical governance overlay, aligning resilience considerations with fiduciary reviews.

Case 3. Global asset manager: Fragility scoring in manager due diligence

A global multi-manager platform allocates capital to over 70 managers across equity, credit, and tangible assets. A fragility scoring layer is added to the traditional due diligence process during the annual review cycle. Each manager is asked to complete a structured assessment covering legal jurisdictional exposure, supply chain reliance, and digital continuity planning. Scores are then weighted by assets under management (AUM) and aggregated into a heat map across the platform.

The results show that while sectoral and geographic diversification appear sound, nearly 40% of the AUM is exposed to operations housed in only two cloud jurisdictions and reliant on maritime transport routes that run through contested waters. One portfolio manager, previously considered a core fixed-income provider, scores in the top decile for fragility due to excessive jurisdictional asymmetry between where the bonds are issued, serviced, and adjudicated.

The CIO does not immediately reallocate capital but requires mitigation plans and creates a structural fragility budget for the next quarter, capping exposure to high-score portfolios and initiating a red-team scenario drill for legal and operational continuity.

This stylized example demonstrates how a fragility scoring rubric could support comparative due diligence among managers.

These implementation snapshots are not prescriptive; they are illustrative. They show how ARMOR-CAP can be introduced gradually and modularly. Institutions may begin with a single screen or scoring rubric and build toward more comprehensive dashboards and overlays. What matters is not the form of adoption but the shift in mindset: Resilience must become a precondition, not an afterthought.

Table 4.9 synthesizes the three examples above, comparing how different ARMOR-CAP tools address distinct risk exposures. It highlights the structural weaknesses that surface, the mitigation steps envisioned, and their corresponding impact on governance and capital strategy. The table offers a template for how diagnostic tools can support differentiated responses across organizational contexts.

Table 4.9. Stylized comparison of ARMOR-CAP diagnostics across three use cases.

Use Case	Primary Tool Used	Key Exposure Flagged	Action Taken	Resulting Impact
Sovereign wealth fund: Infrastructure deal	Sovereign viability screen	Legal regime lacked treaty fallback	Escrow and dual-domicile added	Investment restructured with embedded continuity safeguards
University endowment: Venture portfolio	Fragility dashboard + overlay	Cloud dependency across early-stage tech firms	Mandated digital audits and future disclosure	Improved digital resilience and ongoing monitoring
Global asset manager: Manager due diligence	Scoring rubric + heat map	Hidden fragility across legal, digital, and logistics	Structural fragility budget and mitigation reviews added	Platform-wide fragility cap and red-team simulation initiated

Note: This table distills the key elements of the three fictional use cases, highlighting how different diagnostic tools within the ARMOR-CAP framework can be applied to flag structural fragility. By tracing each scenario from the initial risk exposure to the institutional response, the table illustrates how diagnostic insights might inform governance decisions, allocation safeguards, or oversight practices. It provides a comparative view of how structural risks, often overlooked by conventional models, can be identified, interpreted, and addressed through a consistent analytical lens.

4.9 From Diagnostics to Deployment: Preparing for Resilient Capital Strategy

The diagnostics introduced in this chapter are not meant to sit on a shelf. They are designed for deployment in screening committees, asset allocation meetings, risk reports, and boardroom discussions. ARMOR-CAP is not a philosophical exercise. It is a toolkit for structural visibility, purpose-built for a world in which fragility is no longer rare, and discontinuity is no longer unthinkable.

We have now moved from concept to capability. Chapter 1 outlined the limits of conventional risk metrics. Chapter 2 mapped the contours of modern fragility. Chapter 3 introduced the three diagnostic pillars of the ARMOR-CAP framework. This chapter operationalized them through viability screens, fragility scoring, dashboards, and governance overlays.

But diagnostics alone are not enough. Knowing where fragility resides is only the beginning. The next frontier is to act upon it across mandates, institutions, and capital structures.

In Chapter 5, we begin that transition. The focus shifts from "Can we detect it?" to "Can we mitigate it?" Chapter 5 opens the door to adaptation and redesign, strategies for realigning portfolios, restructuring positions, and embedding structural resilience into the capital allocation process.

4.10 Summary and Transition

This chapter operationalized the ARMOR-CAP framework by translating its conceptual pillars into deployable diagnostics. Through screens, scores, dashboards, and overlays, investors gain the tools to make structural fragility visible and actionable. The five takeaways follow the structure of the framework itself:

- **A**ctivation of the ARMOR-CAP framework begins with diagnostic tools that surface hidden structural exposures before they become losses.
  Viability screens help gate capital deployment by identifying exposures incompatible with basic legal, supply, or operational continuity. These screens allow institutions to challenge the assumption that investability implies survivability.
- **R**eal-world screening, scoring, and stress overlays allow investors to gate, rank, and budget for fragility in ways traditional models cannot. Where conventional risk models focus on volatility and correlation, ARMOR-CAP enables assessment across legal enforceability, supply chain redundancy, and digital continuity. Its diagnostics offer preemptive visibility into risks that compound under stress.
- **M**easurable resilience is now possible through calibrated fragility scores and dashboards that complement, rather than replace, existing risk systems.
  Fragility scoring transforms resilience from a narrative concept into a quantifiable input. Dashboards and overlays provide institutional users with visual cues and comparative tools to monitor structural health in real time.

- **O**rganizations can tailor ARMOR-CAP diagnostics by mandate, region, or strategy, ensuring relevance across sovereign funds, endowments, pensions, and asset managers.
  The framework supports modular implementation. Some institutions may apply a single screen to assess legal compatibility; others may develop full fragility heat maps tied to board-level review. ARMOR-CAP is designed to scale.
- **R**esilience becomes a decision tool, rather than simply a narrative theme embedded directly into how capital is reviewed, allocated, and defended under uncertainty.
  By integrating fragility awareness into governance and portfolio design, institutions can better align fiduciary responsibility with the structural realities of modern capital deployment. Resilience is no longer something to hope for. It becomes something to engineer.

The following chapter advances from detection to adaptation. Chapter 5 examines how investors can restructure portfolios and reposition strategies in response to the fragility diagnostics introduced here. ARMOR-CAP does not stop at identifying where the system may break; it sets the stage for building portfolios designed to hold under pressure.

Chapter 5

Portfolio Integration of ARMOR-CAP

Strategic Priorities of This Chapter

As ARMOR-CAP progresses from a conceptual framework to a practical toolkit, this chapter focuses on how institutions can integrate fragility scoring directly into portfolio construction and management. Rather than replacing traditional risk metrics, the chapter shows how ARMOR-CAP complements them by introducing structural diagnostics that address legal, operational, and jurisdictional vulnerabilities often ignored by market-based models.

The chapter develops practical pathways to convert fragility insights into decision-ready tools. These tools help institutions apply risk thresholds, design overlays, develop dashboards, and embed structural resilience and portfolio design principles into portfolio oversight. In doing so, ARMOR-CAP moves beyond monitoring to become a proactive allocation discipline.

The ARMOR acronym frames the chapter's strategic priorities:

- **A — Apply** structural fragility thresholds to portfolio exposures, transforming risk awareness into consistent decision rules.
- **R — Reweight** and restructure allocations based on identified vulnerabilities, prioritizing capital toward robust systems.
- **M — Monitor** fragility through integrated dashboards that move beyond static reporting into dynamic oversight tools.
- **O — Organize** portfolio workflows and investment committee (IC) processes around ARMOR-CAP diagnostics, strengthening transparency and accountability.

- **R — Reinforce** portfolio resilience through stress testing, fragility budgeting, and scenario analysis to anticipate system failures before they occur.

These priorities set the stage for the following operational chapters, demonstrating how structural risk measurement can evolve from theory into a repeatable, institutionally viable practice.

The tools introduced here are part of the ARMOR-CAP proposal. They are not drawn from existing institutional practices but designed to anticipate and inform them.

5.1 Diagnostic Thresholds as Strategic Triggers

ARMOR-CAP scoring provides a structured method for quantifying hidden sources of portfolio fragility. Unlike volatility or factor exposures, structural fragility looks beyond price signals to assess how legal frameworks, jurisdictional vulnerabilities, and operational dependencies can undermine investment outcomes. Thresholds are among the simplest yet most powerful portfolio integration tools for addressing these hidden risks.

By applying a consistent scoring boundary across asset classes or strategy sleeves, portfolio managers gain a transparent, repeatable mechanism to flag positions that merit deeper investigation. ARMOR-CAP thresholds do not automatically block investments but function as a critical early warning layer within a portfolio's risk framework, offering a proactive signal before fragility evolves into financial loss.

In practice, these thresholds serve multiple purposes:

- They act as a triage tool to prioritize which holdings or strategies need escalation and review.
- They build staff familiarity with ARMOR-CAP scoring ranges before formal governance triggers are activated.
- They anchor a reference point for tracking structural risk exposures over time.

Table 5.1 presents a stylized scoring band framework for a pilot portfolio test. The color-banded structure shows how institutions might differentiate signals for routine monitoring, required discussion, and formal

Table 5.1. Stylized fragility threshold bands for pilot portfolio testing.

Color Band	Composite Score Range	Interpretive Guidance
Green	0–40	No action; routine monitoring
Yellow	41–70	Discuss at next risk or IC review
Red	71–100	Trigger escalation memo and possible portfolio reweight

Note: This table illustrates a stylized banding framework for pilot ARMOR-CAP thresholds. These color-coded zones help investment teams differentiate between routine monitoring, review discussions, and escalation triggers. The scoring ranges are fictional and are offered as a reference for calibrating pilot programs.

escalation. These examples are fictionalized and intended to serve as a starting reference rather than a rigid rule set.

Beyond pilot bands, institutions may wish to evolve toward domain-specific scoring thresholds that address unique sources of structural fragility. Rather than treating fragility scores as passive indicators, these thresholds can become decision triggers tied directly to institutional processes. For example, a legal asymmetry score above a specific threshold might highlight jurisdictions where contract enforcement is uncertain or inconsistent with the investor's legal base, prompting a halt or a deeper review. Similarly, a digital dependency score that exceeds a defined level—particularly if the exposure is concentrated in a single cross-border cloud vendor—may require a mitigation plan or a system migration contingency.

Table 5.2 expands the pilot concept into a domain-calibrated threshold matrix. Each row links a structural risk type to a specific numeric threshold and a suggested governance response. While these responses are illustrative and not prescriptive, they demonstrate how fragility awareness can be routinized and scaled through a repeatable ruleset. Over time, these governance responses could be customized to reflect institutional size, regulatory obligations, or strategic objectives.

Each row in Table 5.2 represents a different diagnostic input from the ARMOR-CAP framework, calibrated to a structural fragility domain. The "Trigger Condition" column defines the exposure that activates the threshold. In contrast, the "Institutional Response" column offers a non-exhaustive menu of plausible next steps: rebalancing, enhanced due diligence, stress simulations, or even full IC review. This structure ensures that fragility awareness is not left to individual interpretation but is routinized and scaled through a decision ruleset. Importantly, these responses

Table 5.2. Sample fragility thresholds and institutional responses.

Metric or Exposure Type	Threshold Level	Trigger Condition	Institutional Response
Sovereign legal asymmetry score	> 60 (out of 100)	High legal risk in non-aligned jurisdiction	Investment halted pending legal due diligence
Digital dependency score	> 50 if cloud is single-vendor	Concentration risk in cross-border data access	Require mitigation plan or data migration options
Supply chain fragility score	> 40 in high-tension regions	Supplier chokepoint in contested jurisdiction	Increase hedging or diversify vendor exposure
Overall fragility composite score	> 30	Cumulative risk exceeds governance threshold	Investment committee review before allocation proceeds
Fragility delta (change over time)	> +15 in one quarter	Rapid deterioration in structural resilience	Flag portfolio for risk overlay and stress simulation

Note: This table presents stylized fragility thresholds that can be calibrated to institutional mandates. Each row links a specific type of structural exposure (legal, supply chain, or operational) to a numerical fragility score and a corresponding governance response. These thresholds do not dictate investment decisions but enable preemptive action by making structural fragility visible and actionable before stress events occur.

are not fixed; they reflect a proposed governance logic, not a regulatory requirement or industry norm.

By embedding fragility thresholds into portfolio workflows, Table 5.1 illustrates how institutions could begin to institutionalize structural risk, not as an afterthought but as a core allocation discipline.

Institutions that adopt a threshold structure like this will develop a shared, institution-wide language for interpreting structural fragility. By embedding these thresholds into portfolio workflows, organizations can move from a purely reactive stance to a proactive allocation discipline, documenting, reviewing, and, when needed, intervening in exposures that threaten the portfolio's structural resilience.

The following section builds on these threshold principles by exploring the integration of structural constraints directly into the portfolio construction process, aligning investment allocations with the viability signals revealed by ARMOR-CAP.

5.2 Portfolio Construction with Structural Constraints

Building on the structural diagnostics introduced in Chapter 4, this section explains how fragility scores can be converted into explicit optimization constraints, reshaping portfolios based on risk, return, and operational viability. Traditional portfolio construction optimizes return per unit of financial risk, typically defined by volatility, correlation, or drawdown metrics. However, these models assume continuous systems, including functioning markets, enforceable contracts, and uninterrupted data flows. ARMOR-CAP accepts this premise but tests whether it holds under stress.

In this reframed optimization, fragility scores introduce both hard and soft constraints that reshape the feasible set. Assets with high legal asymmetry, digital exposure, or supplier concentration may be capped, penalized, or excluded unless mitigation features exist, such as dual-jurisdictional legal coverage, multi-cloud backups, or vendor diversification. This does not eliminate opportunity; instead, it proposes adaptation before fragility hardens into failure.

Constraints can take several forms:

- *Exposure caps*: Limit maximum weights for high-fragility positions.
- *Penalty functions*: Apply fragility-based discounts unless offset by resilience indicators.
- *Scenario overlays*: Run simulations of system discontinuities and reshape allocations accordingly.

Unlike volatility limits, which focus on market behavior, these constraints reflect operational viability under non-market stress. In a hypothetical scenario, a cyberattack on a major cloud provider could trigger a fragility downgrade within ARMOR-CAP scoring models, prompting a reallocation away from vulnerable technology holdings until continuity is assured. Similarly, a diplomatic breakdown might raise sovereign compatibility scores for affected jurisdictions, resulting in temporary gating overlays.

Table 5.3 illustrates how a stylized portfolio could be constructed with and without ARMOR-CAP constraints. While the unconstrained optimization favors high-return assets regardless of structural exposure, the constrained version preserves diversification while reducing reliance on brittle systems. The table compares two portfolio optimization outputs: one

Table 5.3. Stylized portfolio construction with vs. without ARMOR-CAP constraints.

Asset	Optimized Weight (No Constraints)	Optimized Weight (With ARMOR-CAP)	Constraint Triggered
Sovereign bonds (non-aligned)	15%	5%	Legal regime fragility
Cloud-dependent tech firm A	12%	6%	Digital continuity risk
Logistics REIT (Asia port)	10%	4%	Chokepoint exposure in contested waters
Domestic utilities	10%	10%	None
U.S. Treasuries	25%	25%	None
Resilient infrastructure ETF	18%	30%	Benefited from structural reallocation

Note: This table contrasts a standard return-maximizing portfolio with one incorporating ARMOR-CAP fragility overlays. The constrained version limits exposure to assets with high structural risk, such as legal misalignment, vendor dependency, or critical chokepoints, illustrating how fragility-aware constraints can reshape capital allocation without abandoning core financial objectives.

traditional and one constrained by ARMOR-CAP fragility overlays. Both cases aim to maximize return per unit of risk, but only the second portfolio accounts for structural viability. The unconstrained portfolio selects high-return assets that score poorly on legal alignment, supply chain redundancy, or digital continuity. In contrast, the ARMOR-CAP-constrained version incorporates soft caps and penalty functions tied to fragility scores. These limits prevent overexposure to vulnerable jurisdictions, critical infrastructure bottlenecks, or vendor-dependent platforms.

The result is not simply a reshuffling of weights. The structurally constrained portfolio actively reduces exposure to assets that could become inaccessible or nonfunctional under real-world stress scenarios. This may result in a modest trade-off in near-term return expectations, but it introduces resilience features that traditional models overlook. Table 5.3 thus illustrates how ARMOR-CAP constraints reshape portfolio feasibility, not as a post-crisis reaction but as an anticipatory redesign of capital structure.

While these portfolio overlays strengthen risk management, it is worth stepping back to clarify a deeper difference. Traditional frameworks often focus on financial resilience, recovering prices after a market shock. In contrast, ARMOR-CAP emphasizes operational resilience, whether the

Table 5.4. Comparing financial resilience and operational resilience.

Traditional Resilience Thinking	**ARMOR-CAP Resilience Thinking**
Focus on: price recovery after a market shock	Focus on: viability of investee companies during structural disruptions
Assumes: shocks are external and temporary	Recognizes: shocks can arise from internal fragilities (e.g., legal, jurisdictional, supply chain)
Typical tools: portfolio hedges, factor exposures	Typical tools: sovereign compatibility screening, redundancy scoring, Geostrategic Resilience Rating (GRR) metrics*
Goal: rebound in asset prices	Goal: continuity of cash flows and operational survival

* This metric is described later in this chapter.

Note: This table contrasts traditional financial resilience with the operational resilience emphasized by ARMOR-CAP. While conventional tools focus on managing losses after crises, ARMOR-CAP prioritizes the continued functionality and investability of portfolio components under structural stress. This reframing shifts the central question from recovery potential to operational viability during disruptions.

portfolio's investee firms can actually survive system stress in the first place. This distinction is crucial, as Table 5.4 highlights.

5.2.1 *Fragility-adjusted Sharpe ratios*

One proposed extension of the ARMOR-CAP framework is the concept of a *fragility-adjusted Sharpe ratio*,[1] a simple way to internalize structural

[1]The fragility-adjusted Sharpe ratio introduced here is a novel adaptation explicitly developed for the ARMOR-CAP framework. It builds on the foundational logic of the traditional Sharpe ratio, which evaluates excess return relative to volatility. Still, it adds a penalty factor tied to an asset's or portfolio's structural fragility score. This approach contextualizes investment returns within risk environments that account for more than simple volatility, resonating with broader trends in performance measurement. It draws inspiration from Taleb's (2012) conceptualization of fragility and antifragility, which emphasizes sensitivity to stressors and the importance of robust systems in the face of uncertainty. The perspective is further informed by Getmansky, Lo, and Makarov's (2004) analysis of risk measurement and operational risk, which highlights the limitations of traditional risk metrics and the significance of non-market risks such as illiquidity, serial correlation, and operational failures in assessing hedge fund performance. Additionally, the work of López de Prado (2018) is relevant for its application of machine learning

risk into familiar performance metrics. The traditional Sharpe ratio evaluates excess return relative to volatility. But volatility assumes continuous markets and uninterrupted liquidity. In fragile environments, a smooth return stream can mask deep exposure to systems that are only conditionally accessible.

To adjust for this, institutions can apply a fragility penalty to the Sharpe numerator, reducing effective return proportionally to an asset's or portfolio's fragility score. For example,

$$\text{Fragility Adjusted Sharpe Ratio} = \frac{R_p - R_f - \lambda F_p}{\sigma_p}$$

where:
R_p = portfolio return,
R_f = risk-free interest rate,
λ = fragility penalty coefficient,
F_p = portfolio fragility score (0–100 scale),
σ_p = portfolio standard deviation.

Alternatively, this metric can be expressed as

$$\text{Fragility Adjusted Sharpe Ratio} = \frac{\text{Adjusted Return}}{\sigma_p}$$

where Adjusted Return = $R_p - R_f - \lambda F_p$.

This adjustment does not replace the Sharpe ratio. Instead, it contextualizes it. A high Sharpe ratio for a portfolio with high fragility may indicate overstated rewards. A lower Sharpe ratio in a low-fragility portfolio may reflect genuine durability under stress. This simple augmentation helps align performance evaluation with long-term resilience, particularly within institutional mandates where continuity is as important as return.

Table 5.5 provides a numerical example illustrating how fragility penalties alter portfolio rankings, highlighting that higher Sharpe ratios do

---

techniques to detect nonlinear risks and regime changes, offering practical frameworks for managing complex investment environments. Together, these sources provide a foundation for thinking beyond traditional risk metrics and underscore the importance of incorporating a wider range of risk factors in performance evaluation.

Table 5.5. Comparing traditional and fragility-adjusted Sharpe ratios.

Portfolio	Return (R_p)	Risk-Free Rate (R_f)	Standard Deviation (σ_p)	Traditional Sharpe	Fragility Score (Fp)	Penalty Coefficient (λ)	Adjusted Return	Fragility-Adjusted Sharpe
A	8.0%	2.0%	10.0%	0.600	30	0.05	4.5%	0.45
B	7.0%	2.0%	8.0%	0.625	10	0.05	4.5%	0.56
C	6.5%	2.0%	7.0%	0.643	5	0.05	4.25%	0.61

Note: This table provides a numerical example showing how fragility penalties shift portfolio rankings, reinforcing that higher Sharpe ratios do not always imply greater structural resilience.

not always imply greater structural resilience. For our three hypothetical portfolios, the fragility-adjusted Sharpe ratio is calculated as follows:

For Portfolio A:

- $R_p = 8\%$, $R_f = 2\%$, $F_p = 30$, $\lambda = 0.05$, $\sigma_p = 0.10$
- Adjusted Return = 8% − 2% − (0.05 × 30) = 4.5%
- Adjusted Sharpe = 4.5%/10% = 0.45

For Portfolio B:

- $R_p = 7\%$, $R_f = 2\%$, $F_p = 10$, $\lambda = 0.05$, $\sigma_p = 0.08$
- Adjusted Return = 7% − 2% − (0.05 × 10) = 4.5%
- Adjusted Sharpe = 4.5%/8% = 0.56

For Portfolio C:

- $R_p = 6.5\%$, $R_f = 2\%$, $F_p = 5$, $\lambda = 0.05$, $\sigma_p = 0.07$
- Adjusted Return = 6.5% − 2% − (0.05 × 5) = 4.25%
- Adjusted Sharpe = 4.25%/7% = 0.61

Once again, the goal is not to discard Sharpe ratios but to contextualize them, recognizing that risk-adjusted return has little meaning without continuity-adjusted viability.

5.3 From Allocation to Governance: Embedding Resilience in Oversight

The scenarios that follow are not case studies of implementation. They are strategic simulations designed to explore how portfolios might adapt when key structural thresholds are breached. Drawing on diagnostics introduced in Chapter 4, each example tests the consequences of operating under legal obstruction, digital shutdowns, or geopolitical constraints. These aren't stress tests in the traditional financial sense; they ask a different question: How should portfolio structure evolve when core functions, such as capital mobility, data access, or supplier continuity, are compromised?

Today's governance structures (i.e., investment policy statements, risk oversight charters, and ESG dashboards) are still built around market-based risk concepts, including volatility, credit quality, and liquidity. However, structural fragility rarely appears in these documents. A board seldom asks: What is our exposure to digital infrastructure failures? To jurisdictional unpredictability? To operational concentration? Without these questions, there are no answers. And without answers, capital is deployed on blind trust.

The ARMOR-CAP framework introduces a new class of governance indicators, distinct from return statistics or compliance flags. These indicators ask whether the systems supporting asset value are viable, diverse, and secure under stress conditions. Examples include:

- *Dependency concentration*: Are more than 25% of portfolio assets reliant on a single legal regime or jurisdictional interpretation?
- *Continuity readiness*: Are there playbooks or tested procedures for key failure modes (e.g., sanctions, cyberattacks, and regulatory revocation)?
- *Sovereign alignment audits*: Have legal dependencies been reviewed for compatibility with the institution's headquarters, investors, or mission?

These metrics do not replace fiduciary judgment. But they create visibility (i.e., structured, repeatable questions that elevate resilience from a reactive impulse to a governance function). Just like financial stress testing after the 2007–2008 Global Financial Crisis, once structural diagnostics are built into governance materials, they change how institutions prioritize and make decisions. Fragility becomes a formal constraint, not an informal concern.

Table 5.6 outlines how ARMOR-CAP metrics can be systematically embedded into board and IC governance structures. The goal is not to eliminate fragility outright but to ensure that exposures are identified, contextualized, and subjected to disciplined decision-making. Institutions can

Table 5.6. Mapping ARMOR-CAP metrics into governance functions.

ARMOR-CAP Metric	Governance Integration Point	Illustrative Oversight Action
Sovereign legal compatibility	Annual board risk review	Request a legal audit of cross-border enforceability
Digital infrastructure exposure	Investment committee due diligence rubric	Require third-party cloud redundancy disclosure before approval
Supplier/logistics chokepoints	Quarterly risk report to board	Scenario analysis of exposure under shipping lane closure
Fragility composite score	Monthly portfolio manager review	Mandate remediation plan if score exceeds threshold
Resilience audit trail	ESG or fiduciary subcommittee reporting	Demonstrate operational continuity compliance for material exposures

Note: This table shows how ARMOR-CAP metrics align with key governance functions across institutional workflows. Each fragility measure corresponds to a distinct oversight setting, such as board reviews, committee rubrics, or reporting cycles, accompanied by an example of the action it might trigger. This alignment enables institutional investors to integrate resilience screening into their fiduciary processes without overhauling their governance structures.

align structural risk monitoring with their existing fiduciary and governance processes by mapping each ARMOR-CAP diagnostic, such as sovereign legal compatibility or digital infrastructure risk, to a specific oversight touchpoint. This structure reinforces accountability: when fragility scores trigger remediation plans or digital vulnerabilities prompt enhanced disclosures, oversight shifts from passive review to proactive intervention. Ultimately, embedding ARMOR-CAP into governance cycles fosters more informed portfolios and resilient mandates, where fragility is surfaced early, deliberately reviewed, and consistently acted upon.

5.3.1 *Real-world case: Maersk and the NotPetya attack*

One of the most illustrative governance failures in fragility oversight occurred during the 2017 NotPetya cyberattack on Maersk. Although considered one of the world's most operationally advanced shipping companies, Maersk was brought to a standstill globally when a single malware attack shut down its entire digital infrastructure, including port operations, container tracking, and communication systems. The firm's heavy reliance on a uniform IT system across jurisdictions, without meaningful segmentation or local failover plans, meant that a single exploit cascaded globally. The event resulted in hundreds of millions of dollars in direct losses and systemic ripple effects on global trade. A governance approach like the one proposed by ARMOR-CAP, which focuses on digital infrastructure concentration and jurisdictional exposure, could have flagged the core risk, even if the exact method of attack could not have been predicted.

5.3.2 *Regulatory tie-in: EU CSDDD and SEC cyber disclosure rules*

Regulators are beginning to mandate structural risk governance forms aligned with the practices proposed in the ARMOR-CAP framework. The EU's Corporate Sustainability Due Diligence Directive (CSDDD) requires companies to map and mitigate risks within their supply and operational chains, formalizing resilience screening as a compliance function. In the U.S., the SEC's cybersecurity rules, issued in 2023, require public companies to disclose material incidents and detail the governance structures for overseeing cybersecurity risks. Both regulatory regimes shift fragility oversight from optional diligence to a legal requirement. The ARMOR-CAP framework proposes a roadmap for converting these mandates into actionable governance tools, particularly in contexts where geopolitical and operational fragility are increasingly intersecting.

5.3.3 *ARMOR-CAP governance triggers and escalation pathways*

In addition to real-world lessons and regulatory frameworks, institutions can embed proactive escalation procedures through ARMOR-CAP's governance triggers.

No matter how precise, a fragility score is useless without a defined consequence. The purpose of ARMOR-CAP scoring is not only diagnostic but also decisional: to alert, inform, and activate institutional governance. Here, the focus is on how institutions route high fragility scores to appropriate decision points, triggering escalation protocols, committee review, or strategic adjustments.

The core design principle is governance alignment. Each fragility band (green, yellow, and red) must clearly map to a set of predefined responses:

- What happens when a portfolio component enters the red zone?
- Who is notified?
- What documentation or analysis is required?
- When is a holding or approval suspended?

Without these linkages, scoring ends up as a compliance exercise rather than a strategic signal. In their work on operational risk practices, Power (2007) and Mikes (2009) warn that risk dashboards often fail, not because the data are wrong, but because organizations frequently lack effective protocols for response when a warning indicator appears.

To combat this, institutions deploying ARMOR-CAP can implement a trigger framework, which translates score outputs into formal governance actions. These may include:

- escalation memos to legal, risk, or compliance teams;
- IC deferral or approval conditioning;
- board-level disclosure or internal audit review.

Table 5.7 presents a stylized trigger framework that maps fragility score bands to corresponding institutional actions, escalation paths, and documentation requirements.

The exact governance pathways may vary depending on the asset class and institutional structure. For example:

- A public pension plan may route red-zone scores to its internal risk committee for review by the IC.
- A sovereign wealth fund may require escalation to a policy advisory council if scores remain elevated for multiple quarters.
- An outsourced CIO platform may suspend mandate additions until an external consultant reviews the flagged fragility.

In all cases, the effectiveness of routing depends on procedural clarity and auditability. Governance bodies must know:

- when scores cross a line,
- what response is expected,
- and whether that response was documented.

Table 5.7. Governance triggers by ARMOR-CAP fragility band.

Fragility Band	Score Range	Action Required	Escalation Path	Documentation Flag
Green	0–60	No action required	None	Logged automatically
Yellow	61–80	Review and secondary validation recommended	Risk team or GRC review	Memo or flagged review
Red	81–100	Escalation required before approval or retention	IC or board escalation	Formal escalation memo

Note: This table presents a stylized framework showing how fragility scores map to pre-agreed institutional actions. It is designed to be tailored to institution type, oversight structure, and risk tolerance. *This table is fictionalized and stylized for illustrative purposes.*

The ARMOR-CAP trigger system builds on literature emphasizing risk governance routines and decision hygiene. Tufano (2011) notes that most financial failures arise not from the absence of data, but from failures to act on available data, often due to vague accountability. Embedding fragility triggers into internal control agendas and risk memos is a recognized practice that improves institutional reflexes and enables proactive responses before stress events fully materialize.

Within a fully developed or pilot implementation of the ARMOR-CAP framework, score-triggered actions could, in principle, inform performance management and policy reviews. Under such a structure, multiple red-band scores within the same sector might indicate the need for macro reallocation, manager re-evaluation, or strategic hedging.

By creating pathways from signal to action, fragility scoring becomes more than a monitoring tool, it becomes a decision infrastructure.

5.4 Stress Testing Structural Fragility

The mini-cases and illustrative tables in this section are fictionalized but institutionally plausible. They are designed to illustrate how ARMOR-CAP diagnostics, dashboards, and fragility budgeting can be applied in real-world contexts. While inspired by standard institutional practices and recurring fragility patterns, these examples do not depict actual firms, transactions, or individuals unless explicitly cited.

While traditional stress tests examine how portfolios respond to market shocks (e.g., rate hikes, spread widening, and liquidity freezes), these exercises typically assume functioning legal systems, stable jurisdictions, and continuous digital access. The ARMOR-CAP framework proposes a complementary form of stress testing that begins not with asset prices but with the underlying infrastructure enabling those prices.

Structural fragility stress tests simulate systemic breakdowns, not just market disruptions. For example, what if a jurisdiction revokes legal protections overnight? What if export controls sever access to cloud services, as seen in recent U.S. restrictions on Chinese entities, such as Inspur Group? What if physical chokepoints (ports, undersea cables, and borders) are blocked due to sanctions or sabotage, as occurred during pandemic-era shipping crises? These scenarios are increasingly plausible, as evidenced by events such as U.S. Entity List designations, Russian asset seizures, and cross-border infrastructure disruptions (Taleb, 2012; U.S. Department of Commerce, 2025).

The ARMOR-CAP framework proposes a method for institutions to pre-simulate the operational consequences of structural failure modes. These simulations go beyond value-at-risk (VaR) or scenario drift models by forcing institutional actors to consider structural questions proposed in the ARMOR-CAP framework, such as:

- Can we operate legally under this new jurisdictional regime?
- Are we exposed to data transfer disruptions under evolving digital sovereignty laws?
- Do we have contractual or physical redundancy if this vendor or region is compromised?

These questions should not be confined to compliance silos. They must also be considered in portfolio design, risk budgeting, and governance oversight.

The growing complexity and regionalization of global supply chains have heightened concerns about structural fragility. Recent analyses, including works by the World Bank (2023) and the United Nations Conference on Trade and Development (UNCTAD, 2023), document how multipolar geopolitical pressures, data governance conflicts, and physical chokepoints, such as ports and shipping lanes, have eroded longstanding assumptions of continuity. These findings provide an empirical policy backdrop for the domain-specific stress scenarios modeled here.

Table 5.8. Sample structural fragility stress test framework.

Domain	Stress Scenario	Exposure Identification	Viability Question	Response Strategy
Legal	Sanctions freeze assets in jurisdiction	Cross-border bond holdings in targeted country	Are legal claims enforceable under new regime?	Restructure via SPVs or re-domiciliation
Digital	Cloud provider subject to export restrictions	Core systems hosted on sanctioned vendor	Can operations continue under new data sovereignty laws?	Deploy multi-cloud or sovereign-cloud fallback
Physical	Port shutdown in contested maritime region	Infrastructure and shipping REITs	Can goods or services be rerouted or resourced?	Diversify logistics or enter derivative hedges

Note: This table illustrates how structural fragility scenarios can be organized across legal, digital, and physical domains. Each row presents a stylized trigger event (e.g., contract unenforceability, data localization mandates, or port closures) paired with diagnostic questions that help investors evaluate portfolio readiness. This matrix is designed as a flexible template: institutions can adapt it to different geographies, asset classes, or mandate types while maintaining consistent oversight of structural risk.

Table 5.8 shows that structural fragility scenarios can be constructed and evaluated across legal, digital, and physical dimensions, each with distinct triggers, exposures, and continuity plans. This matrix is designed as a flexible template, allowing institutions to adapt it to different geographies, asset classes, or mandate types while maintaining consistent oversight of structural risks.

Stress testing within the proposed ARMOR-CAP framework does not replace macro scenario modeling. Instead, it is meant to complement it by probing vulnerabilities that are often assumed away. Critically, these stress tests can be run at multiple levels: across an entire institution, a specific portfolio, a sector, or even at the individual counterparty level. And they are most effective when repeated routinely, not as a compliance checkbox but as a diagnostic discipline.

By rehearsing failures before they occur, institutions are more likely to remain operational when systems bend or break. In this way, the stress testing approach proposed in ARMOR-CAP is less about prediction than preparedness.

5.4.1 *Mini-case: The Swiss asset manager and the unexpected data sovereignty clampdown*

This fictionalized case was developed to illustrate the fragility of digital infrastructure and jurisdictional compliance risks as framed in the proposed ARMOR-CAP framework.

In 2021, a mid-sized Swiss asset management firm specializing in ESG-themed ETFs found itself in regulatory quicksand after a regional data sovereignty law in Southeast Asia came into effect with little notice. The firm had launched a new ESG fund targeting ASEAN-listed equities, marketed to investors across Europe and Asia. Unknown to the firm's legal and operations teams, a substantial portion of its order routing and analytics platform used to execute trades and rebalance portfolios was hosted in a U.S.-based cloud provider that did not meet the region's new compliance threshold for local data residency.

Within 72 hours of the law's enforcement, the firm's local custodian notified it that certain portfolio services were being suspended pending a compliance review. Traders were locked out of order flow, portfolio rebalancing was delayed, and investors received terse notices that certain functions were "temporarily paused due to jurisdictional processing constraints." The reputational damage was swift, and the operational cost of reconfiguring the tech stack and custodian links ran into millions.

What makes this case instructive within the ARMOR-CAP framework is not the law itself. It's the absence of stress testing for digital infrastructure viability. The firm had performed standard market stress tests, including interest rate spikes, liquidity droughts, and currency volatility. But it never asked a simple structural question: What happens if data localization laws change? Nor did it run a scenario where digital continuity is treated as a sovereign risk.

Had a stress test aligned with ARMOR-CAP principles been conducted, even using simple yes/no diagnostics, it likely would have flagged:

- single cloud provider dependency,
- no documented compliance path under local tech regulation,
- lack of a fallback service continuity plan for digital execution.

And the firm could have staged a mitigation response: either diversifying vendors, restructuring local access rights, or delaying market entry until compliance scaffolding was in place.

This case underscores a core ARMOR-CAP principle: Operational fragility becomes a material financial risk when legal, digital, or geopolitical assumptions break, especially if those assumptions were never explicitly surfaced, tested, or mitigated in advance.

5.4.2 *Mini-case: The Nordic pension fund and the Taiwan contingency drill*

This stylized case reflects how institutional investors might approach geopolitical fragility diagnostics. It is not based on a specific entity or portfolio.

A large Nordic pension fund managing over €100 billion in diversified global assets undertook a comprehensive fragility audit as part of its investment governance overhaul. One of its new mandates, modeled on the diagnostic principles proposed in ARMOR-CAP, was to test operational viability under geopolitical disruptions. Specifically, it is a scenario involving heightened tensions across the Taiwan Strait.

Rather than focusing solely on market contagion (e.g., technology sell-offs or currency volatility), the fund's stress test asked more profound questions: What if semiconductor supply chains are interrupted? Which holdings are contractually dependent on chip deliveries through Taiwan? What legal and logistical workarounds exist?

Using dependency maps and legal exposure audits, the fund identified six portfolio companies ranging from European auto manufacturers to U.S.-listed cloud infrastructure firms that heavily relied on Taiwan-based semiconductor fabrication and had weak or nonexistent backup arrangements.

Instead of divesting, the fund engaged with the firms' investor relations and risk committees to demand clarity on continuity planning. In some cases, the companies enhanced their disclosures or shifted portions of their sourcing to alternative suppliers in South Korea or the U.S. In other instances, the fund applied position caps and adjusted risk-weighting models until redundancy was demonstrated. No major market event occurred that year, but the structural posture of the portfolio had changed.

This case illustrates the proactive intent of the ARMOR-CAP framework: using diagnostics not to react to a crisis but to preemptively reshape exposure. Resilience does not require avoiding fragility altogether. It requires confronting it early enough to adapt.

5.4.3 *Building a fragility scenario matrix*

The framework emphasizes operational viability rather than price movement. It is intended to be a repeatable structure for building fragility overlays into institutional workflows. While the events and questions are illustrative rather than exhaustive, they demonstrate how stress testing under the ARMOR-CAP framework shifts the focus from volatility and contagion to function and continuity.

5.5 Risk Budgeting in a Fragility-Aware Framework

Traditional risk budgeting allocates risk capital across asset classes, managers, or factors using volatility, tracking error, or VaR metrics. These measures rely on assumptions of continuous pricing, functional markets, and institutional access to data and liquidity. However, they often fail to capture systemic fragility, which behaves like an unpriced option, that is, a latent exposure that only materializes when critical infrastructure or legal scaffolding fails.[2]

The ARMOR-CAP framework proposes reframing risk budgeting by introducing a second axis: fragility load. Rather than focusing solely on how much volatility a position contributes, it asks: how structurally vulnerable is this exposure if the system becomes impaired? This dual-lens budgeting model enables portfolio teams to anticipate better compounding risks across jurisdictions, suppliers, and digital infrastructure (volatility and fragility).

Table 5.9 presents a stylized example of how fragility budgeting bands could be structured across different layers of a portfolio, helping institutions impose consistent resilience thresholds without overhauling their asset allocation models.

Importantly, structural fragility is not additive in the way volatility is. A portfolio may appear diversified based on volatility but could be overly reliant on a single digital stack, legal regime, or logistics node. That makes fragility nonlinear and clustering-prone, with risk pockets that do not register on standard dashboards until a threshold is breached.

[2]See Ilmanen (2011) for related discussions on the sources of risk and return, including less obvious or "hidden" risks such as illiquidity and tail risk.

To capture this, the ARMOR-CAP framework proposes integrating fragility budgeting bands (FBBs), categorical thresholds that define acceptable fragility contributions at the asset, strategy, and portfolio levels. Table 5.9 presents a stylized fragility budgeting scale structured around five bands, each represented by a numerical fragility score, a corresponding interpretation, and a suggested course of action. These bands are not based on empirical calibration but are designed to provide institutions with a repeatable diagnostic framework for translating ARMOR-CAP scores into portfolio governance decisions. As fragility scores increase, the guidance shifts from routine monitoring to mandatory remediation or potential exclusion, mirroring how credit limits or liquidity risk thresholds function in traditional risk management settings.

The goal is not to avoid all fragility but to qualify and structure it. Budgeting bands enable institutions to incorporate resilience into investment design without forfeiting high-return opportunities. This framework provides a scalable approach to balancing structural exposure with fiduciary discipline.

Institutions can calibrate these bands to match their governance philosophies. For example, a sovereign wealth fund subject to geopolitical constraints may set stricter portfolio-wide limits. At the same time, a venture investor in frontier markets may tolerate higher fragility at the asset

Table 5.9. Example of fragility budgeting bands in portfolio design.

Tier	Fragility Band Range	Interpretation	Action
Asset-level	0–30	Minimal structural fragility; no constraints	No action required
Strategy-level	31–60	Moderate fragility; justify with offsetting redundancies	Require documentation of fallback infrastructure
Portfolio segment	61–80	High fragility; exposure may be tolerable if diversified	Apply exposure cap or conditional approvals
Total portfolio	81–100	Extreme fragility; correlated systems failure risk	Reduce, restructure, or disqualify unless remediated

Note: This table presents a stylized fragility budgeting framework using score-based thresholds across four portfolio tiers: asset, strategy, segment, and total portfolio. Each band is linked to a fragility score range, an interpretation of structural risk, and a recommended course of action. The table is designed to help institutions translate ARMOR-CAP diagnostics into repeatable governance decisions.

level, provided systemic spillover risk remains contained. This proposed budgeting model is not prescriptive; it is diagnostic. It does not say to invest in fragile assets; it says to know what's embedded before you do and to price or structure accordingly. Just as institutions have grown accustomed to carbon budgets and liquidity stress tests, fragility budgets provide the scaffolding to operationalize structural resilience without dismantling existing investment processes.

5.5.1 *Mini-case: Fragility budgeting alters a cross-border allocation*

This composite case illustrates how fragility budgeting, modeled on the ARMOR-CAP framework, can reshape institutional investment decisions. It does not depict a real institution.

Suppose a large Canadian pension plan was evaluating a new allocation to emerging market private credit, specifically a fund focused on infrastructure projects in Sub-Saharan Africa. The opportunity was attractive: a targeted internal rate of return (IRR) of 15%, low expected correlation to developed market credit, and senior secured positions with multilateral guarantees.

Traditional risk screens raised no red flags. Credit risk, volatility, and currency exposure were all within acceptable ranges. But the proposed allocation failed to serve as a fragility diagnostic. Legal claims relied on arbitration in a single jurisdiction that had recently imposed limits on recognizing foreign judgments. The fund's digital reporting platform depended on a sole vendor based in a country with documented surveillance risks. The infrastructure investments were physically clustered along a single transport corridor and were prone to political disruption.

Under a diagnostic process aligned with ARMOR-CAP principles, the investment received a fragility score of 82, placing it in the "Extreme fragility" band as defined by the institution's internal budgeting framework (see Table 5.9). While the risk-return profile might be compelling, the position exceeded the fragility cap for the plan's emerging markets sleeve.

Rather than abandon the opportunity, the investment team pursued structural remediation by:

- negotiating dual-jurisdiction enforcement rights to mitigate legal concentration risks;

- relocating reporting infrastructure to a sovereign-compliant cloud jurisdiction;
- adding a political risk insurance derivative linked to transport corridor disruptions.

These actions systematically reduced the fragility score to 54, placing the position within the plan's "moderate" fragility band and clearing the final investment committee review.

This case reinforces a core principle of the ARMOR-CAP framework: Fragility budgeting does not reject high-return strategies. Instead, it forces clarity before commitment. Table 5.9 outlines a stylized set of fragility budgeting bands, organized by score range and mapped to specific tiers of portfolio oversight—asset-level, strategy-level, segment, and total portfolio. Each band pairs a numerical threshold with an interpretation of structural vulnerability and a recommended governance action. For example, scores above 80 trigger a review or restructuring, while scores below 30 require no intervention. These bands function similarly to credit limits or liquidity caps but are calibrated to fragility risk rather than historical volatility.

Table 5.10 provides a step-by-step breakdown of the structural remediation process the investment team may undertake. Spanning six weeks, it documents how targeted legal, digital, and operational interventions progressively reduced the fragility score from 82 to 54. Each action (i.e., contract renegotiation, cloud migration, and derivative hedging) is tied to a specific fragility domain and shown to lower the aggregate score by measurable increments. This timeline illustrates the feasibility of fragility mitigation and its value as a structured workflow. This diagnostic-to-decision pipeline enables resilient capital deployment without sacrificing return potential.

5.6 Benchmark-Relative Fragility Scoring

A fragility score alone offers little strategic guidance. Its power emerges when placed in context: How does this portfolio compare to peer institutions? Has its fragility improved since last quarter? Are current exposures materially more vulnerable than the benchmark model used in strategic asset allocation reviews?

Table 5.10. Timeline of fragility remediation for cross-border allocation.

Week	Action Taken	Fragility Impact
Week 1	Initial fragility diagnostic conducted (score: 82)	High fragility flagged – exceeded portfolio band
Weeks 2–3	Legal team negotiates dual-jurisdiction arbitration clause	Legal risk reduced; score improves to 72
Weeks 3–4	The reporting infrastructure has been moved to a sovereign-compliant cloud provider	Digital exposure reduced; score improves to 63
Week 5	Political risk insurance with outage-triggered derivative added	Operational redundancy added; score drops to 54
Week 6	Final investment committee review and approval	Score within budgeted fragility band

Note: This table summarizes the staged interventions used to reduce the fragility score of a high-risk private credit investment. It tracks specific actions (legal restructuring, digital infrastructure upgrades, and insurance overlays) and links them to corresponding score reductions. The timeline illustrates how structural risk can be remediated incrementally through targeted steps aligned with the principles of fragility budgeting.

To unlock these insights, ARMOR-CAP supports benchmark-relative scoring. Institutions can assess their portfolios by comparing ARMOR-CAP scores against:

- internal model portfolios (e.g., baseline allocation frameworks),
- external benchmarks (e.g., peer institutions or consultant-generated composites),
- historical reference portfolios (e.g., last year's allocation, pre-COVID baseline).

This approach transforms fragility scoring into relative resilience positioning, helping boards and CIOs understand whether their portfolios are fragile and more fragile than expected.

Table 5.11 presents a stylized benchmark comparison dashboard, highlighting how fragility scores can be evaluated across actual portfolios, peer composites, and historical baselines.

Benchmark-relative fragility mapping draws on traditions in performance attribution and active risk budgeting, which analyze returns and

Table 5.11. Fragility benchmark comparison dashboard (stylized view).

Portfolio Component	Jurisdictional Score	Operational Score	Legal/ Structural Score	Composite Score	Gap vs. Baseline	Action Flag
Actual portfolio	76.4	81.2	73.5	77.0	+7.2	Review
SAA benchmark	69.5	75.0	70.2	69.8	—	—
Peer average (SWFs)	71.0	77.5	72.0	73.5	+3.5	Watchlist
Historical (Q1 2022)	65.3	72.4	68.1	68.6	+8.4	Escalate trend

Note: This table illustrates a fictionalized comparison between a live portfolio and three reference benchmarks. It presents domain-level ARMOR-CAP scores, gaps versus the baseline, and governance interpretation flags. This table is fictional and stylized for illustrative purposes.

risks relative to a benchmark and elements of governance scorecards for assessing risk management effectiveness. In credit risk, for example, stress testing frameworks often compare stressed outcomes to baseline conditions using adverse-to-baseline deltas rather than reporting only standalone stressed outputs. Similarly, ESG frameworks increasingly use relative exposure metrics to distinguish high-emitting industries or firms from others within the same industry (Ilhan, Sautner, & Vilkov, 2021).

These benchmark comparisons allow institutions to focus on the following:

- *Prioritize areas of divergence*: For example, a spike in legal fragility relative to a baseline may signal contract enforceability risks that need review by the legal team.
- *Justify escalation decisions*: When boards ask, “Why this deal, now?”, score gaps offer audit-ready documentation.
- *Track trends over time and across strategies*: The high fragility of real assets compared to liquid credit may drive rebalancing or hedging decisions.

Institutions may also segment benchmark comparisons by portfolio sleeves, asset classes, or regional exposures. Doing so supports multidimensional resilience oversight and avoids masking risks through portfolio-level averages.

Benchmarking fragility is not about imposing uniformity. It is about providing CIOs and boards with the relational context they need to act decisively and transparently.

5.7 Fragility Dashboards: Turning Diagnostics into Decisions

While benchmark-relative comparisons provide a governance baseline, institutions must also analyze how fragility accumulates across asset classes through multi-asset overlays.

Resilience assessments often suffer from abstraction. Investment committees are briefed on cyber risks, legal asymmetries, or geopolitical tensions, but those conversations rarely translate into decision-ready tools. The ARMOR-CAP framework proposes fragility dashboards (i.e., visual frameworks that consolidate risk diagnostics into a structured, interpretable format). They assess *viability* under stress, tracking key indicators of structural exposure before capital is deployed.

Unlike performance dashboards, fragility dashboards are designed not to explain past outcomes but to challenge forward-looking assumptions. Can this strategy survive a cloud outage in a blacklisted jurisdiction? What happens if cross-border data transfers are suspended? Are there fallback mechanisms in place if primary suppliers are sanctioned? These are not speculative questions. They are preconditions for continuity.

ARMOR-CAP dashboards typically include three classes of diagnostic modules:

- jurisdictional stress modules, which assess legal enforceability and access under sovereign change;
- supply chain dependency modules, which map upstream and downstream fragility nodes;
- continuity modules, which evaluate the resilience of IT, logistics, and legal infrastructure.

Each module uses a common scoring rubric (e.g., green/yellow/red or a numerical scale) and is refreshed quarterly, semi-annually, or upon material changes. While early adopters might start with simple spreadsheets, more advanced use cases could involve integrating ARMOR-CAP-style dashboards into portfolio management systems or investment committee materials.

Table 5.12 illustrates a sample fragility dashboard as it might appear in an investment committee review, showing the diagnostic modules, scores, and associated mitigation triggers. Using standardized metrics, it consolidates structural risk exposure across legal, operational, and supply chain domains. Each module is paired with an escalation or mitigation trigger to ensure accountability and follow-through on decisions.

A key benefit of fragility dashboards is their versatility. They can be deployed:

- as pre-trade overlays, blocking proposals until remediation is documented;
- in quarterly risk memos, identifying trends in systemic exposure over time;
- during board-level governance reviews, offering transparency into non-financial risks.

Importantly, these dashboards are not static. As geopolitical landscapes shift, tech stacks evolve, and regulations change, the dashboard modules and thresholds must adapt. What matters is not the specific score but the discipline of tracking exposure that markets do not price.

Table 5.12. Example ARMOR-CAP fragility dashboard for investment committee review.

Diagnostic Module	Key Indicator	Score	Flagged Action
Jurisdictional stress	% of assets exposed to legal non-alignment	28%	Seek legal audit for top 5 positions
Supply chain dependency	Concentration in <3 suppliers per product	High	Engage investment team to map alternatives
Operational continuity	% cloud exposure to export-controlled zones	41%	Implement multi-cloud fallback
Composite fragility score	Weighted average across all modules	62	Trigger full risk committee review

Note: This table presents a stylized fragility dashboard designed for investment committee use. Each module is scored independently and tied to a recommended action or escalation. The goal is to convert structural exposure diagnostics into decision-ready tools before capital is committed.

5.7.1 *Dashboard evolution in practice*

This stylized case illustrates how fragility dashboards might evolve within a large institutional investor. It does not describe a specific organization.

In this example, suppose a European insurance group initially relied on a manual checklist, a 12-question form that portfolio managers completed as part of their annual due diligence process. Questions included prompts such as: "Is the core cloud provider based in a jurisdiction with export control risks?" and "Is there an enforceable legal contract across borders?" These binary yes/no responses were recorded but rarely linked to downstream investment decisions.

Over time, two developments might push the institution to reassess this approach. The first might be a cyber incident affecting a third-party vendor that exposed digital vulnerabilities that had previously gone unexamined. Second, it might be new EU regulations requiring disclosure of operational continuity measures creating a compliance-driven need for more structured fragility tracking.

By the third year, the checklist might be replaced with a real-time fragility dashboard integrated into the investment management platform. The updated system aggregated multiple sources of structural exposure data, might include:

- real-time geopolitical updates mapped to portfolio holdings,
- supplier concentration indices segmented by asset class,
- sovereign compatibility assessments based on legal regime and enforcement risk.

Board-level risk reviews would now not begin with Sharpe ratios or market beta but with visualizations of structural fragility, highlighting how the portfolio might respond to scenarios involving geopolitical fracture, digital fragmentation, or jurisdictional disruption.

The dashboard would evolve from a simple compliance artifact into a strategic business tool, driving insights and proactive decision-making. It would evolve into a strategic diagnostic layer that supports forward-looking scenario planning, enables capital reallocation under stress conditions, and reinforces fiduciary oversight aligned with both resilience goals and regulatory expectations.

5.8 Portfolio Overlay Implementations: Scoring Without Mandate Disruption

For institutions seeking diagnostic insights without immediate governance impact, portfolio overlay implementations offer a natural next step beyond pilot sleeves. This model applies ARMOR-CAP scoring across the whole book, spanning public and private assets, multiple managers, and geographies, but without triggering formal escalation pathways or altering IC workflows.

The architecture of ARMOR-CAP deliberately draws from military planning doctrines and decision frameworks. Concepts such as commander's intent, rules of engagement, and the Observe–Orient–Decide–Act (OODA) loop inform its escalation logic and override governance. These parallels are not metaphorical. Fabozzi & Stenholm (2025) outlines that asset management and military operations share essential operational DNA: both demand disciplined responses to shifting threats, institutionalized learning from post-action reviews, and structured delegation that empowers frontline judgment without eroding control.

Figure 5.1, which draws on this analogy, visually positions ARMOR-CAP's escalation triggers within the broader continuum of portfolio risk engagement, similar to how commanders assess battlefield conditions and adjust engagement thresholds. Just as combat teams require doctrine to decide when to escalate force or abort missions, institutional investors require codified thresholds to override or recalibrate resilience scoring. This military-strategic framing enhances the robustness and legitimacy of escalation protocols in mission-critical capital deployment.

The benefit is twofold. First, the scoring framework pushes upstream fragility surveillance, embedding risk diagnostics directly into investment workflows before final decisions. Second, it enables structured, auditable responses through predefined override protocols when thresholds are breached.

1. Institutions gain a comprehensive 360-degree view of where fragility is concentrated across legal, jurisdictional, and operational dimensions.
2. Investment teams develop early familiarity with score behavior and domain definitions before escalation thresholds trigger formal governance actions.

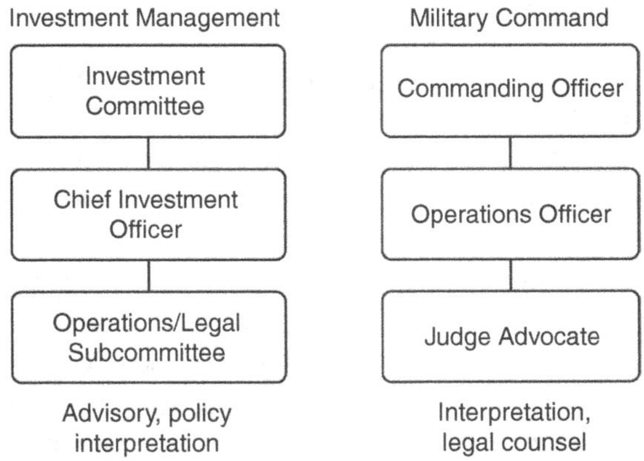

Figure 5.1. Strategic parallels between military doctrine and ARMOR-CAP escalation logic.

Note: This stylized diagram draws on military command frameworks, such as the OODA loop and rules of engagement, to position ARMOR-CAP's escalation triggers within a broader operational resilience context. It underscores how institutional override decisions mirror tactical battlefield responses under uncertainty.

This approach resembles early ESG risk rollouts, where environmental exposure scores were used in dashboards but not yet embedded in mandate language or portfolio construction (Amel-Zadeh & Serafeim, 2018). Similarly, internal VaR models often began as shadow overlays before being formalized in policy.

In the ARMOR-CAP context, overlay implementations help institutions:

- validate domain weights and scoring methodologies across all assets;
- compare fragility patterns by asset class, region, or portfolio manager;
- train investment staff and consultants on interpreting scores and submodules;
- identify risk concentrations not captured by volatility, liquidity, or credit metrics.

The absence of mandatory escalation allows these implementations to act as strategic mirrors, reflecting where resilience is strong, weak, and systematically absent.

5.8.1 *Illustrative institutional insights*

Consider the following stylized examples drawn from hypothetical scenarios to further illustrate the potential insights from a portfolio-wide ARMOR-CAP overlay. If institutions were to apply a full-book overlay, they might uncover patterns worth discussing before any formal escalation triggers are embedded.

For example, a hypothetical endowment could find that, while its hedge fund exposure shows low traditional market risk, its operational fragility scores consistently fall within the yellow band due to reliance on offshore administrators and legacy IT vendors. A public pension might discover that its seemingly "diversified" real asset program is disproportionately exposed to jurisdictions with weak bilateral treaty protections, especially in infrastructure and agricultural holdings.

In these stylized cases, an ARMOR-CAP overlay would function as a diagnostic signal generator, prompting deeper internal discussion even without immediate policy consequences. Over time, future pilot users might find that portfolio-wide overlays surface unexpected patterns, such as the following:

- Mid-risk composites (scores in the 60–80 range) are more common in operational domains than in legal ones.
- Jurisdictional fragility in private markets is often unrecognized by traditional due diligence.
- Some asset managers are resisting score publication due to reputational concerns, signaling limited score literacy and transparency readiness.

These observations could eventually inform calibration cycles, training programs, and investment committee risk appetite workshops, supporting a broader resilience culture.

While overlays help build familiarity, institutions aiming for deeper discipline will look to link scores directly to governance triggers. The following section explores how trigger-based rollouts can accomplish this.

Table 5.13 provides a stylized example of how a full-portfolio ARMOR-CAP overlay might appear, illustrating composite fragility scores across asset classes without yet activating formal escalation pathways.

5.9 Resilient Portfolio Design Principles

While the preceding sections have described structural scoring, overlays, dashboards, and scenario testing, these tools ultimately serve a broader goal: designing resilient portfolios, rather than simply optimizing them.

Table 5.13. Example of a full-portfolio ARMOR-CAP overlay (stylized output).

Asset Class	Allocation (%)	Jurisdictional Score	Operational Score	Legal/ Structural Score	Composite Score	Color Band
Developed equities	28	48.5	52.1	49.3	50.0	Green
Private equity	22	66.4	73.2	61.5	67.0	Yellow
Infrastructure debt	12	79.2	75.3	80.7	78.4	Yellow
Sovereign bonds	18	42.0	37.5	41.3	40.3	Green
Hedge funds	10	59.4	63.7	55.8	59.6	Green
Real estate	10	72.8	77.4	71.2	73.8	Yellow

Note: This stylized dashboard shows composite fragility scores by asset class in a multi-asset institutional portfolio. No formal triggers are active, but score bands flag emerging jurisdictional and operational risk concentrations. Data and bands are fictionalized and stylized for illustration.

Resilience goes beyond diversification by focusing on how portfolios function under discontinuity, stress, or system disruption. Drawing on ideas from complexity theory, network analysis, and military doctrines, a resilient portfolio design anticipates that fragility is a permanent feature of the environment rather than a tail risk to be hedged away.

This design principle includes four core features:

- *Functional redundancy*: Critical exposures should have alternative pathways or substitute assets available if systems break down, ensuring that essential portfolio functions can continue under stress.
- *Modularity*: Portfolios should be segmented or compartmentalized to contain disruptions within a limited sleeve or strategy, rather than propagating shocks across the entire allocation.
- *Adaptive allocation*: Asset weights and exposures should be continuously monitored and recalibrated using structural fragility signals, rather than relying solely on historical risk-return correlations.
- *Strategic optionality*: Portfolios should deliberately preserve capital, governance rights, and liquid resources to seize opportunities following systemic disruptions rather than fully committing to rigid mandates.

These features should be systematically reviewed and documented before stress events occur to help practitioners move from principles to practice. Investment teams and boards can better align portfolio design

Table 5.14. Checklist for resilient portfolio design.

Resilience Feature	Checklist Questions
Functional redundancy	Do we have alternative exposures or substitutes for critical portfolio positions if infrastructure fails?
Modularity	Are portfolio sleeves sufficiently separated so a shock in one does not cascade across the entire book?
Adaptive allocation	Are structural fragility signals integrated into regular rebalancing or allocation reviews?
Strategic optionality	Do we maintain dry powder, flexible mandates, or governance rights to capitalize on post-crisis openings?
Scenario playbooks	Have we rehearsed response pathways for jurisdictional, operational, or legal discontinuities?

Note: This table summarizes key diagnostic questions for embedding resilience systematically in portfolio design. It is fictionalized and illustrative, providing a starting point for discussions among boards, investment committees, and portfolio managers. Institutions can adapt or expand this checklist to suit their governance cultures and risk appetites.

with ARMOR-CAP's structural scoring framework by translating resilience goals into concrete, repeatable questions. The checklist, presented in Table 5.14, offers a fictionalized illustrative template to guide that discussion.

Institutions can incorporate external geopolitical resilience measures alongside these principles. The Geostrategic Resilience Rating (GRR), described in the previous chapter and developed by J. H. Whitney Data Services, provides a forward-looking geopolitical and jurisdictional robustness score. By integrating GRR insights, a resilient portfolio design can prioritize exposures robust to geopolitical or regulatory shocks more effectively, complementing ARMOR-CAP's domain scoring and enhancing the practical toolkit for structural risk readiness.

These resilience features align with the broader ARMOR-CAP scoring framework by transforming diagnostic signals into practical allocation principles. In this view, a resilient portfolio is not simply diversified by geography or asset class but is robust to failures in infrastructure, legal systems, or geopolitical regimes. The following section builds on these concepts by exploring how resilience design can be embedded directly into formal allocation mandates and oversight policies.

5.10 Next Steps and Applications

Having established the principles and a checklist for resilient portfolio design, this section explores the following practical steps for advancing ARMOR-CAP from a conceptual framework to a candidate for pilot testing. While ARMOR-CAP remains a proposal, investment teams and boards can begin discussing ways to experiment with its components in current governance cycles, stress tests, or allocation reviews. These applications are not prescriptive, but they offer starting points for institutions to build familiarity with structural fragility concepts and adapt them to their investment cultures.

The following chapter will build on these portfolio-level foundations by exploring how ARMOR-CAP scoring could be operationalized at the mandate and policy design levels. It will examine ways to embed structural resilience criteria into investment policy statements, manager due diligence protocols, and allocation guardrails, supporting a shift toward long-term strategic preparedness rather than reactive risk control.

5.11 Summary and Transition

This chapter translates the ARMOR-CAP framework from a conceptual risk diagnostic to a set of practical portfolio tools. Introducing scoring thresholds, portfolio overlays, dashboards, stress-tested allocation constraints, and resilient design features showed how structural fragility signals can become part of routine portfolio management. These innovations strengthen traditional risk processes without replacing them, adding a resilience dimension that positions capital for higher survivability under structural stress events.

The chapter's key messages align with the ARMOR acronym:

- **Apply** structural risk thresholds to highlight exposures that would otherwise remain invisible.
- **Reweight** portfolios using constraints anticipating system discontinuity and operational breakdown.
- **Monitor** exposures through dashboards and scenario overlays to make structural risk actionable.
- **Organize** governance processes to interpret fragility signals consistently, even before mandatory triggers are imposed.

- **Reinforce** resilience by embedding ARMOR-CAP metrics into portfolio oversight and asset allocation.

The following chapter will build upon these portfolio-level techniques by moving into formal governance and policy frameworks, showing how ARMOR-CAP can be embedded into institutional codes, mandates, and strategic oversight.

Chapter 6

Embedding ARMOR-CAP into Institutional Governance

Strategic Priorities of This Chapter

The preceding chapters showed how ARMOR-CAP can be integrated at the portfolio level through thresholds, overlays, dashboards, and allocation constraints. However, true resilience requires embedding these tools into institutional governance: the policies, mandates, oversight committees, and fiduciary processes that ultimately direct capital. This chapter shifts the focus from portfolio construction to institutional design, exploring how fragility scoring can evolve from a diagnostic tool to a durable governance framework.

The chapter highlights how ARMOR-CAP's scoring architecture, escalation logic, and interpretive standards can be woven into investment policy statements (IPSs), due diligence protocols, and board-level oversight routines. It also discusses how training, culture-building, and phased adoption timelines help establish these tools as a repeatable discipline rather than a one-time experiment.

The chapter is guided by the following strategic priorities, framed around the ARMOR acronym:

- **A — Align** institutional governance processes with structural fragility diagnostics.
- **R — Recode** the investment policy language to reflect escalation pathways and override protocols.

- **M — Monitor** scoring adoption through continuous literacy-building and calibration cycles.
- **O — Operationalize** trigger-based thresholds within investment committee and board decision structures.
- **R — Reinforce** governance culture to treat structural fragility, return, and volatility as a first-class risk dimension.

By addressing these priorities, this chapter helps institutions evolve from risk awareness to risk governance, ensuring that ARMOR-CAP principles become part of their long-term resilience architecture.

6.1 Introduction to Governance-Based Adoption

Portfolio-level scoring and overlays, while necessary, are not sufficient to safeguard institutional capital. They help identify vulnerabilities, prioritize review, and build familiarity with structural risks, but they remain advisory unless integrated into formal governance. Governance-based adoption entails transitioning ARMOR-CAP from an analytical add-on to a core element in the decision-making processes for fiduciaries, boards, and investment committees.

This step is critical because many of the structural risks highlighted by ARMOR-CAP (e.g., legal enforceability, jurisdictional compatibility, and operational dependencies) exist outside the normal language of portfolio construction. They reside in mandates, side letters, IPSs, and manager due diligence frameworks. Without incorporating ARMOR-CAP's signals into these decision documents, even the best diagnostics will remain a sidelined exercise, disconnected from where actual approvals and risk budgets are determined.

Governance-based adoption, therefore, involves a coordinated redesign of escalation pathways, accountability structures, and overriding rights. It requires not only data but also a culture that supports engaging with those data through consistent, transparent processes. In this way, ARMOR-CAP becomes a routinized part of institutional oversight, transitioning from theoretical resilience to a practical framework for decision discipline.

The following sections detail how to link ARMOR-CAP scoring with trigger-based escalation routines, embed structural risk criteria into investment mandates, and strengthen board-level literacy to ensure consistent interpretation of these tools. Through this progression, institutions can transform structural fragility from passive observation into a governed, tested, and repeatable response capability.

6.2 Trigger-Based Rollouts: Linking Fragility Scores to Decision Consequences

Overlay scoring may raise awareness, but institutional behavior only shifts when scores trigger action. In trigger-based rollouts, ARMOR-CAP scores are formally embedded into governance routines, such as investment approvals, retention reviews, or asset-level deferrals. This marks the turning point where fragility diagnostics are no longer mere risk reports but become an actual decision infrastructure.

In designing these trigger-based systems, institutions may draw lessons from military-inspired command frameworks, such as rules of engagement and pre-committed override pathways. These override protocols define who has the authority to challenge a fragility score, under what conditions, and with what documentation trail. Such clarity reduces the risk of decision paralysis during a stress event. By codifying score override mechanics in advance, governance boards can ensure consistency, accountability, and transparency, even in crisis situations.

Unlike diagnostic-only overlays, trigger-based deployments require:

- pre-agreed thresholds for score escalation;
- clear ownership by specific governance bodies (e.g., chief investment officer, or CIO, risk team, and investment committee);
- documentation templates for memos and escalation records.

This approach parallels the evolution of stress testing in banking, where test outcomes became directly linked to capital planning decisions and risk-weighted asset (RWA) adjustments, giving them concrete regulatory consequences (Board of Governors of the Federal Reserve System, 2019).

Trigger-based deployments often begin with soft enforcement, requiring investment committee discussion when exceeding a yellow-band threshold, before moving on to hard thresholds, such as automatic deferral of red-band exposures or escalation to board-level audit review.

Figure 6.1 illustrates how ARMOR-CAP fragility scores can flow through institutional escalation pathways. It uses a stylized decision tree

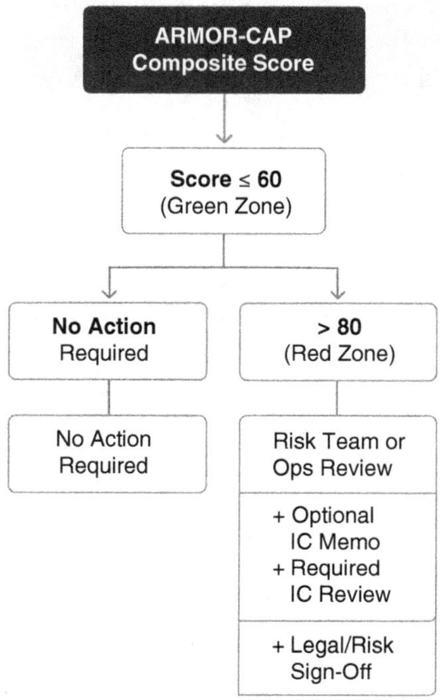

Figure 6.1. Stylized decision tree for ARMOR-CAP score escalation in trigger-based governance models.

Note: This decision tree shows how fragility scores move through institutional governance pathways. Score thresholds configure triggers, which are routed to appropriate oversight channels based on escalation type and asset classes. The figure is fictionalized for illustrative purposes.

to show how threshold breaches are routed to the appropriate governance bodies depending on asset class, domain flag, and score band.

6.3 Case Insights from Trigger-Based Models

In a fictionalized example constructed for illustrative purposes, the Northeast Teachers Retirement System (NTRS) is depicted as embedding ARMOR-CAP thresholds into its private equity re-underwriting process. Whenever an existing position became eligible for reinvestment or expansion, it was re-scored. If the composite fragility score exceeded 85, the position required a formal IC sign-off even if performance targets were met.

In the first quarter following implementation, this trigger halted three capital commitments totaling $450 million. One involved a logistics platform heavily reliant on unvetted vendors within a red-band jurisdiction. The IC ultimately approved the investment only after reworking vendor contracts and establishing escrow clauses. This illustrates that triggers need not necessarily be vetoes. They are friction devices that improve strategic discipline.

Trigger-based rollouts can also be used to illustrate questions of score ownership. In a hypothetical endowment scenario, an operational risk alert flagged a red-band exposure, but the investment team deemed it "not material." The absence of a clearly defined escalation owner delayed the simulated response, leading to a notional policy revision that incorporated escalation tracking into the quarterly Governance, Risk, and Compliance review.

As Mikes and Kaplan (2016) note, the success of risk governance depends not only on metrics but also on interpretive routines (i.e., how signals are read, challenged, and documented).

The escalation system embedded into ARMOR-CAP mirrors the principles of military command-and-control frameworks. Fabozzi & Stenholm (2025) note that asset management and military strategy rely on clearly defined chains of command, codified decision thresholds, and documented return on equity (ROE) to prevent chaos during high-pressure situations. Just as combat field officers must operate under well-understood escalation rules, investment committees must codify override protocols to preserve consistency and avoid *ad hoc* risk reactions.

6.4 Mandate-Embedded Implementation: Codifying Fragility into Institutional Design

While no institution has formally adopted ARMOR-CAP, this book presents the framework for the first time—the final stage of institutional adoption envisioned here involves embedding fragility diagnostics into foundational governance and capital allocation documents. In this scenario, ARMOR-CAP scoring would appear in IPSs, asset allocation mandates, manager due diligence templates, and oversight protocols.

A resilient investment mandate should explicitly incorporate structural fragility measures, much like how risk-based capital rules or environmental, social, and governance (ESG) guardrails are integrated today. This could involve defining minimum resilience criteria, pre-committed escalation protocols, and periodic reviews of fragility scores as part of managerial oversight. The intention is to make structural viability a first-class input to capital allocation, rather than merely a secondary consideration. By embedding these elements into investment policy statements, due diligence templates, and board charters, institutions can shift from reactive stress responses to proactive resilience planning.

The logic behind this proposed evolution is simple: Fragility scoring becomes most effective when it shapes real decisions. Embedding thresholds, escalation logic, or review triggers directly into the mandate language elevates ARMOR-CAP from a risk monitoring tool to a disciplinary mechanism within institutional design.

This conceptual pathway draws upon precedent. Risk-based capital rules under frameworks like Solvency II, minimum ESG standards in European pension law, and cyber risk escalation policies in operational resilience frameworks illustrate how diagnostic metrics can evolve into binding constraints, shaping investment approvals, portfolio rebalancing, and manager retention.

The following examples and tables are fictionalized to demonstrate how such an adoption pathway could look in practice. Table 6.1 presents stylized IPS clauses arranged by their degree of governance commitment,

Table 6.1. Stylized IPS clauses reflecting ARMOR-CAP integration.

Clause Type	**Sample Language**	**Governance Consequence**
Discretionary scoring	"Resilience scores may be considered when evaluating private market investments."	Optional; no binding action
Trigger-based review	"Allocations scoring above 80 on the ARMOR-CAP scale require investment committee review."	Required discussion and memo
Mandate-level constraint	"No new allocation may be approved if the ARMOR-CAP fragility score exceeds 85, unless approved by the board risk committee."	Enforceable veto with override protocol
Strategic rebalancing rule	"If 20% or more of portfolio assets fall into the red band, CIO must submit rebalancing plan within 45 days."	Forward-looking governance action

Note: This table presents stylized examples of IPS language that could accompany adoption of ARMOR-CAP. These examples illustrate hypothetical levels of policy commitment, ranging from soft guidance to enforceable mandates. All language in this table is fictionalized and illustrative. It does not represent real policy language used by any institution. These clauses reflect how a future ARMOR-CAP adoption could be structured.

from discretionary use to enforceable mandates, to illustrate how ARMOR-CAP scoring might be reflected in institutional policy language.

6.4.1 *Fictionalized case: IPS integration at Halcyon College Endowment*

To illustrate how ARMOR-CAP might be codified in practice, consider the fictional case of Halcyon College Endowment, a stylized institution with $8.2 billion in assets. In this hypothetical example, Halcyon revises its IPS to include the following rules:

- All private market allocations must receive ARMOR-CAP scoring before approval.
- Allocations scoring in the red band (>85) require legal and board risk committee review.
- Red-band holdings must be reviewed annually, with a score-based rationale for retention or exit.

The fictional board chair in this example cites the scoring tool as enabling "structural due diligence" that complements but does not replace financial and operational reviews. The change follows a simulated governance failure, where an offshore investment presented legal enforceability risks not captured by traditional risk assessment tools. This stylized case is not drawn from any real institution, but it reflects the logical trajectory of scoring systems that evolve from awareness tools to governance anchors.

6.4.2 *Considerations in mandate integration*

Prospective adopters of ARMOR-CAP would need to resolve several challenges before integrating these metrics into formal mandates, including the following:

- Who owns score generation, challenge, and override rights?
- How frequently should thresholds and bands be reviewed?
- Should legacy assets be grandfathered, and under what exceptions?

Effective integration of non-financial metrics in hybrid governance systems requires both binding thresholds, which ensure accountability, and discretionary interpretation frameworks, which help avoid rigidity and allow for adaptive responses to diverse stakeholder needs. Research on hybrid organizations and contemporary governance models highlights that embedding these standards into organizational codes—the shift from dashboard reporting to formal design—is a critical step for durable, diagnostic governance. This institutionalization makes metrics not just visible for performance monitoring but central to decision-making and ongoing management.

6.5 From Practice to Policy: Scaling ARMOR-CAP Across Institutions

The tools introduced in this chapter (e.g., fragility budgeting, diagnostic dashboards, and stress testing overlays) are not abstract extensions. They are actionable frameworks for embedding resilience into day-to-day decision-making. When systematically applied, these tools transform ARMOR-CAP from a conceptual framework into a repeatable discipline for evaluating structural resilience before capital is committed.

Adapting a resilience framework such as ARMOR-CAP across various institutional settings requires acknowledging the profound differences in mission, scale, and governance traditions. The same scoring framework for a sovereign wealth fund may not work for a corporate pension or a university endowment. Rather than enforcing a single rulebook, practitioners should focus on the principles of modularity and accountability, ensuring local adaptation while preserving the comparability of fragility signals. Such flexibility is essential to building durable adoption pathways.

Yet, the real test of resilience lies in internal alignment and institutional heterogeneity. For the framework to be practical, it must scale across various contextual asset classes, investment mandates, and governance structures, which were not originally designed with structural fragility in mind. Sovereign wealth funds face distinct geopolitical exposure patterns compared to corporate pension plans. Risk-parity strategies may mask jurisdictional risks in ways that private equity portfolios cannot. Multi-asset mandates require unified diagnostics that span equities, credit, infrastructure, and digital ecosystems.

This section addresses that challenge: How can a common fragility framework be implemented across diverse institutions without compromising its analytical integrity? Modularity is the starting point; accountability is what makes it work. From overlay teams to investment policy inserts to manager screening criteria, ARMOR-CAP offers a toolkit that enables the transition of resilience from concept to capital discipline, without requiring a reinvention of portfolio theory.

6.6 Scoring Literacy and Internal Training

Effective deployment of ARMOR-CAP requires more than just infrastructure; it requires interpretive fluency across investment, risk, and operational teams. Without internal training, even well-calibrated fragility scores risk being misunderstood, ignored, or resisted.

The premise is straightforward: For fragility scores to influence real-world capital decisions, all stakeholders must share a baseline understanding of the scoring logic, domain structure, threshold meaning, and escalation triggers. This mirrors the early phases of enterprise risk management (ERM) rollout, where scorecard tools often outpaced the organizational capacity to effectively use them (Mikes, 2009; Power, 2007).

Therefore, training for ARMOR-CAP should be viewed not as a back-end implementation detail but as a core element of rollout governance. Across stylized early adopters, this literacy-building phase often preceded even pilot deployment.

Table 6.2 summarizes these scoring literacy competencies by governance role, illustrating how different stakeholders might build baseline and advanced fluency.

6.6.1 *Scoring resistance is often literacy resistance*

In a series of fictional illustrations developed to demonstrate potential applications of the ARMOR framework, investment committee members are portrayed as initially resistant to red-band scores—not because they disputed the data, but because they lacked fluency in interpreting what the scores represented. In these illustrative cases, a yellow score in a single domain was mistakenly treated as an automatic stop rather than an optional review trigger.

This form of resistance is well-documented in behavioral governance literature. Power (2007) describes "ritualized compliance" as a phenomenon where risk and performance metrics are adopted in form but may be ignored in practice, due to interpretive uncertainty or organizational politics. As with prior governance frameworks, ARMOR-CAP requires a shared interpretive culture to make diagnostic metrics genuinely effective.

Table 6.2. Stylized scoring literacy matrix by governance role.

Governance Role	Baseline Literacy	Advanced Fluency
Investment committee	Understand composite score bands; interpret green/yellow/red; read fragility dashboard summaries	Evaluate threshold implications; challenge override memos; approve rebalancing based on diagnostic insights
Risk team	Navigate domain scoring modules; track escalation logs	Recalibrate scoring weights; simulate impact of changes in submodules; lead override review
Operations & legal	Recognize legal and operational fragility domains; identify red-band contracts	Lead due diligence reviews; implement scoring as part of onboarding
Consultants & advisors	Interpret dashboard outputs for clients; flag anomalies	Propose score-driven mandate changes; construct strategy overlays
Portfolio managers	Access and interpret asset-level scores; monitor scoring trends	Embed scoring thresholds into internal underwriting models

Note: This table outlines the baseline and advanced competencies required to interpret and act on ARMOR-CAP scores, tailored by stakeholder role. These domains are fictionalized and illustrative of the internal readiness gaps that would be typically addressed before implementation. This stylized matrix is fictional and intended to guide the design of training programs. It does not represent actual institutional practices.

6.6.2 *Building that culture: Sample training elements*

To prepare for deployment, stylized training programs in fictionalized settings often include:

- mock investment committee memos using fabricated scores;
- flashcards for domain-specific terminology;
- escalation flow simulations (e.g., "what happens when a composite score hits 88?");
- score audit trails for past investments (using real data applied retroactively);
- peer discussions on override rationales;

These approaches reflect the growing recognition that fragility scoring is not merely quantitative but organizationally embedded and socially negotiated (Mikes & Kaplan, 2016).

Table 6.3. Stylized 24-month deployment timeline for ARMOR-CAP rollout.

Phase	**Timeframe**	**Key Activities**
Exploration & education	Months 0–3	Internal workshops on fragility concepts; dashboard demos; initial scoring FAQ
Pilot sleeve deployment	Months 3–6	Limited scoring rollout to a thematic or private sleeve; no governance triggers
Portfolio overlay	Months 6–12	Full-portfolio scoring across legal, operational, and jurisdictional domains
Trigger-based activation	Months 12–18	Score thresholds assigned to governance actions (e.g., IC memo, deferral review)
Mandate integration	Months 18–24	Scoring logic embedded in IPS language; override protocols formalized

Note: This table presents a fictionalized rollout pathway across five phases of ARMOR-CAP deployment. The timeline is stylized to show how a hypothetical institution might stage education, pilot scoring, and governance integration over two years. It is not based on any actual institutional experience. This timeline is illustrative only and is intended to help institutions conceptualize phased adoption. The sequence and timing are fictionalized and should be tailored to specific organizational readiness.

Institutions may also need to invest in narrative-building skills for fragility interpretation in parallel with technical training. Score outputs can easily become isolated technical artifacts unless investment committees and senior leaders learn to tell a cohesive story about what these signals mean for strategic resilience. Training programs should combine quantitative literacy with a shared language to communicate structural risk, ensuring consistency across oversight tiers.

Table 6.3 presents a fictionalized 24-month timeline showing how ARMOR-CAP might be gradually introduced, from internal education to full mandate integration, to assist implementation teams in visualizing a phased deployment process.

6.6.3 *Mini-case: CedarRock Asset Management—Training meets governance*

This case is fictionalized and intended for illustrative purposes only. It does not depict any real institution or individuals.

CedarRock Asset Management, a $75 billion institutional manager based in Toronto, initiated a scoring-literacy campaign in anticipation of launching a diagnostic tool modeled after ARMOR-CAP. The internal risk committee believed that adopting a fragility-scoring overlay could help future-proof investment governance in the face of growing geopolitical, legal, and operational risks.

Yet, the firm's first internal simulation, based on mock scores across 14 strategies, was muddled. Some senior portfolio managers assumed that yellow-band scores would *automatically block* investment approvals, while legal reviewers misinterpreted high jurisdictional fragility scores as a requirement to halt compliance sign-off. Worse, a client-facing consultant circulated a summary slide that misstated red-band implications, causing reputational friction with a sovereign wealth client.

In response, CedarRock's chief operating officer paused the rollout and commissioned a 60-day internal training sprint. The initiative included:

- short "score logic" primers for each department;
- interactive escalation flow exercises based on stylized cases;
- a mock investment committee memo exercise featuring a red-band override scenario.

By the time the formal dashboard was launched, both the risk and investment teams had co-created escalation language. They updated the investment committee charter to reflect review rights without veto implications. The internal audit team later cited the literacy initiative as a model for *pre-emptive operational risk mitigation.*

Overall, this illustrative case portrays how CedarRock ultimately treats scoring not as a mere technical input but as a shared governance language, an approach that is used here to exemplify how investment and oversight cultures might be unified under the ARMOR framework.

6.6.4 *Mini-case: NorthSound Municipal Retirement Board—When everything scores red*

This case is fictionalized and intended for illustrative purposes only. It does not depict any entity, individuals, or internal policy.

The NorthSound Municipal Retirement Board (NSMRB), overseeing $23 billion in public pension assets, initiated a portfolio-wide fragility scoring pilot modeled after frameworks such as ARMOR-CAP. Using a beta-version dashboard, all 312 direct and indirect holdings were scored across three submodules: legal enforceability, operational continuity, and jurisdictional reliability.

The board had expected a normal distribution of scores; however, the first quarterly report revealed that 47% of assets scored in the red band. Alarmed, the CIO questioned whether the model was over-calibrated or if the portfolio was genuinely fragile. Meanwhile, the investment team grew frustrated with the lack of actionable differentiation, arguing that the signals did not aid in prioritizing governance responses.

During a working session with external consultants, it became clear that the scoring model had imported threshold assumptions from a different risk regime framework initially built for private credit portfolios. NSMRB's high allocation to infrastructure assets in developing markets had triggered legal fragility flags, but these were already under active management review via other controls.

The board paused the use of the red/yellow/green flags and convened a cross-departmental recalibration committee. That group:

- revisited the weightings applied to each fragility domain,
- adjusted the red-band threshold upward for long-duration real assets,
- introduced a new "watch list" zone between the yellow and red bands to help stage action items.

The outcome not only improved scoring but also signified a shift in governance expectations. In a follow-up session, the board chair could have fairly noted, "Scoring should not just highlight risk. It should help us sequence our attention."

6.6.5 *Mini-case: DeltaQuay Foundation—Mandate meets resistance*

The following is a fictionalized case for illustrative purposes. It does not depict any actual foundation, individuals, or investment decisions.

The DeltaQuay Foundation, a $2.1 billion philanthropic allocator with a hybrid governance model, attempted to codify ARMOR-CAP–inspired fragility scoring directly into its IPS. The CIO, previously working on ESG integration in a European pension context, saw structural fragility metrics as a logical next layer of fiduciary accountability.

The revised IPS draft included language stating that:

- no new private allocation could be approved if its fragility score exceeded 85;

- any red band holding would require an override memo signed by the audit and risk committee;
- the CIO would provide a quarterly distribution map detailing fragility exposures across the portfolio.

However, the proposal encountered immediate resistance.

Legal counsel warned that codifying a new, proprietary scoring model into the IPS without ensuring long-term auditability could pose a compliance risk. Several board members, especially donor-affiliated trustees, viewed the override requirement as "second-guessing" the CIO's judgment. A key consultant also flagged concerns that scoring outputs, while directionally helpful, could vary materially based on small data changes or evolving definitions.

Rather than forcing implementation, DeltaQuay backtracked. The CIO reframed fragility scoring as an internal monitoring tool to prepare IC memos, not dictate action. They also funded a pilot with their private equity consultant to develop domain-specific metrics for managerial review.

Eighteen months later, the foundation adopted many of the same escalation processes but using nonbinding protocols rather than embedded mandates. The experiment ultimately shifted from codification to cultural change, a trajectory that the CIO later described as "evolution through exposure, not edict."

6.7 Comparative Implementation Paths by Institution Type

Not all institutions will approach ARMOR-CAP integration in the same way. Variations in governance design, investment philosophy, and stakeholder expectations require tailored implementation models. A sovereign wealth fund with geopolitical mandates will face different fragility vectors and accountability thresholds, from a university endowment focused on long-term thematic exposures. This section aims to delineate these divergences, illustrating how scoring can be adapted to align with existing oversight cultures and operational capacity.

Table 6.4 compares five allocator types, each characterized by distinct governance structures, risk tolerances, and implementation postures, to

Table 6.4. Stylized implementation pathways by institution type.

Institution Type	Likely Entry Point	Key Governance Features	Escalation Model
Sovereign wealth fund	Jurisdictional scoring overlay	State-aligned oversight; geopolitical sensitivity	Cabinet- or ministry-level flagging thresholds
Public pension plan	Pilot sleeve in private credit	Board-led IC; public disclosure obligations	Scoring triggers for IC memos and board review
University endowment	OCIO consultant overlays	Investment committee + CIO; preference for discretion	Advisory scoring in memos; optional override
Insurance general account	Legal enforceability focus	Heavily regulated; actuarial-driven allocation mandates	Compliance-triggered escalation logic
Foundation/ charity	Grant-linked investment scoring	Hybrid boards; reputationally sensitive allocations	Red-band pause triggers; override via legal

Note: This table presents fictionalized comparisons of how five allocator types might phase in ARMOR-CAP, depending on their governance structures and strategic priorities. It is illustrative only and does not reflect actual institutional practices. Each row represents a stylized generalization based on common features. Not all institutions of a given type will follow the same path. Governance culture, rather than the legal form, often drives scoring behavior.

highlight the institutional variability in the deployment of fragility diagnostics. Although fictionalized, these pathways reflect patterns commonly observed in the staged adoption of ESG scoring, risk overlays, and operational risk escalation frameworks.

This diversity of implementation paths underscores a broader governance insight: Resilience overlays cannot succeed as off-the-shelf products. As Power (2007) observes, risk governance frameworks are most effective when they reflect internal political realities, not merely formal policies. ARMOR-CAP should be treated as modular and institution-responsive. Its building blocks—scoring literacy (Section 6.6), override protocols (Section 6.2), and threshold calibration (Section 6.1)—must be synchronized with each institution's governance culture, regulatory environment, and decision-making cadence. Table 6.4 offers stylized entry points, but practical implementation depends on alignment with local norms and risk tolerance.

As highlighted in Fabozzi & Stenholm (2025), the "rules of engagement" that make asset managers effective in volatile markets are often institution-specific. Implementation must be tightly synchronized with internal culture, mission clarity, and operating cadence. This reinforces the need for ARMOR-CAP to be modular and flexible, not as a static playbook but as a doctrine of engagement adapted to each allocator's governance terrain.

While Section 6.5 discussed training and literacy, this section pivots toward execution mechanics. Which tools help institutions in managing fragility escalations, documenting overrides, monitoring scoring trends, and assessing readiness? The following artifacts—fictional but grounded in best practices—illustrate the establishment of institutional processes around ARMOR-CAP without defaulting to one-size-fits-all templates.

6.8 Expanding Implementation Tools and Governance Protocols

The transition from awareness to action demands metrics and a discipline of structural resilience embedded into decision frameworks. If institutions explore operationalizing ARMOR-CAP, the most valuable lessons often arise from what is implemented and *how* it is reviewed, challenged, and refined. This section introduces four stylized governance artifacts that can help reinforce transparency, accountability, and internal learning throughout the scoring process.

6.8.1 *Stylized escalation audit trail*

Escalation triggers, such as red-band scores or domain-level fragility thresholds, are only practical when they are logged, reviewed, and linked to actual governance outcomes. Several fictionalized implementations include an audit trail dashboard that tracks scoring escalations over time to promote transparency and institutional learning.

As shown in Table 6.5, the audit trail records each escalation event, including asset-level identifiers, trigger thresholds, response actions, and sign-off authorities. This fictionalized table is modeled after the tools used in regulatory risk reporting and enterprise risk management (Power, 2007).

Table 6.5. Stylized escalation audit trail log.

Date	Asset/Sleeve	Triggered Score	Domain Flag	Action Taken	Approved by
Jan 2025	Private Credit Fund A	87	Legal	Memo escalated to IC	CIO
Feb 2025	Infrastructure Sleeve	92	Jurisdiction	Halted new deployment	Risk subcommittee
Mar 2025	Global Equity Fund X	84	Operations	Override filed	Head of risk

Note: This fictionalized log illustrates how a pension plan or endowment might track scoring-based escalations, including who triggered, reviewed, and approved each action. The entries are illustrative and do not reflect actual institutional cases. *This artifact does not reflect real institutional data or implementation.*

To: ________ (e.g., Investment Committee or Oversight Body)
From: ________ (Name and Title of Preparer)
Date: ______
Re: Red-Band Score Override – ________ (Investment Name/ID)

Score Summary:

- **Overall Fragility Score:** ___ (Red-band threshold: ___)
- **Triggering Risk Domain:** ___ – Score: ___ (domain score exceeding threshold)

Rationale/Justification:
Provide a clear explanation for why an override is warranted. Include context on the investment, reasons the ***red-band*** *score is being overridden, any mitigating factors or risk management actions, and justification for proceeding despite the high fragility score. This section should be concise yet sufficiently detailed to support the decision.*

Governance Sign-Offs: *(all listed parties must review and approve)*

- **Portfolio Manager (PM)** – Reviewed & Approved
- **Risk Officer (Risk)** – Reviewed & Approved
- **Chief Investment Officer (CIO)** – Reviewed & Approved
- **Investment Committee (IC)** – Reviewed & Approved

Figure 6.2. Stylized red-band score override memo template.

Note: This fictionalized memo template illustrates how an investment team might justify moving forward with a red-band holding, subject to IC or governance review.

6.8.2 *Override memo template*

In hypothetical institutional scenarios illustrating how ARMOR-CAP or similar diagnostic overlays could operate, fragility scores that exceed red-band thresholds are assumed to require formal override procedures to ensure transparency and governance alignment. First, Figure 6.2 presents

Table 6.6. Stylized override escalation log.

Date	Asset/Sleeve	Triggered Score	Domain Flag	Action Taken	Approved by
Jan 2025	Private Credit Fund A	87	Legal	Memo escalated to IC	CIO
Feb 2025	Infrastructure Sleeve	92	Jurisdiction	Halted new deployment	Risk subcommittee
Mar 2025	Global Equity Fund X	84	Operations	Override filed	Head of risk

Note: This fictionalized table tracks override requests triggered by red-band ARMOR-CAP scores. It records the affected sleeve or asset, the flagged fragility domain, the action taken, and the approval authority. It is illustrative only and does not reflect any real institution or scoring event.

Table 6.7. Stylized score evolution for one portfolio sleeve.

Time Period	Composite Score	Legal Fragility	Operational Fragility	Jurisdictional Fragility
Q1 2024	82	88	75	83
Q3 2024	78	84	72	78
Q1 2025	72	80	68	70

Note: This fictionalized table shows how composite and domain-level scores might change across three time periods. These patterns are illustrative and not based on real-world data. This stylized scoring evolution can help governance teams determine whether red-band exposures are being addressed over time.

a standardized form of the stylized override memo template that can be used by investment teams to request approval to proceed despite elevated fragility signals. Second, Table 6.6 shows a fictionalized escalation log that tracks override events over time, including trigger thresholds, actions taken, and governance sign-offs. Together, these tools support both case-by-case decision-making and portfolio-level accountability.

6.8.3 *Stylized score evolution timeline*

Once override protocols are in place, institutions must still evaluate whether fragility exposures are being actively addressed over time. Trend visibility, at both the domain and composite levels, is critical. This section introduces a fictionalized scoring evolution table (Table 6.7) that tracks the change in fragility scores of a single portfolio sleeve across

Table 6.8. Stylized organizational readiness diagnostic.

Governance Domain	Sample Readiness Indicators
Governance structure	IC charter includes diagnostic escalation pathways
Scoring literacy	At least one session per quarter is held for PMs and risk teams
Data integration	Legal and operational fragility data are centralized and reviewable
Override protocols	Drafted override memo template and sign-off matrix
Transparency standards	Dashboard pilots shared with the audit or compliance committee

Note: This fictionalized diagnostic tool helps institutions gauge their preparedness for the ARMOR-CAP rollout across five dimensions. It is not drawn from any specific institutional framework.

three periods. Such visualizations help governance teams assess whether red-band risks are being resolved, sustained, or deepened, and whether escalation mechanisms are working as intended.

6.8.4 *Organizational readiness diagnostic*

Before implementing a diagnostic overlay such as ARMOR-CAP, institutions must assess their internal capacity to absorb and act on the insights generated. Scoring frameworks that outpace an organization's data integration, literacy, or governance readiness can result in superficial adoption or operational resistance. Table 6.8 presents a fictionalized self-assessment tool to help institutions evaluate their preparedness across five governance dimensions. While illustrative, the diagnostic reflects common pre-implementation checks used in enterprise risk management and strategic transformation programs.

6.9 The Road Ahead: Evolving Governance with ARMOR-CAP

Although this chapter detailed how to embed ARMOR-CAP into institutional governance through scoring, escalation protocols, and mandate design, the path forward will not be linear. Institutions will face competing pressures: preserving traditional investment freedoms while responding to a world where structural fragility can compound portfolio risk beyond what volatility measures reveal.

Moving forward, ARMOR-CAP should be seen as a modular toolkit, rather than a one-size-fits-all directive. Its concepts—jurisdictional compatibility, digital continuity, and supply chain resilience—may initially serve as diagnostic overlays but will gain influence as more allocators witness unpriced fragility events. Strengthening internal literacy, coordinating escalation playbooks, and aligning governance charters with these tools will allow institutions to gradually adapt ARMOR-CAP, consistent with their culture and mission.

As structural risks evolve, the ARMOR-CAP framework will also need to grow. Future iterations could incorporate new risk dimensions (e.g., climate physical hazards, cybersecurity partnerships, or evolving geopolitical controls), building on the same modular, accountable principles. This forward-looking flexibility is what makes ARMOR-CAP not merely an overlay but a governance doctrine ready to adapt to the next decade of institutional risks.

6.10 Summary and Transition

This chapter bridged portfolio-oriented scoring with full institutional adoption, showing how governance documents, escalation routines, and override frameworks can transform ARMOR-CAP from a diagnostic experiment into a durable discipline.

- **Align** governance charters, committee structures, and escalation procedures with ARMOR-CAP metrics.
- **Recalibrate** investment policy statements and mandate documents to include resilience criteria.
- **Mobilize** training and scoring literacy initiatives to build interpretive capacity and shared accountability.
- **Operationalize** escalation thresholds to seamlessly flow into day-to-day approvals and oversight.
- **Reinforce** a governance culture where structural fragility is managed proactively rather than reactively.

Together, these actions build the foundation for Chapter 7, which will transcend institutional processes to explore cross-institutional collaborations and market-wide resilience patterns that can further reinforce structural stability throughout the financial ecosystem.

Chapter 7

Operationalizing Resilience Across Mandates

Strategic Priorities of This Chapter

Structural fragility may be diagnosed at the level of assets, strategies, or portfolio exposures, but diagnosis alone does not equal institutional resilience. The tools introduced in previous chapters—fragility budgeting, dashboards, and stress testing overlays—are not abstract extensions. They are operational scaffolds. This chapter proposes how these scaffolds can be adapted to specific institutional mandates without requiring wholesale redesign. The goal is to embed ARMOR-CAP-style diagnostics into the investment process upstream of risk realization and downstream of strategy design. This approach responds to a world where structural, geopolitical, and infrastructural shocks increasingly bypass traditional market-based signals.

This chapter unfolds across five interlocking themes:

- **A — Adaptation by Mandate.**
  Fragility manifests differently for sovereign wealth funds, insurers, pensions, endowments, and family offices. Each requires its own diagnostic emphasis.

- **R — Role-Specific Interfaces.**
  The structure of dashboards and fragility overlays must align with each institutional actor's decision authority and governance model.

- **M — Modularity Without Disruption.**
  Integration does not demand a systemic overhaul. Structural diagnostics are introduced as overlays to augment existing tools.

- **O — Operational Translation of Scores.**
  Fragility scores can inform actual portfolio decisions through threshold flags, viability screens, or conditional strategy approval logic.

- **R — Resilience as an Institutional Discipline.**
  Resilience becomes a design constraint rather than a buzzword, mapped to fiduciary duties and expressed through accountable, repeatable diagnostics.

7.1 Tailoring ARMOR-CAP to Institutional Mandates

While ARMOR-CAP offers a universal diagnostic framework for structural fragility, its practical application must be calibrated to the institutional context in which it operates. Different types of capital allocators, such as sovereign wealth funds (SWFs), pensions, endowments, insurance general accounts, and family offices, face distinct operational constraints, regulatory obligations, and governance philosophies. Applying the framework rigidly risks either overcomplicating decision-making or diluting its intent. Tailoring is not only a matter of preference; it's also a matter of fiduciary realism.

This chapter applies the three diagnostic pillars introduced in Chapter 3 (sovereign compatibility, supply chain resilience, and operational continuity) to institutional contexts. While the pillars remain consistent, their relative importance and implementation vary based on mandate type, regulatory exposure, and capital structure.

SWFs often embed geopolitical considerations in their mandates. A fund based in a politically neutral jurisdiction may prioritize diversification of strategic alliances, while one aligned with national development goals might screen investments for geopolitical alignment. Tools like ARMOR-CAP, a conceptual framework for assessing geopolitical risk, could theoretically be calibrated to evaluate sovereign compatibility through metrics such as legal reciprocity, data governance alignment, and jurisdictional dependencies. Due to their scale and state affiliations, SWFs could integrate such frameworks into national risk oversight, linking portfolio resilience to economic strategy.

As long-duration investors with fixed liabilities, pension funds operate under stringent regulatory oversight, primarily focused on preserving purchasing power and minimizing downside risk. While traditional risk management frameworks often emphasize market and credit risk, growing attention is being paid to emerging risks such as supply chain fragility and operational resilience, which can significantly impact the viability of infrastructure and private credit investments. Many pension funds have integrated environmental, social, and governance (ESG) considerations into their investment processes, reflecting evolving best practices in responsible investing. To further strengthen risk management, pension funds are encouraged to adopt additional analytical frameworks that address financial viability and broader value considerations. These practices support fiduciary standards by enabling rigorous processes, and outputs such as dashboards and audit trails can be effectively integrated into internal and regulatory reporting (OECD, 2021; CFA Institute, 2021).

University endowments and foundations operate differently, emphasizing long-term alpha generation and reputational stewardship. These investors often embrace innovation but may lack the resources for continuous geopolitical risk modeling. ARMOR-CAP can be streamlined as a pre-screening mechanism at the investment committee level, flagging proposals with embedded fragility that would otherwise go unnoticed. For example, a fund investing in frontier tech startups that heavily rely on non-democratic jurisdictions for manufacturing or server infrastructure might appear to have high growth but is structurally brittle. ARMOR-CAP's value lies in making those fragilities visible before capital is committed.

Insurance companies, particularly those managing general accounts, are subject to strict requirements for balance sheet matching and regulatory capital adequacy. Regulators, such as the International Association of Insurance Supervisors, require insurers to adopt a total balance sheet approach to identify and manage risks arising from asset–liability mismatches and exposures to legal, cyber, or operational risks. In practice, insurers must monitor concentrations of risks, such as clustered exposure to legal systems with retroactive policy risk or to assets in jurisdictions with weak cyber norms. They must also ensure that their portfolios are resilient to operational and legal discontinuities, especially in complex asset classes such as structured credit and real assets.

While proprietary tools or internal diagnostics may be used to flag such fragility concentrations, there is no evidence that frameworks like ARMOR-CAP are formally integrated into statutory capital models, such as Solvency II or NAIC Risk-Based Capital. Insurers are encouraged to align their risk management practices with regulatory requirements, but this does not involve adopting unestablished frameworks into regulatory reporting.

Family offices and foundations often lack the scale or bureaucracy of institutional peers, allowing for faster implementation. ARMOR-CAP functions effectively as a lightweight toolkit for these entities, relying on simple yes/no screens, fragility scoring rubrics, or a single-page dashboard to support quarterly portfolio reviews. What matters is not the tools' complexity but the inquiry's consistency: Is this exposure viable if key systems fail? ARMOR-CAP offers family offices a disciplined approach to risk management that balances flexibility and speed.

Across these investor types, the core design principle is modularity. ARMOR-CAP is not a software product. It is a mindset encoded in repeatable diagnostics. Institutions can start small: screening new strategies for sovereign alignment, adding fragility scores to board reports, or mapping key supplier and jurisdictional dependencies. Over time, these modules can scale to enterprise-level decision-making architectures, allowing for alignment between capital deployment and systemic viability.

Chapter 4 introduced this modularity through viability screens and fragility scoring tools. Here, those same diagnostics are adapted to institutional settings, with thresholds and tools adjusted to reflect fiduciary realities.

Table 7.1 illustrates how the ARMOR-CAP framework can be customized across different types of institutional capital allocators. While the core diagnostic pillars remain consistent (sovereign compatibility, supply chain resilience, and operational continuity), their practical application varies by organizational mandates, governance architectures, and regulatory constraints. For example, SWFs may embed ARMOR-CAP dashboards into national strategic policy reviews. At the same time, family offices may rely on simplified tools to flag fragile exposures during quarterly check-ins. The table highlights the primary use case for each allocator type, the dominant form of structural fragility they must navigate, and the likely mode of implementation. These distinctions emphasize that ARMOR-CAP is not a prescriptive toolset but a modular framework that is scalable and adaptable to the fiduciary context.

The mini-cases in this chapter are fictionalized but institutionally plausible. They are designed to illustrate how ARMOR-CAP concepts such as fragility scoring, escalation triggers, and resilience-layered governance can play out across various investment contexts. While inspired by observed institutional behavior, each case has been anonymized, synthesized, or constructed to avoid referencing any specific organization or

Table 7.1. Customizing ARMOR-CAP by institution type.

Institution Type	Primary Use of ARMOR-CAP	Key Fragility Focus	Implementation Mode
Sovereign wealth funds	Strategic alignment with national objectives	Legal reciprocity, jurisdictional access	Integrated dashboards linked to state policy
Pension funds	Fiduciary duty and long-term liability coverage	Supply chain durability, operational access	Pre-trade overlay and quarterly board reports
University endowments	Risk-adjusted alpha and reputational integrity	Digital stack reliance, supplier fragility	Committee-level screen for new allocations
Insurance general accounts	Regulatory capital matching and balance sheet integrity	Legal enforceability, cyber/IT continuity	Statutory alignment with solvency frameworks
Family offices	Flexibility, long-horizon wealth preservation	Jurisdictional exposure, asset-level fragility	Lightweight dashboard and periodic reviews

Note: This table summarizes how different types of capital allocators tailor ARMOR-CAP to their specific mandates, governance models, and structural fragility exposures. While the framework's core pillars remain consistent, institutions emphasize different diagnostics depending on their strategic goals and regulatory constraints. The table outlines the primary application of ARMOR-CAP for each institution type, the key fragility dimensions they face, and the modes through which the framework could be operationalized.

individual. Their purpose is didactic: to demonstrate how structural fragility becomes actionable in governance frameworks.

One avenue for extending ARMOR-CAP into institutional mandates is to explicitly codify resilient portfolio objectives, distinct from traditional ESG or factor-based screens. As highlighted in prior discussions, resilience is a capacity-based orientation that prioritizes legal enforceability, operational continuity, and sovereign compatibility, rather than a purely values-based framework. Institutions can adapt their investment policy statements (IPSs) to specify that allocations should preserve strategic optionality and critical redundancies, consistent with ARMOR-CAP's structural viability aims. This shift reframes resilience as a performance discipline rather than a moral or branding exercise, complementing, but not duplicating, ESG structures.

7.2 Mapping ARMOR-CAP Diagnostics to Portfolio Design

Resilience cannot remain a boardroom conversation. It must be embedded within the portfolio architecture. This section illustrates how diagnostics for structural fragility (e.g., sovereign, operational, and supply chain risks) can align with portfolio components. The process begins by identifying and integrating exposure vectors with asset classes and investment processes.

While traditional asset allocation focuses on beta exposure, liquidity, and factor tilts, structural fragility analysis overlays these with a resilience lens. The innovation lies not in reweighting based on volatility but in assessing whether underlying infrastructure can function under stress. This complements, rather than replaces, existing models such as ESG or climate risk overlays.

Some examples are as follows:

- *Emerging market sovereign bonds*: Enforceability risk (e.g., contract viability amid political shifts) must be assessed beyond credit ratings and foreign-exchange risk.
- *Digital infrastructure-dependent equities*: The resilience of cloud provider jurisdictions is critical for operational continuity.
- *Private credit tied to infrastructure*: Supply chain chokepoints (e.g., the Suez Canal) represent latent fragility absent from historical data.

Mapping also reveals nonlinear fragility: Portfolios diversified by issuer may share hidden dependencies (e.g., common legal regimes or cloud platforms). Surfacing these allows for targeted exposure adjustments.

Table 7.2 outlines how structural fragility manifests differently across asset classes and how ARMOR-CAP diagnostics can be aligned accordingly. While all asset classes are exposed to some combination of legal, digital, and physical risks, the dominant fragility vector often varies by asset structure, cash flow dependencies, and jurisdictional interfaces. For example, sovereign bonds are sensitive to legal enforceability and cross-border restrictions, while private credit is more exposed to disruptions in supplier networks and embedded operational risks. Venture capital portfolios may appear diversified across themes or sectors. Still, structural fragility arises from unpriced jurisdictional and regulatory volatility, particularly when exits rely on foreign capital markets or hostile regimes. By mapping each asset class to a primary fragility vector and recommending a corresponding ARMOR-CAP diagnostic, the table provides a high-level guide for integrating structural considerations into portfolio construction and due diligence.

Table 7.2. Aligning ARMOR-CAP diagnostics with asset classes.

Asset Class	Primary Fragility Vector	Key ARMOR-CAP Diagnostic Tool	Application in Portfolio Design
Sovereign bonds	Legal enforceability	Jurisdictional stress mapping	Adjust allocation to aligned regimes
Public equities	Digital infrastructure dependency	Cloud/IT continuity audit	Screen for sovereign-hosted platforms
Private credit	Supply chain vulnerability	Supplier network heatmaps	Include redundancy reviews in due diligence
Real assets (RE, Infra)	Geopolitical chokepoints	Cross-border access simulation	Evaluate alternative routing and access models
Structured products (CLOs)	Legal and counterparty concentration	Sovereign-aligned counterparty analysis	Diversify by legal system exposure
Venture capital	Jurisdictional regulatory change	Regulatory volatility overlay	Stress test exit scenarios under shifting tech regimes

Note: This table illustrates the varying structural fragility profiles of different asset classes and identifies the ARMOR-CAP tools most relevant to each. It maps the dominant fragility vector for each asset type (legal, digital, or geopolitical) and links it to a corresponding diagnostic method. These mappings help investors incorporate structural resilience directly into portfolio design, strategy evaluation, and position-level risk management.

These diagnostics do not predict returns; instead, they assess whether the conditions enabling the returns are stable. This perspective is especially relevant as allocators seek to navigate fractured global supply chains, tightening data localization regimes, and rising extraterritorial enforcement. In that environment, fragility becomes a design constraint, not a reactive filter.

The framework anticipates that forward-thinking institutions could embed these overlays as part of a broader shift toward structural resilience in capital deployment. A Nordic pension fund integrates legal exposure heatmaps into all new real asset allocations. In a fictionalized scenario, a Middle Eastern SWF develops a sovereign compatibility dashboard to evaluate venture capital investments, illustrating how ARMOR-CAP diagnostics could be adapted to align with national policy priorities.

ARMOR-CAP provides the structure to normalize these practices across portfolios, ensuring that resilience is not a patchwork of intuition but a systematized layer in portfolio design.

Under the ARMOR-CAP framework, portfolio managers can be evaluated for their resilience-readiness, in addition to standard risk, return, and operational due diligence. This means assessing whether their strategies have structural redundancies, robust legal frameworks, and contingency resources to continue operating during systemic interruptions. Adding this layer to multi-manager oversight complements traditional skill evaluation by explicitly screening for fragility exposure at the manager level, strengthening overall platform resilience.

Mini-case: A Canadian pension fund reconsiders its infrastructure allocation

This fictionalized case was constructed for illustrative purposes based on patterns observed in institutional infrastructure review practices.

In 2025, a major Canadian pension fund was evaluating a $500 million allocation to a consortium building a renewable energy transmission corridor through Eastern Europe. On paper, the investment passed all traditional tests: strong projected internal rate of return (IRR), low leverage, experienced operators, and multilateral financial backing. The ESG scores were positive; no red flags appeared in the initial country risk models.

However, applying ARMOR-CAP fragility diagnostics revealed a different profile.

Using supplier dependency heatmaps and cross-border access overlays, tools described earlier in this chapter, the investment team identified three potential red flags:

1. The primary power conversion facility relied on a single grid interface located in a NATO-adjacent country with escalating diplomatic tensions.
2. The legal contracts governing the off-take agreements were enforceable only in a local court system known for political interference.
3. The cloud-based control system was hosted on infrastructure routed through a third-party provider in a jurisdiction under evolving EU data protection scrutiny.

These vectors (i.e., geopolitical chokepoints, legal asymmetries, and digital dependencies) would elevate the portfolio's composite fragility score beyond the infrastructure sleeve's tolerance threshold.

Rather than abandon the project, the team in this fictional case study could have adjusted the situation as follows:

- The off-take contracts could be revised to include international arbitration clauses.
- A secondary grid interface could be added, allowing for power rerouting during crisis scenarios.
- The cloud services provider could be replaced with a European sovereign cloud vendor compliant with local digital laws.

In this illustrative scenario, the project's fragility score would fall below the portfolio's acceptable threshold following these adjustments.

The lesson is simple: Risk-adjusted return is incomplete if it ignores structural fragility. By embedding ARMOR-CAP diagnostics early in the investment review process, institutions can preserve access to high-return opportunities without compromising viability under stress.

Table 7.3 presents the before-and-after fragility scores for the fictional Canadian pension fund infrastructure investment described in the preceding mini-case. The table disaggregates the overall fragility profile into three distinct exposure vectors (i.e., jurisdictional legal risk, supply chain/access chokepoints, and digital infrastructure dependency). It quantifies the percentage reduction after applying targeted mitigation strategies. These adjustments included contractual enhancements, infrastructure redundancy, and the migration of digital dependencies to a new jurisdiction. The table illustrates how ARMOR-CAP diagnostics can guide

Table 7.3. Fragility score remediation: Canadian pension infrastructure case.

Fragility Vector	**Pre-Mitigation Score**	**Post-Mitigation Score**	**% Reduction**
Jurisdictional legal risk	85	60	–29%
Supply chain/access chokepoint	78	50	–36%
Digital infrastructure risk	73	46	–37%
Composite fragility score	**79**	**53**	**–33%**

Note: This table presents the fragility scores for the fictional Canadian pension fund infrastructure project before and after targeted mitigation steps. Scores are shown for each ARMOR-CAP vector (legal, supply chain, and digital), demonstrating how tailored interventions reduced fragility. The overall composite score drops by 33%, bringing the investment within the infrastructure sleeve's modeled tolerance range.

remediation planning by translating structural interventions into quantifiable score reductions, enabling alignment between portfolio resilience goals and institutional tolerance thresholds. The case reinforces ARMOR-CAP's role as a diagnostic tool and a mechanism for proactive intervention, turning fragility insights into design solutions.

7.3 Integrating Fragility Scoring into Governance and Oversight

As resilience becomes a recognized pillar of institutional strategy, it must also be translated into the language of governance. Boards, risk committees, CIOs, and external auditors require more than conceptual frameworks; they need clear, repeatable metrics that signal when exposure is acceptable, mitigation is necessary, and escalation is needed. Fragility scoring offers a pathway to build that structure.

One pathway to achieve this cross-allocator resilience is through resilience benchmarking consortia. As envisioned in the ARMOR-CAP proposal, these consortia would share anonymized fragility scores, escalation patterns, and policy responses among member allocators. This structure promotes consistent standards, highlights systemic blind spots, and builds a common language for structural risk governance, strengthening the broader ecosystem.

Unlike market risk or credit risk, fragility cannot be captured with a single volatility number or rating. It requires a multidimensional assessment that includes jurisdictional dependencies, operational continuity, supply chain redundancy, and legal access under stress. While there is no single, widely accepted framework for structuring and benchmarking fragility across managers or portfolios, the investment industry is increasingly developing tools to assess these risks systematically. Leading approaches include stress-testing, scenario analysis, and the integration of ESG and climate risk factors into portfolio construction (see, for example, Giese, Nagy, & Lee, 2021, on ESG integration, and industry best practices on operational and supply chain risk).

The most crucial function of fragility scoring in a governance context is thresholding. Investment committees and fiduciary boards could define *ex ante* fragility tolerance bands as they define duration buckets or tracking error limits. For example, a composite fragility score over 70 might trigger a full board review, while a score below 40 could be considered within normal limits. These thresholds are not regulatory requirements; they represent a proposed fiduciary practice designed to reduce blind spots in structural exposures.

ARMOR-CAP dashboards and fragility scoring outputs can also support structured discussions during risk reviews. Rather than reactively asking "Where did the risk come from?" boards might proactively ask "What are we currently exposed to that cannot survive systemic interruption?" This shift in emphasis from backward-looking attribution to forward-looking viability reflects the demands of navigating geopolitical complexity and digital interdependence.

Table 7.4 illustrates how fragility scoring can be operationalized through structured governance thresholds. The table proposes a four-tier system categorizing composite fragility scores into risk bands: Low (0–39), Moderate (40–59), High (60–74), and Critical (75–100). Each band corresponds to a recommended governance action and the level of oversight responsible for it. For example, exposures with low fragility scores may proceed under standard review by portfolio managers. In contrast, high scores would require a formal mitigation plan and follow-up from the risk committee. At the extreme end, critical scores would trigger the suspension of deployment and escalation to a fiduciary body such as a board of trustees. This framework brings structure and accountability to

Table 7.4. Governance thresholds based on ARMOR-CAP fragility scores.

Fragility Score Range	Risk Classification	Recommended Governance Action	Responsible Oversight Body
0–39	Low	Proceed under standard review	Portfolio manager/ risk team
40–59	Moderate	Include resilience commentary in approval memos	Investment committee
60–74	High	Require mitigation plan and follow-up reporting	Risk committee
75–100	Critical	Suspend deployment and escalate to full board or fiduciary review	Board of trustees/ oversight board

Note: This table presents a sample threshold system for fragility scores, showing how they can be mapped to specific governance actions. Scores are classified into four bands—low, moderate, high, and critical—with increasing requirements for mitigation and oversight. The framework ties each threshold to a responsible decision-making body, from portfolio managers to full fiduciary boards.

fragility management, linking diagnostic insights directly to institutional decision-making processes. By embedding fragility thresholds into investment review workflows, ARMOR-CAP provides a repeatable method for aligning oversight practices with structural risk tolerance.

Several institutions are beginning to explore how structural fragility could be integrated into governance processes. In a fictionalized example, a Dutch pension scheme includes fragility thresholds in its asset manager's request for proposals, asking managers to document resilience scores alongside risk-adjusted return projections. Similarly, a North American university endowment incorporates fragility scoring into its strategy review templates, particularly for alternative investments with embedded jurisdictional exposure, demonstrating how the ARMOR-CAP framework might be applied. The benefit isn't just diagnostic insight; it's governance clarity.

ARMOR-CAP enables boards and committees to go beyond narrative-driven oversight by creating a shared vocabulary around fragility. They gain a structure for asking difficult questions, assigning responsibility, and ensuring that structural exposures are not hidden beneath performance metrics.

Mini-case: A U.S. endowment flags a legal fragility before deployment

This fictionalized case was built to reflect common practices in U.S. endowment governance when handling legal and data-related risks.

The investment committee of a mid-sized U.S. university endowment was preparing to approve a $75 million allocation to a private equity fund focused on AI-enabled logistics platforms in Southeast Asia. The strategy—characterized by high growth, early mover advantage, and strong co-investor participation from respected global names—appeared attractive.

The due diligence memo included traditional risk metrics, track record data, and a clean ESG report. However, the endowment had recently adopted an ARMOR-CAP-inspired fragility scoring overlay as part of its governance modernization process. The fragility dashboard issued by the internal risk team showed a composite score of 76, well above the committee's alert threshold of 60.

The source of the risk? The fund's two anchor investments relied on AI server farms located in a jurisdiction undergoing regulatory changes regarding foreign data access. Under a proposed law, foreign investors could lose remote visibility into performance data, legal rights could be subordinated to local content laws, and the repatriation of profits might require multi-tiered approvals. The private equity sponsor had not flagged this, as it assumed these risks were immaterial given the contractual structures.

But the ARMOR-CAP dashboard told a different story: The legal fragility vector was red, and digital access was flagged as "contingent." Based on a board-defined policy, the allocation was paused and escalated to the risk oversight subcommittee.

That escalation can lead to:

- a renegotiation of limited partner rights with a special arbitration clause;
- a requirement that all future portfolio companies mirror data into a compliant European jurisdiction; and
- a trigger for a quarterly fragility review report tied to capital calls.

The endowment can ultimately approve the allocation but only after reshaping the deal terms to reduce operational and legal exposures.

The lesson is that governance escalation is not a bureaucratic brake—it's a resilience safeguard. Fragility scoring provides boards with the structure to say not just "yes" or "no," but "not yet—fix the fragility first."

Mini-case: A European foundation misses structural exposure
This fictionalized case was developed to highlight gaps in fragility governance and risk detection within international private credit investments.

A large European charitable foundation committed €100 million to a private credit fund focused on financing mid-sized logistics companies operating along the East African coast. The fund sponsor had a strong track record, and the investment aligned with the foundation's dual return–impact mandate. Board approval was swift, driven by performance projections and ESG alignment scores.

But there was no fragility screening, jurisdictional audit, or ARMOR-CAP-style overlay.

Six months later, the region's largest port operator, used by three of the fund's core borrowers, was abruptly nationalized following a shift in political leadership. Debt service froze. Collateral valuations plunged. One borrower went into restructuring, and another defaulted entirely. The fund's valuation dropped 12% in a single quarter.

It wasn't just the operating environment that changed; no one had asked what might happen *if* the regime changed. The legal enforceability of contracts, sovereign infrastructure alignment, and backup access mechanisms were never discussed at the board level. No dashboard flagged jurisdictional fragility. No escalation mechanism was triggered. And by the time questions were asked, capital had already been deployed.

A simple fragility scorecard would have flagged all three top exposures as "high risk." However, without a protocol to surface those signals, the board acted on narrative confidence rather than operational viability.

The absence of governance is not neutral. It's directional, as demonstrated in this mini-case. When fragility is not framed, scored, or surfaced, capital flows toward systemic assumptions that may not hold.

The last two cases present a stark contrast. In the first, a predefined governance threshold tied to a fragility score triggered escalation, reshaping investment terms and preventing exposure to a foreseeable legal constraint. In the second, the absence of a structured diagnostic or escalation protocol left a well-intentioned allocation vulnerable to a political regime shift—an avoidable loss that became institutionalized. Together, they illustrate the governance value of ARMOR-CAP, not as an additional reporting burden but as a mechanism to discipline capital deployment in environments where structural risk is rising and conventional due diligence may be blind to it.

7.4 Building an Institutional Fragility Dashboard

As ARMOR-CAP tools move from theory to implementation, the institutional fragility dashboard is one of the most potent yet underutilized applications. Unlike dashboards that track financial returns or compliance checklists, the ARMOR-CAP dashboard integrates cross-functional data to deliver a real-time snapshot of legal, operational, and geopolitical structural exposures. Its goal is not to predict market movements but to answer a more basic question: Can this institution continue functioning under systemic disruption?

At its core, the fragility dashboard consolidates outputs from the three pillars of ARMOR-CAP:

- *Sovereign compatibility*: Flagging exposures to legal systems, data regimes, or enforcement norms misaligned with institutional domicile or fiduciary responsibilities.
- *Supply chain resilience*: Identifying critical supplier nodes or chokepoints lacking redundancy or exposed to sanctions, transit risk, or political interference.
- *Operational continuity*: Scanning digital and physical infrastructure for single points of failure, whether it's a concentrated cloud service provider or a geographically exposed logistics hub.

Over time, a standardized ARMOR-CAP scoring regime could also feed directly into market-based pricing signals, such as how credit ratings and ESG metrics influence spreads and asset valuations. Incorporating structural fragility scores into benchmarks or passive allocation rules could accelerate resilience incentives, rewarding portfolios and issuers with demonstrated operational and jurisdictional robustness.

When implemented thoughtfully, a modern dashboard can serve as an overlay on existing risk, compliance, or ESG systems, eliminating the need to rebuild internal infrastructure. The primary value of such a tool is its ability to integrate information across organizational silos, drawing inputs from investment teams, legal counsel, cybersecurity, operations, and procurement. This integration enables a more unified and actionable view of potential fragilities, moving beyond fragmented insights from individual departments.

Table 7.5 presents a model dashboard layout designed to operationalize ARMOR-CAP diagnostics across institutional portfolios. The table is structured around the framework's three primary fragility categories—sovereign compatibility, supply chain resilience, and operational continuity—and a composite score aggregating overall exposure. The dashboard specifies each category's representative metrics, internal data sources, escalation thresholds, and governance actions. These thresholds are not intended as fixed rules but as illustrative parameters that institutions might adapt based on their mandates, oversight structures, and risk tolerances. For example, sovereign misalignment above 25% of assets under management (AUM) could trigger escalation to the risk committee. At the same time, excessive concentration in a single cloud provider

Table 7.5. Sample ARMOR-CAP institutional fragility dashboard structure.

Fragility Category	Example Metrics	Data Source	Threshold	Governance Action
Sovereign compatibility	% of AUM exposed to misaligned jurisdictions; treaty gaps	Legal + compliance teams	>25% misaligned AUM	Escalate to risk committee
Supply chain resilience	# of critical suppliers with no alternative; transit exposure zones	Procurement & ops	>3 chokepoints	Trigger supplier redundancy review
Operational continuity	Cloud provider concentration, data localization risk	IT + cybersecurity	>60% single-cloud	Require a migration plan or sovereign hosting audit
Composite fragility score	Weighted average across all categories	Dashboard engine	>65 composite score	Trigger full fragility mitigation protocol

Note: This table outlines a sample institutional dashboard for tracking structural fragility using ARMOR-CAP. It specifies example metrics for the three pillars, identifies typical internal data sources, and assigns escalation triggers based on hypothetical thresholds. The dashboard integrates category-level insights with a composite score, offering a scalable template for embedding fragility awareness into governance.

might prompt an audit of hosting arrangements. The composite fragility score provides a normalized benchmark for portfolio-level decisions, guiding whether mitigation or reallocation is warranted. This structure shows how the ARMOR-CAP framework can be converted from conceptual diagnostics into repeatable governance workflows.

This kind of dashboard not only centralizes awareness but also makes fragility auditable. Board members can ask: What is our current sovereign compatibility rating? CIOs can run reports showing score improvement over time. Operational teams can simulate score shifts under geopolitical scenarios. Most importantly, fragility exposure becomes trackable, making it a standard part of performance rather than a narrative afterthought.

Some large investors have already started implementing ARMOR-CAP-style dashboards. An SWF in the Middle East now integrates legal-asymmetry scores into its pre-trade memos. A U.S. insurer embeds cloud dependency risk into its internal ratings process. A global asset manager has assigned a fragility review ownership to the chief operating officer's office, ensuring operational blind spots are addressed institutionally and not left to investment teams alone.

By formalizing fragility monitoring through dashboards, ARMOR-CAP delivers what so many resilience initiatives lack: repeatability. Not just one-off red-team exercises, but ongoing structural visibility embedded into capital allocation itself.

Mini-case: A fragility dashboard averts a crisis in real time
This finalized case was synthesized for this chapter based on plausible scenarios where real-time fragility alerts could influence final-stage capital deployment.

A global asset manager based in London was preparing to allocate $400 million to a regional infrastructure fund with assets in Southeast Asia. The fund held long-dated stakes in toll roads, port terminals, and logistics parks, many of which were tied to infrastructure corridors of the Belt and Road Initiative (BRI). The investment committee was aligned. The risk team had signed off. And ESG reviews came back positive.

But just 48 hours before the capital call, the firm's recently launched ARMOR-CAP fragility dashboard issued a system alert: Three of the fund's core assets were governed under bilateral treaties with limited legal reciprocity, and all of them relied on digital infrastructure operated by a Chinese cloud provider recently flagged in EU parliamentary discussions about sanctions enforcement.

Because the fragility dashboard was embedded within the pre-trade governance process, the alert automatically escalated to the CIO and legal counsel. Within hours, a follow-up review revealed:

- no contractual fallback if the local enforcement regime was suspended;
- no legal guarantee of data access continuity in the event of EU–China digital restrictions;
- no contingency plan for port or toll road rerouting if partner countries realigned politically.

The CIO paused the allocation and called an emergency meeting of the risk and operations subcommittees. To make the allocation acceptable, the asset manager could restructure the deal terms as follows:

- An international arbitration clause could be inserted into all operating agreements.
- Cloud redundancy could be added using a sovereign-aligned provider domiciled in say, Singapore.

- The sponsor could be required to develop a legal fallback plan in case of treaty suspension.

Suppose the final fragility score on the revised position as a result of these three actions dropped from 78 to 47. That would clear internal approval thresholds.

Suppose subsequently, EU legislation passed, expanding scrutiny of digital infrastructure providers linked to foreign intelligence risks. Competitors who had not flagged the exposure would have to unwind positions at a discount.

As can be seen from this mini-case, dashboards are not window dressing. When embedded adequately in governance workflows, fragility diagnostics can preempt missteps that are invisible to conventional risk, legal, or ESG reviews. The power of ARMOR-CAP is not perfectly captured in its timely disruption of flawed assumptions.

7.5 Embedding ARMOR-CAP into Investment Policy Statements

For ARMOR-CAP to function as more than a tactical overlay, it must be encoded into the governing DNA of institutional investment, beginning with the IPS. The IPS defines the strategic, operational, and risk parameters within which capital is allocated. It outlines fiduciary duties, return expectations, risk budgets, and governance structures. Yet, most IPS documents remain silent on fragility, implicitly assuming system continuity, legal enforceability, and uninterrupted market access. ARMOR-CAP challenges that assumption.

Integrating ARMOR-CAP into the IPS enables institutions to signal to internal stewards, external managers, and oversight bodies that resilience is not a suggestion but a prerequisite. By codifying sovereign compatibility, supply chain resilience, and operational continuity as structural criteria for deployment, the IPS becomes an instrument of forward-looking governance.

Table 7.6 presents a stylized example of how an institutional IPS might be revised to incorporate ARMOR-CAP diagnostics. The table contrasts standard IPS language, typically focused on volatility, liquidity, and credit metrics, with a version introducing resilience criteria based on structural fragility assessments. In the ARMOR-CAP-informed version, traditional financial risk constraints are complemented by requirements for

Table 7.6. Example of IPS clause before and after ARMOR-CAP integration.

Clause Component	Traditional Language	ARMOR-CAP-Informed Language
Investment criteria	Strategies must meet risk-return expectations within volatility and liquidity bands.	Strategies must meet risk-return expectations and demonstrate resilience under discontinuity scenarios, including legal, supply chain, and operational stress.
Risk considerations	Portfolio volatility shall not exceed *X*%, and credit exposure shall be diversified.	Portfolio shall maintain fragility scores below governance-defined thresholds. Exposure to legal asymmetry, digital chokepoints, or concentrated supply chains must be documented and mitigated.
Governance escalation	Strategies flagged as high-risk must be reviewed by the risk committee.	Allocations with fragility scores above 70 must be escalated to the full board with mitigation plans reviewed quarterly.
Reporting requirements	Quarterly performance and compliance reports to be submitted.	Quarterly fragility dashboards and stress test updates to be submitted alongside performance reviews.

Note: This table compares a traditional IPS clause with one revised to reflect ARMOR-CAP principles. The updated language integrates fragility scoring, escalation thresholds, and resilience documentation into investment, risk, and reporting protocols. It demonstrates how structural fragility can be codified within governance frameworks rather than acknowledged as an externality.

legal viability, supply chain redundancy, and operational continuity. Fragility scores are proposed as a new governance dimension, with thresholds that can trigger escalation and mitigation protocols. The updated clause language also formalizes the use of fragility dashboards and stress test updates in regular reporting cycles. While purely illustrative, this comparison demonstrates how institutions can embed ARMOR-CAP into their policy architecture, aligning investment guidelines with the realities of geopolitical risk, infrastructure dependence, and systemic vulnerability.

Some institutions are beginning to explore how structural fragility, such as exposure to geopolitical, legal, and supply chain risks, could be formally addressed within their governance frameworks. For example, in a hypothetical scenario, a U.S. state pension plan might amend its IPS to require mapping of sovereign risk exposures for all new private investments. Similarly, a European insurance group could integrate screening criteria for supply chain dependencies into its guidelines for illiquid assets, triggering a governance review when certain risk thresholds are crossed. In both cases, the IPS functions as a living document that evolves in response to changing geopolitical, legal, and digital realities.

The OECD (2024) Guidelines on Corporate Governance of State-Owned Enterprises advocate for robust and adaptive governance frameworks, emphasizing transparency, accountability, and effective risk management. However, the guidelines do not prescribe specific screening or mapping methodologies for risk or investment processes.

Mini-case: A fictional Nordic pension fund embeds fragility scoring in its IPS

This fictionalized case is presented for instructional purposes but reflects governance patterns that may emerge as institutional allocators adapt to structural fragility risks.

In 2025, a Nordic public pension fund initiated a comprehensive review of its IPS in response to board-level concerns over rising geopolitical instability, particularly in technology infrastructure. Although the fund already maintained a sophisticated ESG framework and a robust enterprise risk system, the CIO recognized that systemic fragility, particularly legal and operational dependencies, was not explicitly accounted for in its existing policy.

Working with internal teams and external advisors, the fund proposes an IPS revision that introduced the following structural fragility thresholds:

> "All new private market and infrastructure investments must demonstrate resilience under jurisdictional, operational, and supply chain stress scenarios. Allocations with fragility scores above 65 must undergo legal review and be accompanied by a documented mitigation plan before investment committee approval."

Suppose six months later, the revised IPS was put to the test. The investment team reviewed a co-investment opportunity in a European fiber-optics firm expanding into Africa and Central Asia. The deal appeared attractive, with strong valuations, clean sponsor materials, positive ESG ratings, and alignment with long-term infrastructure goals.

However, fragility diagnostics flagged three risks:

- The firm's expansion relied on a telecom license that could be revoked without appeal.

- Its cloud infrastructure was fully hosted in a diplomatically volatile jurisdiction.
- Key suppliers were listed under U.S. export restrictions.

The resulting fragility score was 72, exceeding the IPS-defined threshold. Following the policy, the risk committee could initiate a structured mitigation process. The sponsor could possibly agree to:

- migrate data hosting to a neutral jurisdiction;
- include arbitration clauses under Swiss law;
- dual-source critical digital components.

Suppose that these measures reduced the fragility score to 54, bringing the investment within policy limits. One year later, a licensing regime change in one of the original jurisdictions resulted in access revocation for a competing firm, an exposure the pension fund avoided.

This scenario illustrates why codification matters. The fund transformed resilience from an informal concern into a binding governance requirement by embedding fragility scoring into its IPS. In this case, the value of ARMOR-CAP was not theoretical; it was operational.

Table 7.7 outlines a staged progression in how institutional IPS can evolve to incorporate fragility-aware language. The framework begins with traditional language that omits structural risk entirely and moves through intermediate phases of narrative awareness, procedural requirements, and threshold-based governance triggers. At the highest level of maturity, IPS language fully embeds ARMOR-CAP diagnostics as a standard condition for capital deployment, linking structural viability to investment approval.

Table 7.8 complements the language evolution in Table 7.7 by mapping how institutional processes mature alongside policy changes. It describes five stages of governance development, each defined by the IPS posture, the presence of fragility triggers, and illustrative actions. At the lowest stage, fragility is entirely ignored; at the highest, ARMOR-CAP dashboards drive automated governance responses that condition capital release on structural viability.

Codifying fragility awareness into the IPS yields multiple benefits:

- It clarifies structural expectations for external managers.
- It empowers risk and compliance teams with documented escalation pathways.

- It reduces ambiguity during shocks, offering pre-agreed thresholds for intervention.

Most importantly, it transforms ARMOR-CAP from a tactical tool into a strategic standard, anchored in the institution's legal and fiduciary core.

As Tables 7.7 and 7.8 illustrate, the progression from narrative awareness to fully embedded fragility thresholds is not merely a shift in language; it is a shift in institutional design. As IPS language evolves, so too do the governance mechanisms that determine when risk must be escalated, which bodies must intervene, and how structural vulnerabilities are addressed before capital is deployed. This section outlines how fragility-aware governance matures alongside IPS development, translating diagnostic insight into structured oversight actions.

Governance triggers and the maturation of resilience oversight

A pattern emerges across Tables 7.6, 7.7, and 7.8: The shift from informal or advisory language to threshold-based governance mechanisms is not merely semantic but operational. The true power of resilience-layered IPS frameworks lies in their ability to define expectations and consequences. That is, when fragility is detected, what happens next?

In Level 0 or Level 1 IPS documents (as shown in Table 7.7), governance responses are often left to individual interpretation. Legal asymmetry or supply chain vulnerability might be noted but rarely escalated; however, when institutions reach Level 3 or Level 4, where quantified fragility scores are codified, predefined triggers activate governance responses: legal review, mitigation plan submission, or even full board escalation.

Table 7.9 illustrates how governance escalation protocols mature alongside the institutional adoption of the fragility-aware IPS. It shows the evolution from informal or nonexistent triggers in traditional IPS frameworks to structured, quantifiable escalation mechanisms anchored in fragility scoring thresholds. As institutions progress through the IPS maturity curve—from Level 0 (Traditional) to Level 4 (Embedded ARMOR-CAP)—governance actions shift from discretionary analyst commentary to automated board-level escalation tied to pre-defined score bands and systemic risk triggers.

Tables 7.4 and 7.9 provide a governance toolkit for embedding ARMOR-CAP into institutional oversight. Table 7.4 defines the fragility

Table 7.7. Evolution of IPS language to integrate structural resilience.

Stage	IPS Language Focus	Fragility Awareness	Governance Implications
Level 0: Traditional	"Investments will be assessed based on return expectations, standard deviation, and liquidity metrics."	Absent	Fragility not considered; system continuity assumed
Level 1: Narrative aware	"Investments should consider geopolitical and operational risks where material."	Implicit, anecdotal	Addressed *ad hoc* by individual reviewers; no escalation or scoring required
Level 2: Procedural	"All illiquid strategies must include a section discussing operational and legal continuity assumptions."	Proceduralized but unsystematic	Governance reviews inconsistently applied; disclosures without thresholds
Level 3: Threshold-based	"Investments with fragility scores >65 must undergo formal legal review and mitigation before approval."	Quantified and policy-linked	Triggers structured oversight processes; escalation embedded in IPS
Level 4: Embedded	"Resilience scoring is required for all asset classes. ARMOR-CAP thresholds form part of pre-trade approvals."	Fully embedded in investment and risk systems	Institutionalized governance; resilience metrics required for capital approval

Note: This table traces how IPS language evolves from generic risk metrics to resilience-based governance. It identifies five levels of fragility integration, from *ad hoc* awareness to formalized thresholds and embedded scoring. The goal is to show how institutions can codify structural risk into their decision-making architecture over time.

score bands and their corresponding governance actions, enabling investment committees and boards to make informed decisions based on structural viability. Table 7.9 complements this by mapping how escalation mechanisms mature across IPS development stages, showing that resilience governance is not merely a matter of score interpretation but of institutional design. These tools offer a blueprint for transforming fragility awareness into enforceable policy actions.

Table 7.8. Institutional maturity model for IPS resilience integration.

Stage	Label	IPS Character	Governance Trigger	Example Action
1	Reactive	IPS silent on structural fragility	None	Investments approved on return metrics alone
2	Aware	Language includes narrative references to geopolitical risk	Informal alerts by staff reviewers	Analyst flags concern in an appendix
3	Proceduralizing	Requires qualitative commentary on continuity risks	Optional review at risk committee	Legal continuity note included with approval memo
4	Threshold-linked	IPS includes quantified fragility thresholds	Required escalation to risk or board level	Score >65 requires documented mitigation
5	Embedded (ARMOR-CAP)	Fragility scoring institutionalized across asset classes and teams	Auto-escalation based on dashboard output	Capital cannot be deployed until fragility score falls within limits

Note: This table presents a five-stage model for institutional adoption of fragility-aware IPS governance. It links IPS posture with governance triggers and practical actions. The framework helps institutions benchmark their progress toward fully embedded structural resilience practices.

This escalation logic transforms ARMOR-CAP from a diagnostic lens into a governance tool. Without clearly defined governance responses, fragility scoring may remain cosmetic. With them, it becomes institutional muscle, automatically activating accountability in proportion to structural exposure.

As shown across IPS clause revisions, escalation thresholds, and institutional maturity curves, the formal integration of fragility governance is not an abstract exercise but an operational safeguard. ARMOR-CAP provides the language, thresholds, and escalation logic to turn fragility awareness into fiduciary discipline. Institutions are prepared to translate policy into practice with resilience now embedded in IPS mandates and governance workflows. The next step is implementation: aligning dashboards, diagnostic tools, and cross-functional oversight to ensure documented and actionable structural risk.

Table 7.9. Escalation triggers by IPS maturity level.

IPS Level	Maturity Description	Trigger Type	Escalation Mechanism
Level 0	Traditional	None	No escalation language; risk addressed informally
Level 1	Narrative aware	Advisory notes	Analyst-level commentary without required action
Level 2	Procedural	Qualitative review required	Optional risk committee input; no threshold enforcement
Level 3	Threshold-linked	Quantified fragility threshold	Mandatory legal review or mitigation for scores >65
Level 4	Embedded ARMOR-CAP	System-based scoring with auto-flags	Automatic escalation tied to pre-trade and board approvals

Note: This table tracks how escalation mechanisms evolve as IPS governance becomes more structurally resilient. It highlights the shift from informal or qualitative triggers to system-based thresholds linked to ARMOR-CAP diagnostics. The model reinforces that policy maturity is not merely about language but about how institutions respond to real-time risk signals.

Governance escalation can be summarized as follows. The evolution of IPS governance is not about adding complexity. Instead, it's about adding clarity, consequence, and control. These five principles summarize how resilience oversight transforms from passive awareness to institutional discipline:

- *Link language for escalation*: Fragility terms in the IPS must connect directly to who is accountable and what actions are triggered.
- *Move from commentary to thresholds*: Governance effectiveness increases when escalation is based on scores or trigger levels, not narrative disclosures.
- *Design governance to match risk exposure*: Decisions at higher fragility levels should automatically be routed to higher levels of oversight.
- *Automate enforcement, not just measurement*: Fragility diagnostics' value lies in activating institutional procedures without discretion.
- *Treat governance design as part of the risk architecture*: IPS clauses, thresholds, and structured oversight triggers should be considered integral components of the institution's operating model, not legal boilerplate.

In addition, collaborative platforms could coordinate joint stress-testing and scenario-planning exercises across multiple allocators, creating shared data pools and comparative benchmarks for structural fragility. These joint initiatives would strengthen trust and improve calibration while fostering a more transparent and robust market environment.

7.6 Expanding Dashboard Visualization: Stylized Implementation Examples

To further illustrate how institutions can operationalize fragility monitoring through dashboard tools, consider stylized wireframes or grayscale mock-ups representing the core features of an ARMOR-CAP-aligned resilience dashboard. These visual tools help decision-makers synthesize multi-dimensional risk data into a coherent view.

- *Risk heatmaps by region or vendor tier*: These highlight geographical or supplier-specific concentrations of fragility, coded by severity bands (e.g., red for acute exposure, yellow for moderate, and green for stable).
- *Viability alerts and scoring bands*: Panels flag critical stressors such as sovereign risk deterioration, energy supply insecurity, or legal exposure from shifting regulatory regimes. These alerts are scored using ARMOR-CAP benchmarks and coded to track over time.
- *Escalation triggers and threshold warnings*: The dashboard includes escalation thresholds (e.g., breach of fragility index > 75), with visual cues such as red blinking indicators or automated notifications to governance bodies.

These dashboards are not merely data visualization exercises but serve a governance function. Implementing best practices suggests updating dashboards on a rolling basis (e.g., monthly), integrating them with institutional risk appetite statements, and reviewing them regularly with oversight committees. The most effective designs tie dashboard thresholds to decision rights. For example, this would trigger portfolio reviews, halt new exposures in flagged regions, or escalate reports to board-level subcommittees.

Table 7.10 maps the distribution of ARMOR-CAP responsibilities across key institutional roles (portfolio managers, risk officers, investment committees, and boards). It shows how no single function features fragility diagnostics but requires a layered, role-specific approach to governance.

Table 7.10. Stylized fragility dashboard panels and escalation logic.

Panel	Dashboard Focus	Visual Element	Scoring Threshold	Escalation Trigger
A	Sovereign compatibility heatmap	Choropleth map showing legal alignment by jurisdiction	>25% AUM in red-coded regions	Escalate to legal and compliance review
B	Viability alert bar chart	Bar chart for each fragility domain (legal, cyber, and supply chain)	Any domain scoring >70	Flag for investment committee inclusion
C	Composite fragility index timeline	Line graph showing fragility score over time (vs. benchmark)	Slope > +10 points QoQ	Trigger portfolio rebalancing review
D	Threshold warnings summary	List of flagged exposures with color-coded severity tags	≥3 red tags in a single region or asset class	Escalate to CIO or board-level oversight

Note: This table illustrates how ARMOR-CAP responsibilities are distributed across institutional governance layers. Each role engages with a specific diagnostic input and has defined escalation or response duties when fragility thresholds are met. By embedding accountability at multiple levels, institutions can ensure that resilience oversight is distributed and disciplined.

For each actor, the table identifies their primary accountability, the ARMOR-CAP data or output they engage with, and the type of action they are expected to take when fragility thresholds are approached or breached. This cross-functional alignment ensures that structural risk is neither siloed nor overlooked but addressed at the appropriate organizational level with the right governance tools.

These escalation principles come to life when embedded in real-time decision systems. They are most visible through fragility dashboards aligned with institutional governance roles.

Beyond passive signal-sharing, future iterations of ARMOR-CAP could support sector-level crisis coordination protocols and shared escalation pathways. By jointly defining what score thresholds or scenario triggers should prompt a sector-wide response, institutions can create a more resilient financial ecosystem that reacts faster and more coherently to systemic shocks.

7.7 The Next Phase: Institutionalizing Resilience in Practice

Integrating fragility awareness into governance is no longer a conceptual frontier; it is fast becoming an institutional imperative. Yet, embedding resilience into IPSs and designing tiered governance responses through dashboard infrastructure is only the beginning. The next stage is institutionalization: embedding ARMOR-CAP principles into the culture, decision-making processes, and oversight rhythms of asset owners, allocators, and fiduciary stewards.

As risk architectures evolve, institutions must move beyond episodic adoption of resilience tools. The goal is not to create another layer of compliance but to embed reflexive resilience into the machinery of capital allocation. This requires coordination across legal, investment, operations, and risk teams to ensure that fragility signals, triggered by geopolitical shifts, legal asymmetries, or infrastructure risks, lead to decisions, not just dashboards.

Looking forward, several trends will shape how ARMOR-CAP is implemented and adapted:

- *Cross-functional governance will become the standard.* Investment decisions will increasingly require documented input from legal, cyber, and operational risk officers, especially when structural fragility thresholds are breached.
- *Pre-trade diagnostics will become as routine as volatility screens.* Institutions will implement filters to block or flag exposures by asset class, fragility index, sovereign compatibility scores, or supply chain viability.
- *Resilience benchmarking will be developed.* Just as ESG benchmarks evolved to track carbon and governance exposures, new resilience indices will compare portfolio durability across peers, funds, and strategies.
- *Codification will feed automation.* As fragility clauses mature within IPS documents, automation engines can directly tie them to system-based alerts and pre-programmed escalation logic.

The path ahead is clear: Resilience will not simply be monitored. It will be enacted instead. The policies, clauses, and thresholds described in this chapter offer a scaffolding. The institutional discipline to act on them (reflexively, repeatably, and across asset classes) will define resilience leadership in the decade ahead.

While coordination and information sharing strengthen collective resilience, they raise concerns about excessive uniformity, potential collusion, or antitrust scrutiny. ARMOR-CAP adopters must balance the benefits of cooperation with safeguards that preserve fair competition and protect against herd-driven vulnerabilities.

7.8 Summary and Transition

This chapter advanced the operational core of ARMOR-CAP by showing how structural fragility becomes governable through policy codification, automated escalation, and dashboard-linked oversight. Institutional oversight shifts from discretionary judgment to structured enforcement when fragility metrics are embedded in IPSs and aligned with governance triggers. In this framework, resilience is no longer an advisory theme. Instead, it becomes a measurable, monitorable, and enforceable condition of capital deployment.

Five strategic takeaways define the chapter's contribution:

- **Automate escalation across governance layers.**
  Threshold-based triggers should route decisions to legal, investment, or board-level review, replacing narrative commentary with structured, accountable oversight.
- **Reframe IPS mandates to embed fragility metrics.**
  Linking structural viability scores to approval workflows transforms resilience from aspirational guidance into an enforceable investment policy.
- **Measure governance maturity through responsive action.**
  The effectiveness of fragility oversight lies not in having dashboards but in whether alerts lead to timely, documented, and accountable decisions.
- **Operate dashboards as activation tools, not displays.**
  Dashboards should be wired for intervention, triggering preauthorized responses, rather than passively reflecting risk conditions.
- **Realign fiduciary duty around structural resilience.**
  IPS frameworks incorporating ARMOR-CAP extend fiduciary responsibility to cover legal enforceability, supply continuity, and operational viability, alongside traditional financial metrics.

With fragility governance now codified into policies, thresholds, and dashboards, the next step is institutional execution. The following chapter turns from internal governance design to implementation, examining how ARMOR-CAP tools can be integrated into workflows, mapped to specific asset classes, and adapted to the mandates of different allocator types. Operationalizing resilience requires frameworks and field-tested procedures that translate structural diagnostics into investment discipline.

As the following chapter explores mandate design and scoring adoption timelines, these cross-institutional perspectives will remain vital to harmonizing fragility diagnostics without undermining healthy market competition.

Chapter 8

Field Scenarios and Implementation Lessons

Strategic Priorities of This Chapter

The preceding chapters established the ARMOR-CAP framework's architecture, tools, and governance pathways, providing a comprehensive blueprint for embedding resilience into institutional investment processes. However, even the best frameworks encounter practical hurdles when deployed in real organizations. This chapter advances the discussion by immersing the reader in realistic, fictionalized field scenarios, highlighting how ARMOR-CAP might be implemented, tested, challenged, and adapted in practice.

The chapter has four strategic priorities:

- **A — Amplify:** Provide narrative depth by examining extended, plausible case studies that demonstrate ARMOR-CAP in action.
- **R — Reveal:** Uncover the challenges, breakdowns, and "failure modes" arising during implementation, from governance bottlenecks to data coverage gaps.
- **M — Model:** Illustrate how investment teams might interact with ARMOR-CAP processes on the ground through fictional documents, memos, and meeting minutes.
- **O — Orient:** Equip practitioners with lessons learned that can guide calibration of escalation rules, stakeholder education, and portfolio rebalancing decisions in the real world.

- **R — Reinforce:** Strengthen governance structures by embedding lessons from these scenarios into durable policies, procedures, and organizational culture.

This chapter does not describe real institutional experiences. Instead, it uses stylized, hypothetical examples to show how the ARMOR-CAP framework could unfold in practice, including the kinds of iterative and sometimes contentious steps that organizations might face when embedding resilience into daily decision-making.

8.1 Introduction

ARMOR-CAP was designed not as a static checklist but as a living, adaptive framework for managing structural fragility in capital allocation. Previous chapters described its conceptual pillars, scoring systems, diagnostic overlays, and institutional pathways, providing readers with a rigorous toolkit for building resilience into investment practices. Yet, the move from conceptual design to practical deployment is rarely linear. The realities of institutional culture, governance friction, data limitations, and political pressures shape its trajectory.

This chapter applies ARMOR-CAP through stylized, fictionalized cases drawn from energy, finance, technology, and infrastructure. These scenarios do not represent any real institutions or allocations but are designed to illustrate how structural fragility can surface in unexpected ways. Each case demonstrates how ARMOR-CAP scoring, resilience portfolio design principles (as introduced in Chapter 5), and governance overlays might transform risk oversight from passive observation to active mitigation.

Through extended case narratives, the chapter will illuminate how fragility scores move from spreadsheets to investment committee (IC) debates, how thresholds are challenged or ignored, and how new risk frameworks can either gain traction or stall when faced with entrenched incentives. Each scenario will weave in stylized investment memos, boardroom exchanges, scoring dashboards, and escalation decisions to give readers a grounded sense of what ARMOR-CAP looks like "in the wild."

The cases are designed to teach as well as to caution. Where a fictional institution succeeds, the narrative highlights the factors that made that success possible: cross-functional coordination, documentation rigor, or leadership sponsorship. Where a fictional institution fails, the narrative

Table 8.1. Institutional modes of ARMOR-CAP implementation.

Mode	Description	Typical Use Case	Governance Involvement
Pilot sleeve	Apply ARMOR-CAP to a single asset class or strategy (e.g., infra, PE)	Trialing diagnostics in complex private assets	Investment risk or PM team
Portfolio overlay	Apply scoring to the full book without governance triggers	Score awareness, no immediate escalation	Risk team with light PM input
Trigger-based rollout	Link score bands to investment approval or retention workflows	Compliance-aligned scoring with thresholds	GRC and IC integration
Mandate-embedded	Bake scoring into IPS language, mandate design, or onboarding docs	Long-term resilience governance	Board and executive oversight

Note: This table illustrates four hypothetical approaches by which institutions could implement ARMOR-CAP. Each mode differs by its scope, ownership, and strategic intent, offering flexible entry points and learning trajectories. This table is stylized and fictionalized for illustrative purposes.

exposes the root causes: misaligned incentives, data blind spots, or insufficient governance authority.

These scenarios are not meant to be prescriptive but illustrative. They demonstrate that even the most well-designed frameworks succeed only when institutions integrate them into authentic decision-making, backed by a culture of accountability, transparency, and iterative learning.

Recalling the four dominant modes through which institutions might initially deploy ARMOR-CAP is helpful to frame these scenarios. These modes differ in scope, governance, ownership, and escalation pathways, offering distinct entry points and learning trajectories. Table 8.1 summarizes these stylized implementation pathways, which serve as a conceptual map for the following fictional case narratives.

8.2 Evergreen State Pension Pilot: A Stylized Use Case in Infrastructure Investing

Institutional adoption of any new diagnostic tool typically begins with a limited-scope rollout that is targeted enough to contain risk but broad enough to reveal implementation challenges. This section explores a stylized use case featuring the hypothetical Evergreen State Pension (ESP), a fictionalized $120 billion U.S. public pension fund. ESP is modeled after the concerns faced by many large public plans: balancing long-term infrastructure investments with legal and operational exposures that traditional environmental, social, and governance (ESG) and risk frameworks could not fully address.

8.2.1 *Background and rationale*

In this fictional scenario set in 2025, ESP's board of trustees is portrayed as requesting a pilot to test ARMOR-CAP in a focused asset sleeve before considering broader adoption. Infrastructure co-investments were chosen because they involved complex contracts, vendor relationships, and jurisdictional risks, making them a prime candidate for fragility screening. ESP is described as having recently expanded its infrastructure sleeve through co-investments in transportation and energy assets, prompting fictional trustees to ensure these positions could withstand geopolitical shocks and legal asymmetries.

The pilot had three explicit goals:

- Assess whether ARMOR-CAP scoring surfaced risks missed by existing ESG frameworks.
- Test the workflow impact of integrating fragility scoring into IC reviews.
- Evaluate how escalation memos might operate in practice.

8.2.2 *Stylized scoring illustration*

In this fictionalized illustration, ESP selected 14 active co-investments totaling $6.1 billion across transportation and energy infrastructures, primarily in Asia and Latin America. Each deal is reviewed using the ARMOR-CAP diagnostic pillars, with stylized attention to:

- jurisdictional fragility (e.g., bilateral treaty protections, sovereign risk),
- operational fragility (e.g., vendor concentration, digital dependencies),
- legal/structural fragility (e.g., enforceable step-in rights, bankruptcy carve-outs).

As part of this fictionalized illustration, the infrastructure subcommittee is portrayed as collaborating with ESP's legal, risk, and investment teams to apply ARMOR-CAP scores to each co-investment.

One hypothetical case involved a fiber-optic network expansion in Southeast Asia that scored 92.4 on a stylized composite fragility scale, placing it deep in the "red zone."

Key fictionalized fragility drivers included the following:

- The host country was not a party to any bilateral investment treaties with the U.S.
- A single vendor operating under U.S. export restrictions served as a critical supplier.
- Step-in rights were governed entirely by local law with no arbitration fallback.

While this stylized project would have passed the chief investment officer's (CIO) financial hurdle rate, the hypothetical high ARMOR-CAP score is portrayed as triggering a formal escalation.

8.2.3 *Escalation and governance response*

A stylized fictional escalation memo (Figure 8.1) presents a simulated assessment of legal, operational, and jurisdictional exposures for one infrastructure co-investment. In this scenario, the memo recommends deferring further capital deployment until enforceable remedies could be strengthened. ESP's risk committee and legal counsel are portrayed as hypothetically agreeing, concluding that the investment, as imagined, lacked sufficient safeguards if the vendor defaulted or the local government imposed capital controls.

A fictionalized internal committee debate follows. In this scenario, some stylized portfolio managers argue that the deal's projected returns outweigh its structural exposures. The CIO portrayed in this illustration, responds that ignoring a red-zone ARMOR-CAP flag would conflict with the fund's hypothetical resilience mandate. In a narratively constructed narrow vote, the committee is shown deferring the additional capital call and reallocating $250 million to a lower-scoring energy transmission project in Latin America.

The stylized board minutes later noted:

> *"This marks the first time a non-financial structural fragility score altered an approved allocation. While the CIO emphasized risk prudence, members requested a formal review of ARMOR-CAP thresholds to ensure the framework balances flexibility with resilience."*

Evergreen State Pension Infrastructure Co-Investment Pilot

Escalation Memorandum: Fragility Review

Subject: Fiber-Optic Network Expansion – Southeast Asia

Date: June 12, 2024

Prepared by: Office of the Chief Investment Officer

Summary of Findings:

- **Jurisdictional Fragility:** Host country not party to U.S. bilateral investment treaties.
- **Legal Fragility:** Step-in rights under local law only, no international arbitration fallback.
- **Operational Fragility:** Sole vendor subject to U.S. export restrictions.

Composite ARMOR-CAP Score: 92.4 (Red Zone Threshold: >75)

Recommendation:

- Defer additional capital deployment pending legal renegotiation to include enforceable arbitration clauses and dual-vendor guarantees.
- Request further stress-testing of local regulatory risk by external counsel.

Next Steps:

- Present findings to Infrastructure Subcommittee (June 20, 2024)
- Submit board-level risk update (July 1, 2024)

CIO Comment:

"This project's exposure profile cannot be mitigated within our current policy limits. Recommend pause and reallocation."

Figure 8.1. Fictional ARMOR-CAP escalation memo (excerpt).

Note: This figure presents a stylized escalation memo generated through the ARMOR-CAP framework, highlighting how structural fragility triggers formal governance actions. The memo summarizes jurisdictional, legal, and operational vulnerabilities associated with a proposed infrastructure investment and recommends pausing capital deployment pending risk mitigation. It illustrates how diagnostic scores translate into oversight decisions and board-level communications.

8.2.4 *Lessons learned and institutional implications*

In this fictionalized illustration, the stylized pilot is portrayed as yielding a mix of successes and challenges for ESP. On the positive side, the ARMOR-CAP framework surfaced a critical legal enforceability gap that traditional risk models had overlooked. The scenario also demonstrates how a transparent escalation pathway, presented in a stylized board-level risk update, could, in principle, shield an investment team from retrospective second-guessing.

However, the stylized pilot also highlights several hypothetical weak spots:

- gaps in submodule data coverage for private co-investment structures;
- uncertainty regarding ownership of escalation decisions between investment and legal staff;
- concerns about "signal fatigue" if too many investments were hypothetically flagged in the red zone.

In this fictional scenario, ESP is depicted as extending ARMOR-CAP to its private credit and real estate strategies, while adopting a phased rollout to refine score calibration and governance alignment.

Table 8.2 presents a stylized summary of outcomes across infrastructure, private credit, and real estate, capturing:

- institutional profile,
- pilot sleeve,
- scoring emphasis,
- governance trigger used,
- key pilot insight.

These fictionalized findings illustrate how even a cautious conceptual-pilot sleeve deployment of ARMOR-CAP might test an institution's ability to translate fragility signals into defensible capital-allocation choices.

8.3 Atlas University Endowment: From Enthusiasm to Pushback

University endowments often operate with a dual mission: preserving purchasing power over long time horizons while stewarding reputational integrity. The Atlas University Endowment, a fictional $10 billion educational foundation, is used here to illustrate how ARMOR-CAP might be introduced enthusiastically but face institutional resistance during practical implementation. This stylized example is designed to model the internal dynamics of a forward-looking endowment exploring a resilience-focused overlay.

Table 8.2. Stylized summary of ARMOR-CAP pilot deployments.

Institution Type	Pilot Sleeve	Scoring Emphasis	Governance Trigger Used	Key Pilot Insight
Public pension fund	Infrastructure co-investment	Legal & jurisdictional	IC memo + board-level risk update	Deferred capital call due to lack of treaty protections
Sovereign wealth fund	Emerging market debt	Jurisdictional & operational	Portfolio risk committee memo	Identified concentrated custodial and payment systems risk
University endowment	Private equity co-investment	Legal enforceability	None (diagnostic only)	Flagged step-in rights gaps in 2 of 9 co-investments
OCIO platform	Multi-asset models	Composite fragility	Legal & ops escalation team	Reprioritized vendor relationships after red-zone triggers
Insurance general account	Real assets	Operational fragility	IC discussion only	Highlighted cyber/IT risk in real estate data-sharing dependencies

8.3.1 *Background and mandate context*

In this fictionalized scenario set in 2025, the Atlas University Endowment's investment committee is portrayed as exploring resilience overlays to strengthen its ESG framework. Several stylized board members, concerned about geopolitical risks to international private equity and venture capital allocations, are imagined as endorsing ARMOR-CAP as a diagnostic tool. They view its structured scoring as a potential complement to traditional ESG metrics, particularly for uncovering hidden operational and legal exposures in complex cross-border investments.

Given Atlas's commitment to innovation, there is initial enthusiasm, within this stylized context, for piloting ARMOR-CAP on a selection of private equity co-investments with emerging-market components. These hypothetical deals are described as having delivered strong returns but facing increasing exposure to vendor concentration, data localization laws, and legal asymmetries in non-OECD jurisdictions.

8.3.2 *Stylized pilot rollout and score calibration*

In this fictional illustration, Atlas is portrayed as selecting nine active private equity co-investments, totaling $800 million, for a stylized ARMOR-CAP pilot. The hypothetical deals are assessed using ARMOR-CAP's three diagnostic pillars: sovereign compatibility, supply chain resilience, and operational continuity.

Several key stylized friction points are modeled to reflect challenges that a university endowment might encounter in practice:

- *Data completeness*: Many GPs provided limited operational data, complicating the scoring of supplier or digital dependencies.
- *Score communication*: The private markets team viewed ARMOR-CAP scores as "uncertain" compared to familiar ESG ratings.
- *Escalation logic*: Unlike infrastructure portfolios with clear legal frameworks, venture-backed companies operated with layered corporate structures that blurred legal accountability.

Despite these hypothetical challenges, the stylized pilot flags two co-investments as structurally fragile. One fictional case, a high-profile fintech startup operating in a jurisdiction with aggressive data localization policies, is described as receiving an illustrative ARMOR-CAP score of 81, placing it in the red zone.

8.3.3 *Governance, conflict, and decision debate*

In this stylized scenario, the fictional ARMOR-CAP pilot team is portrayed as drafting an escalation memo recommending enhanced legal protections and potentially delaying a follow-on investment. However, the stylized portfolio manager leading the fintech strategy objects in this fictional context, arguing that the legal risk was theoretical and the investment's performance metrics justified immediate reinvestment.

While structurally rigorous, this narrative conflict illustrates a core tension that might arise in real-world settings: ARMOR-CAP signals could potentially challenge or override traditional performance-based allocation arguments. In this stylized debate, the fictional investment committee is depicted as divided:

- Stylized board members and risk staff support delaying the follow-on allocation.
- Fictional portfolio managers express concern about missing market opportunities and disappointing co-investment partners.

In a simulated contentious IC meeting, the CIO is portrayed as proposing a comprise, partially holding back the allocation while legal counsel reviews relevant data provisions. Stylized IC minutes excerpted in Figure 8.2 capture the narrative resolution:

> *"Consensus reached to fund $10 million of proposed $20 million allocation while legal counsel reviews data residency provisions. ARMOR-CAP score acknowledged as a legitimate governance input but not a stand-alone veto."*

8.3.4 *Stylized postmortem and lessons learned*

Three months later, within this stylized scenario, news breaks that the fictional fintech's local regulator has frozen customer data under newly enacted national security laws. This fictional action is portrayed as temporarily paralyzing the company's operations. In this illustrative case, Atlas is described as being partially insulated because of its reduced reinvestment exposure, but it still faced valuation markdowns.

A stylized board-level postmortem is imagined, concluding that while ARMOR-CAP provided an early warning signal, the institution's internal

Atlas University Endowment – Investment Committee Meeting

Date: October 14, 2025

Agenda Item: Follow-on Allocation Request – FinTech Co-Investment

Discussion Highlights:

- ARMOR-CAP composite score of 81 placed investment in red zone
- PM argued business performance metrics outweighed structural concerns
- Board members emphasized fiduciary duty to respect risk frameworks
- Legal counsel noted unclear data residency protections

Decision:

- Partial allocation of $10 million approved (out of $20 million request)
- Additional legal review of data localization and recourse provisions mandated
- ARMOR-CAP score acknowledged as a legitimate governance input but not a standalone veto

Action Items:

- Legal review completion deadline: November 30, 2025
- Resubmit allocation memo to IC for final sign-off after legal review

CIO Closing Comment:

"We are building confidence in fragility scoring, but we cannot treat it as a hard stop until escalation pathways are fully codified."

Figure 8.2. Stylized investment committee minutes (excerpt).

Note: This figure presents a fictional excerpt from investment committee minutes, illustrating how ARMOR-CAP scoring informs, but does not solely dictate, capital allocation decisions. Despite a red-zone fragility score, the committee approved a partial investment pending further legal review. The discussion reflects the evolving role of structural diagnostics in governance, balancing fiduciary duties with practical flexibility as escalation protocols mature.

culture failed to fully act decisively on that insight. Stylized board members note several hypothetical governance shortfalls:

- a gap between fragility scoring and actionable decision thresholds,
- inconsistent portfolio manager training on how to interpret ARMOR-CAP signals,
- the lack of a formal permission structure to override performance incentives when structural fragility emerged.

The Atlas case demonstrates that diagnostic frameworks alone cannot shift culture. Resilience overlays must be accompanied by clear decision

Table 8.3. Key failure modes observed in Atlas University's endowment pilot.

Failure Mode	Description	Mitigation Steps
PM performance bias	PMs prioritized short-term financial returns over structural risk scores	Add fragility thresholds as mandatory IC inputs
Data coverage gaps	GPs lacked operational and legal data detail to support robust scoring	Formalize data disclosures in due diligence questionnaires
Weak escalation authority	No clear owner of escalation decisions for private investments	Define escalation ownership in IC charters
Threshold ambiguity	Red-zone scores lacked explicit enforcement rules	Document hard vs. soft thresholds in investment policy
Inconsistent stakeholder training	PMs and risk teams did not share common ARMOR-CAP language or understanding	Require annual ARMOR-CAP training modules

Note: This table summarizes the key failure modes observed during the ARMOR-CAP pilot of Atlas University's endowment. These issues reflect common challenges when integrating structural fragility scoring into private market allocations. Practitioners can use these lessons to strengthen governance and alignment before a broader rollout.

rules, escalation pathways, and consistent education to build trust and legitimacy across investment teams.

Table 8.3 summarizes the key failure modes illustrated by this scenario, including:

- portfolio manager performance bias,
- data coverage gaps,
- weak escalation authority,
- threshold ambiguity.

In this scenario, Atlas University Endowment is portrayed as taking steps to strengthen its governance by modeling a policy for partial gating of red-zone investments and introducing ARMOR-CAP training modules for all portfolio managers and risk staff.

8.4 Orbis Sovereign Fund: Trigger-Based Rollout in a Geopolitical Environment

Sovereign wealth funds face distinct challenges when implementing structural risk frameworks, especially when their mandates align with national strategic priorities. The fictional Orbis Sovereign Fund (OSF), a $500 billion sovereign investor based in a geopolitically neutral but strategically active jurisdiction, is used here as a stylized illustration of these complexities. In this fictional scenario, OSF's efforts to integrate ARMOR-CAP through a trigger-based rollout highlights how cultural resistance and political considerations might constrain resilience efforts.

8.4.1 *Mandate and governance context*

OSF's stylized mission blends long-term national wealth preservation with strategic domestic development goals. Its fictional portfolio includes global real estate, infrastructure, and technology platforms across multiple jurisdictions. In response to growing geopolitical fragmentation, OSF's risk team is portrayed as proposing ARMOR-CAP to identify fragilities in its cross-border holdings, particularly in contested sectors such as logistics hubs, critical minerals, and data infrastructure.

In this hypothetical scenario, the board is described as approving a pilot with a trigger-based rollout design. ARMOR-CAP score bands are linked to simulated escalation thresholds, including—in the red zone—automatic board-level intervention and possible position rebalancing.

The stylized triggers are defined as follows:

- Green zone (score < 40): Normal monitoring.
- Yellow zone (40–60): Portfolio review triggered.
- Red zone (>60): Board-level risk discussion, with potential hard stop.

8.4.2 *Stylized implementation tensions*

In this fictionalized scenario, rolling out the trigger-based ARMOR-CAP framework at OSF is portrayed as encountering substantial internal resistance:

- Some stylized OSF officials express concern that ARMOR-CAP is a foreign-designed scoring model, potentially conflicting with principles of sovereign self-determination.
- Regional project sponsors are imagined to worry that the red-zone triggers could slow down politically important infrastructure deals.
- Legal teams are described as raising hypothetical concerns that hard-coded triggers might create compliance burdens that conflict with national strategic discretion.

To explore these dynamics, a fictional governance working group, composing stylized representatives from OSF's legal counsel, risk heads, and sovereign affairs advisors, is portrayed as debating for weeks how much authority ARMOR-CAP scoring should have relative to board-level discretion.

8.4.3 *Fictional governance negotiations*

A stylized excerpt from the fictional working group discussion is presented in Figure 8.3 to illustrate the types of internal governance debates that might arise when attempting to integrate ARMOR-CAP in a sovereign wealth fund context.

OSF Working Group Discussion Notes – November 7, 2025 (Stylized Excerpt):

- *Risk director:* "If we override the red-zone triggers repeatedly, the framework will lose credibility."
- *Strategic affairs officer:* "We cannot let a numeric score shut down projects aligned with national policy."
- *Legal counsel:* "We need flexibility but also clear rules or we risk noncompliance with board governance principles."
- *Outcome (fictional):* Agreement to pilot red-zone triggers with a board veto override option, subject to documentation of rationale.

8.4.4 *Stylized pilot rollout results*

In this fictional scenario, OSF is portrayed as applying the trigger-based ARMOR-CAP system to a stylized $15 billion sleeve of cross-border logistics and energy real estate assets. Of 45 fictionalized assets reviewed:

- 12 are described as falling in the green zone (routine monitoring);
- 24 in the yellow zone (portfolio reviews triggered);
- 9 in the red zone, requiring board-level discussion.

In one illustrative red-zone case, a high-profile port investment located in a region with unpredictable political alliances receives a stylized ARMOR-CAP score of 78. ARMOR-CAP highlights hypothetical risks related to sovereign compatibility, local union controls, and contested port governance structures.

Orbis Sovereign Fund – ARMOR-CAP Working Group

Date: November 7, 2025

Participants:

- Risk Director
- Strategic Affairs Officer
- Legal Counsel
- Portfolio Manager, Global Infrastructure

Discussion Highlights:

Risk Director:

"If we override the red-zone triggers repeatedly, the framework will lose credibility. We must protect ARMOR-CAP's signaling integrity."

Strategic Affairs Officer:

"National priorities cannot be subordinated to a numeric model, especially if a project supports diplomatic relationships."

Legal Counsel:

"Without some override documentation, we could be exposed to claims of inconsistent governance under our sovereign charter."

Portfolio Manager:

"We need a practical balance — if an asset is strategically important, fine, but then we must structure legal guarantees to offset its fragility."

Outcome:

- Pilot red-zone triggers will remain active
- Board will retain veto override authority for designated strategic projects
- All overrides must be documented in board risk minutes with supporting legal opinions

Figure 8.3. Stylized working group discussion excerpt (Orbis Sovereign Fund).

Note: This figure captures a fictionalized exchange within an ARMOR-CAP working group at a sovereign fund, highlighting the tension between structural diagnostics and national strategic priorities. Participants debate the risks of overriding red-zone fragility scores, the need to preserve governance integrity, and the role of legal documentation in maintaining accountability. The discussion underscores how override authority can coexist with rigorous documentation and institutional safeguards.

Although such a score would normally trigger a hard stop under the stylized rollout protocol, the OSF board in this fictional narrative is portrayed as overriding the ARMOR-CAP trigger. The rationale is framed in terms of strategic diplomatic considerations. The override is accompanied by modeled governance conditions, including enhanced legal protections, dual-party operational oversight, and quarterly reporting to the sovereign affairs committee.

8.4.5 *Stylized lessons learned*

The Orbis Sovereign Fund case illustrates several key takeaways that may be relevant for sovereign allocators considering structural fragility frameworks:

- cultural friction between sovereign priorities and standardized resilience scoring;
- potential conflicts between geopolitical objectives and independent risk triggers;
- the value of documented override protocols to balance flexibility with accountability.

Table 8.4 summarizes stylized best practices emerging from this hypothetical pilot. These fictionalized insights are designed to help

Table 8.4. Best practices for trigger-based ARMOR-CAP rollouts in sovereign funds.

Practice	Description
Red-zone override documentation	Require a formal board memo explaining the rationale for overriding a hard stop
National priority exception	Identify pre-approved project classes where resilience scoring serves as advisory only.
Strategic affairs integration	Involve sovereign strategic offices early in ARMOR-CAP calibration.
Quarterly reporting	Enhance reporting cadence for assets subject to override
Education and change management	Provide training for sovereign officials on ARMOR-CAP concepts to build trust in scoring.

Note: This table outlines best practices drawn from the Orbis Sovereign Fund's trigger-based ARMOR-CAP hypothetical pilot. These practices highlight how sovereign investors can balance resilience scoring with strategic national priorities. They offer a blueprint for maintaining accountability while preserving flexibility.

other sovereign allocators to think through how fragility scoring systems like ARMOR-CAP might be aligned with national strategic mandates in theory, even if no such implementation has yet occurred in practice.

8.5 Apex Family Office: Lightweight Dashboards in a Nimble Environment

Family offices operate with a unique blend of flexibility and concentrated decision-making authority. The fictional Apex Family Office, managing $2 billion in assets across direct private equity, real estate, and multi-asset strategies, is used here as a stylized illustration of how a lightweight version of ARMOR-CAP might be integrated into a fast-moving investment environment. Unlike large institutions with formal boards and multi-layered investment committees, this fictional office is portrayed as relying on a small circle of decision-makers who value speed and discretion.

8.5.1 *Stylized pilot objectives and dashboard design*

In this fictional scenario, Apex's leadership is portrayed as seeking to improve structural risk visibility into structural risks without disrupting their quick turnaround on investment decisions. To achieve this, they are imagined as adopting a lightweight ARMOR-CAP dashboard, designed with simple yes/no indicators and a high-level fragility scoring system presented on a single page. The objective of this stylized pilot is to embed resilience thinking into quarterly reviews and new investment proposals without adding bureaucratic friction.

Key features of the fictional dashboard include:

- a composite fragility indicator with green/yellow/red flags;
- a one-page summary of legal, supply chain, and operational dependencies;
- a section for brief mitigation notes, if needed.

The intention behind the fictional dashboard was to serve as a conversation starter, not a strict gating mechanism.

8.5.2 *Stylized pilot rollout and early challenges*

In this fictional scenario, the lightweight ARMOR-CAP dashboard is portrayed as being piloted across $500 million in direct private equity holdings. Almost immediately, the Apex team—within this stylized narrative—encounters several illustrative challenges:

- *Over-screening concern*: One promising real estate co-investment is flagged red due to local legal ambiguities and a single-vendor construction contract. In this scenario, the family principal expresses concern that the signal is overly conservative and risks derailing a lucrative, long-standing relationship.
- *Threshold ambiguity*: With only a high-level composite flag, the fictional team struggles to interpret exactly what specifically must be addressed before proceeding.
- *Cultural fit*: The small, relationship-driven Apex team finds the "structural fragility" language unfamiliar compared to their usual deal-screening language.

A stylized investment committee discussion, excerpted in Figure 8.4, captures the underlying tension:

> *"We cannot let a red flag shut us down on a deal with a fifteen-year relationship. The scoring is helpful, but we need the flexibility to apply judgment."*

8.5.3 *Stylized adaptation and mitigation*

To address the fictional concerns raised during the stylized pilot, Apex is portrayed as modifying its lightweight ARMOR-CAP dashboard to better align with its culture and decision-making style. These illustrative adjustments include:

- adding short narrative boxes explaining why a score was flagged,
- replacing the pass/fail framing with a checklist of potential mitigations,
- rebranding the tool as a "Resilience Lens" to reduce perceived friction and improve cultural fit.

This fictionalized adaptation is designed to balance structural discipline with operational flexibility. In the stylized scenario, the previously

Apex Family Office Resilience Lens Dashboard

Date: March 10, 2026

Investment Proposal: Midtown Urban Co-Investment

Composite Fragility Flag: RED

Key Issues Identified:

- Single-vendor construction contract without backup supplier
- Local legal jurisdiction lacks established dispute resolution channels
- Permit processes subject to sudden regulatory change

Mitigation Discussion (Narrative):

"While vendor concentration is high, the relationship is strong, and local partners are experienced. Recommend adding dual-recipient legal recourse clauses and exploring secondary supplier options before final approval."

Next Review:

- Target date: May 15, 2026
- Responsible party: Apex General Counsel

Figure 8.4. Stylized resilience dashboard snapshot (Apex Family Office).

Note: This figure illustrates a fictional resilience dashboard used by a family office to evaluate a proposed co-investment through the ARMOR-CAP framework. The dashboard flags structural vulnerabilities, including vendor concentration, legal uncertainty, and regulatory volatility, prompting a mitigation plan before final approval. It illustrates how fragility scoring can be operationalized in a concise, decision-oriented format that integrates legal, operational, and governance reviews.

flagged real estate deal is brought back to the investment committee after the vendor contract is revised and dual legal recourse clauses are added. As modeled, the fragility flag shifts from red to yellow under the updated dashboard logic.

The fictional family principal, in this scenario, approves the investment, citing improved structural protections and greater confidence in the downside survivability of the asset.

8.5.4 *Stylized lessons learned*

The fictional Apex Family Office case demonstrates that smaller, more agile investors may still benefit from a simplified application of the ARMOR-CAP framework but only if the approach is adapted to their

Table 8.5. Adapting ARMOR-CAP for family office settings.

Adaptation	Description
Narrative notes	Add brief narrative context to scores to support flexible decision-making.
Simplified indicators	Use green/yellow/red flags with supporting commentary rather than numeric thresholds.
Cultural rebranding	Position the tool as a "Resilience Lens" instead of a compliance overlay
Relationship sensitivity	Incorporate longstanding partner relationships as a mitigating factor in risk reviews.
Quick turnaround fit	Design dashboards for quarterly check-ins rather than continuous monitoring.

governance and culture. In this stylized scenario, the following practices emerge as useful guidelines:

- use simpler, narrative-based scoring tools that clarify rather than constrain;
- focus on discussion rather than strict thresholds;
- calibrate dashboards to match their governance style.

Table 8.5 summarizes fictional best practices drawn from the stylized Apex Family Office case, illustrating how smaller, agile investors might tailor ARMOR-CAP tools to align with their governance style.

8.6 Cross-Case Lessons

The preceding case narratives reveal a familiar pattern: Implementing ARMOR-CAP is not simply a technical process but an exercise in governance, culture, and disciplined adaptation. Each fictional institution (e.g., Evergreen State Pension, Atlas University Endowment, Orbis Sovereign Fund, and Apex Family Office) highlighted barriers and breakthroughs as it translated structural fragility diagnostics into operational practice. Taken together, these experiences underscore several cross-cutting lessons for practitioners.

First, clarity of ownership is critical. ARMOR-CAP signals only gain traction when escalation pathways, decision rights, and override protocols are clearly defined. Several case studies revealed confusion regarding

Table 8.6. Cross-case implementation lessons.

Lesson	Implications for Practice
Clear ownership of decisions	Define escalation and override responsibilities to avoid institutional ambiguity.
Calibrated thresholds	Tailor scoring bands and enforcement rules to match institutional risk appetite.
Consistent education & training	Build confidence and consistency through workshops and periodic knowledge refreshers.
Flexible override protocols	Allow reasoned exceptions with proper documentation to preserve strategic flexibility.
Iterative feedback mechanisms	Embed score reviews and scenario testing into governance cycles to maintain relevance as conditions evolve.

Note: This table distills the key lessons from the four fictional case studies in this chapter. These insights highlight critical enablers of successful ARMOR-CAP adoption, from threshold design to governance alignment. Practitioners can use this reference as a checklist when planning or refining their resilience rollouts.

who makes the final decision when a fragility score conflicts with financial performance metrics. Second, threshold design matters. Numeric scores are powerful, but they risk being ignored or applied too rigidly without calibrated, institution-specific thresholds. Flexible frameworks, with documented exceptions and recorded rationales, can help institutions balance discipline with strategic opportunities.

Third, education and communication emerged as essential. Investment teams need a scoring tool, a shared vocabulary, and consistent training to interpret fragility signals. ARMOR-CAP is more effective when all stakeholders, from legal to operations to portfolio managers, trust and understand its purpose. Finally, these scenarios showed that resilience cannot remain a one-time exercise. Institutions must build feedback loops to revisit scores, test escalation protocols, and adapt to evolving geopolitical, legal, and operational realities.

Table 8.6 summarizes these cross-case insights in a concise reference for future ARMOR-CAP pilots and broader implementation efforts.

8.7 Summary and Transition

This chapter advanced the ARMOR-CAP framework from theory to field-level application, highlighting practical challenges and adaptations through realistic, fictionalized case scenarios. These narratives provided a richer sense of how structural fragility scoring functions in different institutional contexts, from large sovereign wealth funds to nimble family offices. The lessons drawn here reinforce the critical ingredients of a durable resilience strategy:

- **Assess** how pilot sleeves and trigger-based rollouts can surface structural vulnerabilities and test institutional governance boundaries.
- **Reveal** hidden conflicts between performance-based incentives and structural scoring, exposing cultural and political resistance to resilience protocols.
- **Map** practical pathways for integrating ARMOR-CAP, including escalation memos, dashboard tools, and threshold calibration methods.
- **Orient** investment teams and stakeholders toward an iterative mindset, recognizing that resilience is a living discipline that evolves with shifting legal, technological, and geopolitical landscapes.
- **Reinforce** the commitment to transparency, clear decision rights, and robust override documentation to ensure ARMOR-CAP signals remain credible and actionable over time.

These fictional scenario-based illustrations will serve as a transition to future discussions, which will explore how ARMOR-CAP principles could influence broader market practices, collaborative stress-testing initiatives, and evolving regulatory standards.

As the discussion now shifts beyond single-institution pilots, Chapter 9 will examine how ARMOR-CAP concepts can be scaled across entire market ecosystems. It will consider the opportunities and challenges of integrating fragility scoring into collaborative initiatives, regulatory frameworks, and industry-wide stress-testing practices.

Chapter 9

Interpreting ARMOR-CAP Scores: Benchmarking, Trajectories, and Strategic Translation

Strategic Priorities of This Chapter

With scoring mechanics established and governance pathways clarified, this chapter questions: What do ARMOR-CAP scores mean in context? Beyond point-in-time thresholds and red-band alerts, practical interpretation requires institutions to track score evolution, benchmark against peers or sleeves, and extract forward-looking insights. This chapter unpacks how scores can be normalized, compared across domains, and converted into board-ready narratives or policy triggers. It also introduces diagnostic formats such as spider charts, heat maps, and trend lines, which help institutions translate complexity into resilience-informed decision-making.

ARMOR-CAP is a proposed framework introduced in this book. It has not been adopted or implemented by any institution to date. All cases, scorecards, dashboards, and governance examples in this chapter are fictionalized for illustrative purposes only.

The five foundational elements of this chapter are as follows:

- **A — Analyze score trajectories, not just thresholds.**
  Fragility is dynamic. Institutions must monitor how scores evolve, not just whether they cross a trigger.
- **R — Reference peer and internal benchmarks.**
  Scores gain meaning when contextualized. Benchmarking across manager sleeves, asset classes, or peers makes diagnostic output actionable.

- **M — Map domain interactions and compound fragility.**
  Legal, jurisdictional, and operational scores may converge or conflict. Understanding overlap improves signal clarity.
- **O — Operationalize interpretation through visual tools.**
  Dashboards, spider plots, and scorecards communicate metrics to boards, investment committees, and external stakeholders.
- **R — Recast scoring as strategic insight, not compliance.**
  When fragility metrics inform allocation, oversight, and mandate design, they become instruments of resilience, not just risk.

9.1 Trajectory-Based Scoring: Movement Over Time

While thresholds are essential for triggering oversight, the movement of ARMOR-CAP scores, whether upward, downward, or stagnant, provides the richest diagnostic signal. Static fragility scores offer only a snapshot; trajectories tell a story. Did a jurisdictional fragility rating improve following regulatory harmonization? Did operational fragility rise across several sleeves after a supplier audit? The dynamic behavior of scores helps distinguish between transient noise and emerging systemic vulnerabilities.

To extract meaning from score trajectories, institutions should track their rates of change, directionality, and volatility. As previously described in Chapter 6 for static thresholds, these dynamic attributes also influence escalation decisions and resource allocation: Rising scores may justify preemptive audit funding, while stabilized scores might support capital deployment. Most importantly, the trajectory of movement informs timing (i.e., when to engage, escalate, or exit).

9.2 Benchmarking and Peer Comparison

ARMOR-CAP scoring becomes more powerful when contextualized. A fragility score of 68 in legal risk may trigger concern, but compared to a peer median of 80 or a prior-year institutional average of 72, it may represent material improvement. Benchmarking enables institutions to situate their fragility exposure in relative terms, comparing not only absolute scores but also performance trends and fragility resilience across sleeves, asset classes, or peer allocators.

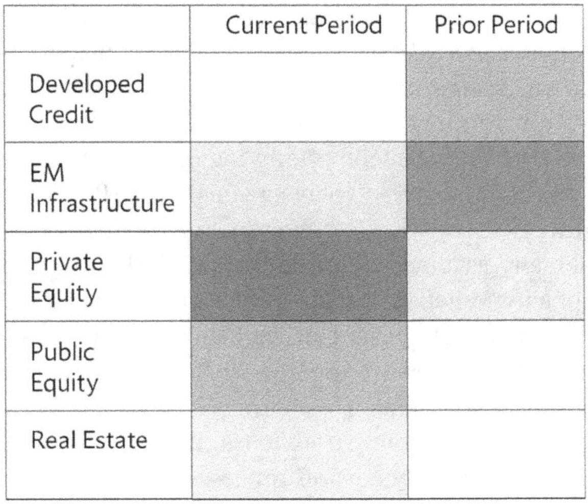

Figure 9.1. Stylized ARMOR-CAP heat map for sleeve-level benchmarking.

Note: This fictionalized figure illustrates how a benchmarking heat map might be used to visualize changes in fragility scores across five investment sleeves, comparing current-period and prior-period data. Shading intensity reflects a simulated alignment or deviation from hypothetical peer benchmarks, purely to demonstrate the ARMOR-CAP concept.

There are three primary modes of benchmarking under ARMOR-CAP:[1]

1. Internal benchmarking, where scores across investment sleeves or business units are compared to identify relative fragility concentrations.
2. Temporal benchmarking tracks how institutional fragility profiles change over time, allowing for retrospective performance reviews.
3. External benchmarking involved anonymized peer comparisons based on shared exposure domains or reporting consortia.

Figure 9.1 presents a stylized benchmarking heat map that compares fragility scores across five institutional investment sleeves over two reporting periods. Each jurisdictional, legal, and operational domain is color-coded and indexed against a fictionalized industry median.

[1]Earlier standardization and comparative frameworks are detailed in Chapter 7, which provides the foundation for these benchmarking modes.

To illustrate how benchmarking might inform institutional diligence under the proposed ARMOR-CAP framework, consider the following entirely fictional scenario. A stylized multi-strategy endowment is constructed solely for illustrative purposes and modeled as if it were applying ARMOR-CAP's benchmarking logic. In this hypothetical example, one private equity sleeve displays a consistent 10–15-point elevation in operational fragility relative to a peer median. Although this difference does not breach any assumed override threshold, the divergence is simulated to prompt a hypothetical due diligence audit. The imagined outcome of this fictitious review suggests that, had such a signal existed in a real-world setting, it might have triggered enhanced internal reporting or a staged reallocation of capital. This narrative is speculative and included exclusively to show how comparative fragility metrics could theoretically influence institutional decision processes under the ARMOR-CAP approach.

9.3 Cross-Domain Fragility and Compound Risk

ARMOR-CAP is designed to disaggregate fragility into domain-specific components, each scored independently (i.e., legal, jurisdictional, operational, and sovereign compatibility). However, real-world fragility rarely respects these boundaries. Risk tends to cluster across domains in complex portfolios, amplifying systemic exposure. What begins as legal uncertainty (i.e., ambiguous enforceability clauses) can cascade into operational breakdowns or trigger geopolitical countermeasures. ARMOR-CAP's value lies in scoring domains separately and illuminating where risks converge and compound. This section builds on the trajectory logic established previously.

Figure 9.2 provides a stylized visualization of domain-level score correlations drawn from a fictional institutional dataset. It highlights how fragility in one domain may forecast movement in others, helping institutions prioritize early interventions.

Understanding these relationships has practical consequences. A jurisdictional fragility score rising independently may merit a localized review. But if that score co-moves with operational and legal fragility, it suggests a structural issue, possibly tied to regional legal regimes, supply chain exposure, or regulatory constraints. This is why some institutions may want to implement compound score triggers, where escalation is based not

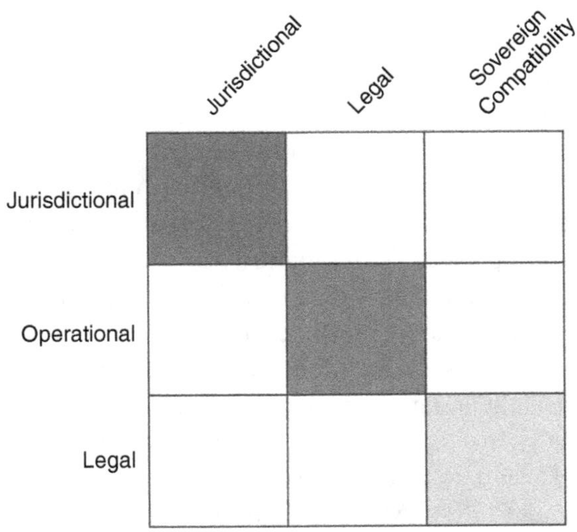

Figure 9.2. Stylized correlation map of ARMOR-CAP domains.

Note: This figure presents a fictionalized correlation matrix showing interdependence among ARMOR-CAP domains (jurisdictional, operational, legal, and sovereign compatibility). Darker shading reflects a stronger positive correlation. Visualization helps identify compound fragility pathways and systemically significant risk intersections.

on individual thresholds but on correlated score movement across domains.[2] Compound fragility is also a key consideration in scenario planning. Institutions can simulate shocks, such as data sovereignty laws, sanctions regimes, or foreign investment reviews, and model how these events might propagate fragility across multiple domains. Doing so transforms ARMOR-CAP from a static scoring engine to a resilience simulation platform, capable of guiding strategic decisions under structural stress.

To illustrate how cross-domain fragility might be diagnosed under the proposed ARMOR-CAP framework, consider the following purely hypothetical example. A stylized sovereign wealth fund, constructed solely for illustrative purposes, is modeled as if it were applying ARMOR-CAP's compound fragility logic. In this fictional case, a review of the fund's African infrastructure sleeve reveals how legal uncertainties can cascade

[2]Portfolio-level illustrations of correlated domain vulnerabilities were introduced in Chapter 8, and this section expands on those ideas.

into operational vulnerabilities and raise potential geopolitical concerns. Although none of the individual domain scores cross a red-band threshold, the conceptual correlation logic embedded in ARMOR-CAP hypothetically flags the confluence of elevated legal, operational, and jurisdictional risks. In this stylized narrative, a simulated cross-functional review identifies that a vendor restructuring involving politically exposed persons introduced legal ambiguity and operational concentration risk. As imagined, the project is temporarily paused and a hypothetical re-engagement process begins with a more risk-adjusted vendor.

This fictional scenario is presented exclusively to demonstrate how compound fragility flags, if such tools were implemented, could inform institutional oversight and governance responses under structural stress. It draws conceptually from multi-vector risk modeling and geopolitical sensitivity protocols, and is intended to clarify how a cross-domain logic might operate under the ARMOR-CAP framework as proposed.

9.4 Visualization and Communication Tools

A well-structured scoring framework is practical only if decision-makers can interpret and act upon it. ARMOR-CAP is designed to diagnose fragility and communicate it across investment teams, governance committees, and institutional stakeholders. To support governance, escalation, and rebalancing decisions, fragility scores must be presented in decision-ready visual formats that balance accuracy with clarity.

ARMOR-CAP provides three core visualization modalities:[3]

1. spider charts for multi-domain fragility profiling;
2. trend lines and band overlays for temporal tracking;
3. scorecard dashboards for integrated assets, sleeves, or institutional communication.

Figure 9.3 presents a stylized ARMOR-CAP spider chart that maps domain-level scores across four categories of fragility. This allows governance teams to see where fragility is most concentrated and to determine whether scores converge or diverge across domains.

[3] Earlier chapters, including Chapter 6, introduced visualization concepts for escalation and monitoring; this section builds on those to support broader governance communication.

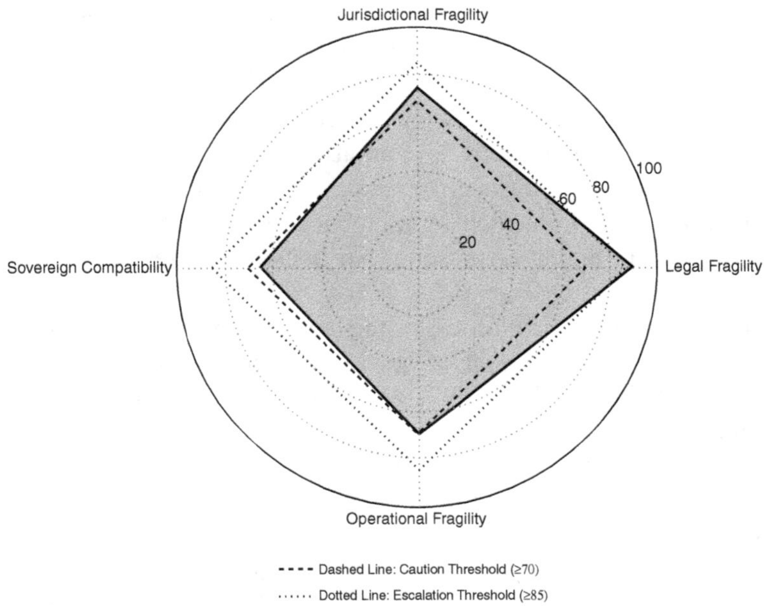

Figure 9.3. Stylized spider chart of multi-domain ARMOR-CAP scores.

Note: This figure illustrates a stylized ARMOR-CAP spider chart used to communicate multi-domain fragility to governance teams. While the composite score remains within acceptable bounds, the legal domain breaches the red-band threshold (score > 85), prompting a mock audit committee to flag the exposure for review. This fictional scenario is generalized from recurring design patterns in institutional dashboard governance and does not reflect actual use by any real institution.

Spider charts are well-suited for board or risk committee settings, where members may not engage with detailed submodule reports but can intuitively understand relative domain weaknesses. These visuals are often supplemented by summary scorecards, which show domain scores, historical movement, and escalation status in a compact table.

To illustrate how visualization tools might guide governance discussions under the proposed ARMOR-CAP framework, consider the following entirely fictional example. A stylized outsourced–chief investment officer platform, created solely for demonstration purposes, is modeled as if it were preparing quarterly review packets containing hypothetical spider charts constructed from conceptual domain-level fragility scores. In this imagined scenario, one thematic emerging-markets sleeve shows elevated legal and jurisdictional fragility, with the legal domain reaching a score of 85 even though the composite fragility score remains below any assumed red-band threshold.

In this purely illustrative narrative, the mock audit committee reviewing the fictional dashboard flags the position for closer examination and, in the simulated governance workflow, the sleeve is hypothetically shifted from overweight to neutral in the following quarter. This scenario is speculative and intended only to demonstrate how visual tools, such as spider charts, might inform governance conversations if the ARMOR-CAP approach were implemented in practice. It does not reflect actual use of the framework by any institution, nor does it represent a historical or ongoing pilot.

Another key visualization tool is the banded score overlay, a line chart showing historical movement of scores with colored bands to indicate escalation thresholds. These tools allow users to track motion, not just magnitude, as discussed in Section 9.1.

Finally, full scorecards offer institutional users a compact way to assess the risk posture of multiple strategies or managers. These dashboards often include composite scores, domain breakdowns, change indicators (indicated by ↑, ↓, and →), escalation flags, and override statuses.

Figure 9.4 presents a fictionalized ARMOR-CAP scorecard dashboard for a sample endowment with five strategy sleeves. It includes composite and domain-level scores, status flags, and directional arrows to aid review.

Visual tools are not merely aesthetic additions; they are enablers of accountability. Power (2007) notes that rendering risk into visible, comparable formats transforms latent uncertainty into actionable governance knowledge. In ARMOR-CAP, visuals convert multidimensional diagnostics into alignment-ready decisions.

Strategy Sleeve	Composite Score	Legal	Operational	Jurisdictional	Sovereign	Direction	Escalation	Override
Public equities	58	55	60	59	56	→	No	N/A
Private credit	72	68	75	71	74	↑	Watch	N/A
Real assets	65	60	62	66	63	→	No	N/A
EM infrastructure	80	88	82	77	79	↑	Review	Pending
Hedge funds	61	58	63	62	61	↓	No	N/A

Figure 9.4. Stylized institutional scorecard for ARMOR-CAP oversight.

Note: This figure presents a fictional dashboard displaying fragility scores across five strategic sleeves. Each row includes composite and domain-specific scores, directional movement indicators, and escalation or override statuses.

9.5 Score Normalization and Calibration Across Institutions

ARMOR-CAP was designed to provide institution-specific diagnostics. This section operationalizes the benchmarking logic introduced in Section 9.2.

A raw operational fragility score of 72 at a small public pension system may not reflect the same underlying risk magnitude as a 72 reported by a sovereign wealth fund with global legal capacity.

Normalization in ARMOR-CAP requires aligning inputs and scaling logic across institutions while preserving local context.[4] This involves the following:

- *Weighting adjustments*: Institutions differ in prioritizing domains (e.g., operational vs. jurisdictional). Cross-institutional comparisons often require rebasing scores to a standard weighting scheme.
- *Data depth correction*: Some institutions may report more granular operational risks (e.g., supplier dependencies), while others aggregate. A normalization layer can adjust for disclosure richness.
- *Band calibration*: Escalation bands (e.g., yellow at 65–74) may require realignment when comparing institutional cohorts with risk tolerances or fragility profiles.

Figure 9.5 presents a stylized scoring calibration chart illustrating how fragility scores are adjusted across three institutional types using a shared benchmark range. It highlights the interpretive shift between raw and adjusted scores for governance purposes.

Fictionalized Case: Smoothing Masks Fragility Inflection: A hypothetical U.S. public pension, modeled for illustrative purposes, applied a three-month smoothing function to ARMOR-CAP's jurisdictional domain scores for a regional infrastructure strategy in Eastern Europe, purely to illustrate how smoothing might influence escalation timing in a fictional scenario. While this reduced short-term signal volatility, it also masked a sharp rise in legal fragility following abrupt regulatory changes regarding foreign tax treatment.

[4] Standardization themes introduced in Chapter 7 serve as a foundation for this normalization discussion.

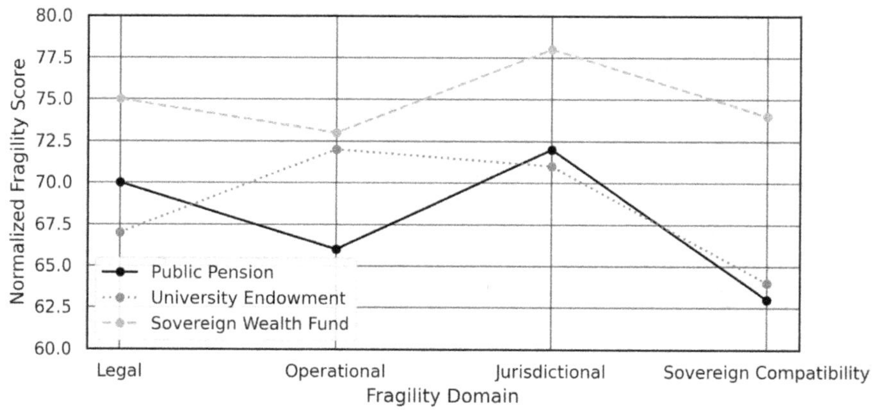

Figure 9.5. Stylized calibration of ARMOR-CAP scores across institutions.

Note: This fictionalized figure shows raw versus normalized scores across three institutional types: a public pension, a university endowment, and a sovereign wealth fund. A unified benchmark overlay helps align escalation interpretations across organizational models.

When the smoothed signal breached the yellow band, a red-band flag would have already been triggered under raw score data. The delay in escalation led to missed mitigation opportunities and required retroactive adjustments to exposure thresholds. *This fictionalized example illustrates a recurring oversight theme: Smoothing filters can inadvertently suppress governance-relevant signals, particularly in dynamic regulatory environments.*

Fictionalized Case: Cross-Institution Normalization Reveals Governance Tension: A fictional, multi-institutional modeling exercise highlights how differing governance structures and risk tolerances could affect calibration choices under the proposed ARMOR-CAP framework. One public pension system exhibits unusually high operational fragility compared to peer institutions, despite having similar strategy exposures. A normalization layer, rebased domain weights and adjusted for data granularity, reveals that the outlier score stemmed from a narrow risk classification scheme, not an actual structural difference. The fictional exercise highlights the importance of governance in score harmonization. *This case is fictional and used to demonstrate how normalization mechanisms can impact score comparability in multi-institutional settings.*

Table 9.1 provides stylized use cases across various governance and investment decisions to illustrate how normalized ARMOR-CAP scores are applied in practice. These examples are fictionalized.

Table 9.1. Stylized use cases of ARMOR-CAP score interpretation.

Use Case	Scenario	ARMOR-CAP Insight	Outcome
1. Termination memo triggered by score surge	A sovereign wealth fund sees a 22-point spike in operational fragility for a regional private equity manager. No red-band threshold is breached, but the acceleration is atypical.	Trendline overlays show prior stability; domain comments cite compliance audit delays.	The CIO drafts a memo recommending reallocation due to score trajectory, not end-point level.
2. Portfolio reweighting based on compound risk	A thematic EM infrastructure portfolio shows moderate increases in legal and sovereign fragility scores. Neither domain independently escalates.	Correlation matrix reveals these domains co-move frequently during FX or nationalization risk events.	The fund decreases sleeve exposure by 15% and earmarks reallocation to developed green infrastructure.
3. Visual flag at quarterly review	An OCIO dashboard spider chart shows asymmetry in sovereign risk exposure—one manager has outlier fragility despite portfolio similarity.	Peer benchmarking reveals this manager is overweight in a nation flagged for sanctions instability.	Board requests manager engagement and initiates override protocol if mitigation plans fail.
4. Override decision reversal via governance memo	A university investment committee plans to override an 87 jurisdictional fragility score in its Latin America credit fund.	Scorecard notes show the rating was driven by a now-repealed decree, with no persistent legal risk.	The override is withdrawn and replaced with a 90-day monitoring trigger with reporting requirements.

Note: The examples below are fictionalized to illustrate how ARMOR-CAP scoring outputs inform governance, oversight, and portfolio decisions. These use cases focus on interpretation—not framework design or implementation and showcase how diagnostic signals drive institutional action.

Normalization also supports governance trust. When boards or oversight committees engage in inter-institutional reviews, such as joint pension boards or national endowment alliances, they require confidence that scores are comparable. This is particularly important when fragility metrics are used in collective rebalancing, co-investment evaluation, or shared environmental, social, and governance (ESG) platforms.

Emerging metrics such as the Geostrategic Resilience Rating (GRR, mentioned in Chapter 4) offer an example of how normalization can extend to geopolitical stress factors. While GRR was initially conceived as a forward-looking resilience indicator rather than an exclusionary filter, its integration into co-investment reviews and fragility dashboards highlights a practical method for benchmarking systemic resilience across institutional types. ARMOR-CAP could harmonize with such external scoring tools to create a more complete, interoperable measure of structural and geopolitical vulnerability.

9.6 Design Principles for Visual Interpretation

If ARMOR-CAP were to be adopted in the future, its visual design principles would need to ensure that fragility diagnostics are communicated clearly, intuitively, and consistently across diverse governance audiences. Scoring systems without intuitive, decision-oriented visuals risk becoming "dashboard clutter" rather than tools for governance. To be effective, ARMOR-CAP visuals must be interpretable under time pressure, accessible to non-technical stakeholders, and structured for repeatability. This section identifies design principles for converting raw diagnostic outputs into actionable insights.

Figure 9.6 highlights common visual formats for ARMOR-CAP scores, emphasizing when each is most effective. (These design ideas build on the visualization frameworks introduced in Chapter 6.)

Institutions should adopt a set of design principles that align diagnostics with governance workflows to ensure ARMOR-CAP visuals support decision-making clarity rather than overwhelm users. The following guidelines synthesize lessons from usability research, institutional risk reporting, and pilot implementations. These are not aesthetic preferences; they are structural features that make fragility scores legible, actionable, and trustworthy:

Visual Format	Best Use Case	Ideal Audience
Spider chart	Compare fragility domains at a glance	Risk committee, strategy teams
Heat map	Track changes across sleeves or time periods	Portfolio managers, operational oversight
Trend line with escalation bands	Visualize score trajectories and escalation risk	CIOs, escalation review panels
Scorecard dashboard	Summarize composite/domain scores across managers or portfolios	Board members, external auditors

Figure 9.6. Visual modalities for ARMOR-CAP communication.

Note: This fictionalized reference chart maps common visual formats—spider charts, heat maps, trend lines, and scorecards—to their use cases and ideal audiences. The figure highlights trade-offs between detail and interpretability.

1. **Match the visual format to the decision context.**
   Spider charts are helpful for multi-domain comparisons; heat maps work best for cross-sleeve or temporal tracking. Composite-score trend lines support escalation reviews. Select visuals based on the question, rather than simply the available data.
2. **Use consistent icons, arrows, and band coloring.**
   Directional indicators (↑, ↓, and →), escalation bands (grayscale equivalents of red, yellow, and green), and override markers (e.g., asterisks or shaded cells) should be standardized across committees. This builds user familiarity and trust.
3. **Minimize cognitive overload.**
   Avoid packing multiple score dimensions into a single chart without explanatory labels or legends. Use white space, bolding, and font hierarchy to emphasize key changes.
4. **Embed context without requiring deep training.**
   Rather than expecting users to remember domain definitions, link each score to a brief descriptor or tooltip-style footnote in digital dashboards. This allows boards and CIOs to interpret results without scorecard fatigue.
5. **Provide summary views before drilling into detail.**
   Most governance users prefer dashboards that begin with composite and red-band flags, then allow for domain-level reviews as needed. ARMOR-CAP recommends a two-tier visual strategy: an executive summary followed by score decomposition.

9.7 Backtesting Fragility Scores: Historical Signal, Not Return Forecasting

ARMOR-CAP scores are not designed to predict alpha. They do not replace performance models or macro outlooks. However, one of their most compelling strengths is the ability to backtest fragility signals against historical disruptions, not to forecast returns, but to assess whether the framework would have flagged structural vulnerabilities before realized stress.

Unlike volatility-based backtests, ARMOR-CAP backtesting is event-oriented. It asks: Did domain-level fragility scores increase prior to governance breaches, ESG failures, or value impairments? The goal is diagnostic validation.

9.7.1 *Three diagnostic approaches to backtesting ARMOR-CAP scores*

If ARMOR-CAP were adopted, backtesting would be essential to building institutional confidence since retrospective analysis can help validate signal reliability and refine escalation protocols in a hypothetical implementation.[5] The goal is not to predict past events perfectly but to assess whether fragility indicators would have offered practical foresight. Institutions can apply several structured methods to evaluate ARMOR-CAP's performance against known stress episodes and governance breakdowns:

1. **Event-Aligned Retrospective Mapping**
   Overlay fragility scores against historical events such as liquidity freezes, governance failures, or regulatory actions. Identify whether ARMOR-CAP scores moved meaningfully in advance. This supports retrospective accountability.
2. **Synthetic Score Reconstruction**
   Using historical data (e.g., supplier diversity, regulatory audit gaps, domicile change), recreate how domain scores would have behaved

[5]Related scenario-based stress test approaches were discussed in Chapter 8, providing complementary methods for portfolio-level validation.

prior to a known fragility event. This is useful for building board confidence or calibrating escalation thresholds.

3. **Pattern Archetype Testing**
   Test whether fragility score "shape" (e.g., a slow incline + a sharp spike) consistently precede governance problems. This supports protocol refinement (e.g., determining when to override or pause).

While backtesting can build confidence in ARMOR-CAP's utility, it must be interpreted with care. The goal is not to establish perfect foresight but to understand how structural fragility signals behave in real-world events. Several practical and conceptual limitations must be acknowledged when conducting retrospective analyses:

- Score availability and granularity vary across institutions, making standardized backtests challenging.
- False positives are a risk: not all fragility spikes lead to disruption, and governance teams must balance signals with discretion.
- ARMOR-CAP is not intended to forecast market events but rather to interpret system-level tension from legal, operational, and jurisdictional precursors.

9.8 Common Pitfalls in Interpreting ARMOR-CAP Scores

As institutional adoption of ARMOR-CAP evolves, so does the risk of misinterpretation, where fragility scores are read too narrowly, taken out of context, or misapplied as deterministic signals. To prevent governance drift or false confidence, this section outlines the most common interpretive errors and how to avoid them.

Table 9.2 summarizes six typical pitfalls and their suggested mitigation strategies. These fictionalized diagnostics are drawn from stylized board reviews and risk committee debriefs across asset owner types.[6]

[6]Earlier discussions of literacy challenges and score comprehension in Chapter 6 relate directly to these interpretive pitfalls.

Table 9.2. Common pitfalls in interpreting ARMOR-CAP scores.

Pitfall	Description	Suggested Mitigation
Band fixation	Treating score bands (e.g., yellow = 65–74) as definitive thresholds rather than risk signals.	Emphasize *trajectory* and rate of change; use bands as discussion triggers, not rule sets.
Overweighting one domain	Assuming a high score in one domain (e.g., legal) is a "go/no-go" signal for strategy approval.	Encourage cross-domain review; require minimum composite analysis before escalation.
Ignoring metadata	Skipping narrative comments or score drivers in favor of just the numeric score.	Require metadata disclosure as part of override or escalation procedures.
Using ARMOR-CAP as a performance proxy	Misusing fragility scores to explain return underperformance.	Reinforce that ARMOR-CAP signals structural exposure, not investment performance.
Loss of resolution in composite scores	Relying only on composite scores, which may mask domain-level fragility.	Break out scores visually (e.g., spider or stacked bar charts) in board dashboards.
Stale escalation logic	Using the same override rules or thresholds across market cycles or asset types.	Calibrate escalation policies annually; review in light of backtest findings.

Note: The cases in this table are fictional and constructed purely for illustrative purposes. They reflect stylized governance missteps that might arise in future attempts to embed structural fragility scoring into institutional oversight processes. These examples draw on simulated workshop scenarios to highlight how misinterpretations of ARMOR-CAP signals could undermine decision-making if not correctly addressed.

9.9 Interfacing ARMOR-CAP with Other Risk and ESG Systems

As institutional investors evaluate resilience tools, a frequent question emerges: How does ARMOR-CAP integrate with existing risk platforms and ESG dashboards? While ARMOR-CAP is not intended as a replacement for market risk models or sustainability ratings, it is proposed to complement them by diagnosing structural fragility vectors often missed by traditional systems. This section explores how ARMOR-CAP interfaces with other analytical frameworks.

Integrating ARMOR-CAP into existing institutional infrastructure does not require replacing legacy risk or ESG systems. Instead, it extends their diagnostic reach, capturing fragility vectors that standard metrics often overlook. Institutions can adopt multiple interfacing models depending on their internal workflows, technical capabilities, and governance architectures. The following three approaches illustrate common pathways for embedding ARMOR-CAP into real-world decision systems:

1. **Layered Interpretation**
   ARMOR-CAP scores are added to traditional analytics to provide an early-warning overlay. For example, a standard volatility or VaR spike may not capture legal fragility in a new jurisdiction, but ARMOR-CAP would. In this model, fragility scores are discussed alongside existing metrics.
2. **Data Exchange Integration**
   In a hypothetical scenario, institutions could embed ARMOR-CAP into internal dashboards to complement existing risk platforms and ESG frameworks. This illustrates how fragility diagnostics might integrate with broader governance systems if adopted. For instance, the legal team may input jurisdictional fragility scores monthly, and these are automatically pulled into the CIO's allocation heat map.
3. **Governance Escalation Interface**
   While traditional systems focus on real-time exposure, ARMOR-CAP informs governance action triggers. Fragility bands, override logs, and scorecards are routed to escalation committees. This separates "market alerts" from "institutional warnings."

9.10 Advancing Structural Fragility Governance

ARMOR-CAP's scoring infrastructure will only be as valuable as the institutional change it supports. As this chapter has shown, embedding fragility diagnostics into workflows demands more than clear visuals or careful calibration; it requires a cultural shift in how non-financial risks are surfaced, interpreted, and acted upon. The forward pathway for ARMOR-CAP will not be measured by perfect scores or algorithmic precision but by its ability to strengthen governance reflexes before crisis thresholds are breached.

Several areas merit continued development:

- Score literacy must deepen across institutional roles. Analysts, risk teams, and board members should learn how scores are generated and what they signal about structural exposures that traditional metrics may overlook.
- Override protocols and documentation standards should mature. As Sections 9.4 and 9.5 highlighted, dashboards and escalation mechanics are only as reliable as the audit trails they produce. Future ARMOR-CAP iterations should support override governance that is both flexible and enforceable.
- Cross-institutional calibration will require caution. While normalization improves comparability, it can also flatten critical institutional nuances. Building a common language for fragility while avoiding a rigid template remains a priority.
- Retrospective scoring should become the routine. As discussed in Section 9.7, analyzing score signals from aftermarket or geopolitical events can improve future alert sensitivity and strengthen institutional trust in ARMOR-CAP's potential as a forward-looking diagnostic.

Ultimately, the mission is not merely better scoring but to have better foresight.

9.11 Summary and Transition

This chapter demonstrated how fragility scores could be rendered, interpreted, and potentially acted upon across proposed institutional workflows. While scoring diagnostics are powerful, their full value will only be realized if they shape decisions through dashboards, override protocols, and governance interfaces in a future adoption scenario. The five strategic takeaways are as follows:

- **Adapt presentation for audience alignment.**
  Effective use of ARMOR-CAP demands tailoring outputs to stakeholder roles, from investment teams to trustees. Design choices, such as scorecards, spider charts, and band overlays, should reflect how decisions are made and who makes them.

- **Refine escalation triggers to avoid score fatigue.**
  Threshold-based triggers must be calibrated to align with an institution's risk appetite. If every signal triggers action, none will. As discussed earlier in this chapter, vigilance must be balanced against noise suppression.
- **Monitor implementation asymmetries.**
  The same ARMOR-CAP score may prompt different actions at different institutions. Variability does not mean failure; it reflects diverse mandates and governance models. However, awareness of this asymmetry is crucial for accurate score interpretation.
- **Optimize calibration across entities.**
  Cross-institutional benchmarking will require normalization of inputs, weights, and band definitions. Earlier sections highlighted how calibration supports trust and interoperability.
- **Reassess tools through backtesting and feedback loops.**
  Fragility scores should not be static. Institutions must revisit score behavior after crises or near misses to refine signal logic and escalation pathways. Resilience is the product of a learning system.

Ultimately, these practices could help prepare institutions to more confidently consider adopting structural fragility diagnostics.

Appendix A

Glossary of ARMOR-CAP Terms and Governance Concepts

This appendix provides standardized definitions for key terms used throughout the ARMOR-CAP framework. It is intended to support consistent interpretation across readers, reviewers, and prospective pilot institutions. Where appropriate, distinctions are made between proposed terminology (specific to ARMOR-CAP) and general governance usage.

ARMOR-CAP Terminology

Term	Definition
ARMOR-CAP	Allocation for Market and Operational Resilience-Capital Allocation Protection. A proposed framework for scoring and escalating structural fragility across institutional portfolios.
Domain score	A fragility score assigned to a specific risk domain (e.g., legal, operational, jurisdictional, or sovereign compatibility), typically scaled from 0 to 100.
Composite score	A weighted average of multiple domain scores for a strategy, mandate, or institution. Used to provide an overall fragility snapshot.
Fragility band	A scoring range (e.g., green, yellow, or red) used to categorize risk severity and trigger escalation thresholds.
Directional movement	The trajectory of a score over time, used to detect deteriorating or improving fragility even if absolute levels remain stable.

Term	Definition
Override protocol	A governance mechanism that allows institutional actors to document and justify why a red-band fragility score does not trigger action.
Escalation trigger	A threshold that prompts review, documentation, or action when fragility scores enter a predefined risk band.
Normalization	Adjusting scores across institutions to account for domain weighting, data granularity, and risk tolerance differentials.
Sovereign compatibility	A fragility domain focused on the alignment (or conflict) between portfolio exposures and the regulatory or political systems in which they are embedded.

Governance and Oversight Concepts

Term	Definition
Fiduciary escalation	The process of surfacing, documenting, and responding to structural risk exposures in a manner consistent with fiduciary duty.
Audit trail	A time-stamped, permissioned record of score movements, override decisions, and governance responses. Central to ARMOR-CAP accountability.
Visual diagnostic	A graphical representation of scores (e.g., spider chart, trend line, and scorecard) used to support institutional interpretation and action.
Red-band override	A documented justification for not acting on a domain or composite score that has entered the red risk band. Typically logged with rationale and timeline.

Portfolio and Investment Management Terms (As Used in ARMOR-CAP Context)

Term	Definition
Sleeve	A sub-component of a larger investment portfolio, typically representing a specific asset class, strategy, or mandate tracked independently for reporting and governance purposes.
Mandate	A formal investment instruction or guideline given to an internal or external manager, defining objectives, risk limits, and constraints.
Allocation overlay	A governance tool or scoring mechanism that sits on top of a traditional allocation model to introduce non-financial risk filters, such as structural fragility.
Strategy approval cycle	The periodic institutional process of reviewing, approving, or reallocating capital to individual investment strategies.
Composite portfolio view	A holistic governance-level view that combines fragility, performance, and exposure data across multiple sleeves or managers.
Scenario testing	The process of evaluating how investment strategies or fragility scores would behave under simulated geopolitical, regulatory, or operational stress conditions.
Pre-trade governance filter	A proposed ARMOR-CAP integration point where a strategy or trade idea is reviewed for fragility scores prior to execution.

Appendix B

Methodology Notes and Data Considerations

This appendix outlines the underlying methodological principles and data structures proposed for the ARMOR-CAP framework. Since ARMOR-CAP is a new and fictionalized diagnostic model introduced by the author, this section clarifies how scores are conceptualized, what data types may be used, and what assumptions are embedded in the system design.

B.1 Scoring Architecture: Conceptual Overview

ARMOR-CAP employs a modular scoring system with four core fragility domains:

- *Legal fragility*: Risks from litigation exposure, regulatory inconsistencies, and contractual enforceability.
- *Operational fragility*: Internal vulnerabilities stemming from staffing, systems, supply chains, or governance infrastructure.
- *Jurisdictional fragility*: Risks arising from cross-border exposure, political instability, tax/legal regime changes.
- *Sovereign compatibility fragility*: Alignment (or lack thereof) with home-country values, ESG commitments, and economic security priorities.

Each domain is scored on a 0–100 scale, with soft escalation bands introduced at 65 (yellow) and hard governance triggers above 85 (red).

Note: These escalation thresholds are adjustable and designed for institution-specific calibration.

B.2 Data Inputs and Score Derivation

ARMOR-CAP does not rely on a single data feed. Instead, it combines multiple qualitative and quantitative signals:

Data Source Type	Example Inputs
Internal documents	Due diligence memos, audit reports, compliance reviews
Public data	Sanctions lists, regulatory disclosures, ESG ratings
Semi-structured narratives	Board minutes, risk memos, investor communications
Third-party intelligence	Political risk monitors, cyber threat feeds, legal case databases
Machine-assisted tagging	NLP tools that extract features from legal agreements or filings

ARMOR-CAP is domain-agnostic: Scores may be derived manually, via algorithmic heuristics, or through hybrid (machine-assisted) models.

B.3 Score Normalization and Peer Calibration

ARMOR-CAP includes optional normalization modules to allow comparability across asset classes, geographies, or institutional types. These can:

- adjust scores for domain weighting differences;
- rebase scores relative to institutional size, complexity, or risk tolerance;
- smooth time-series data to identify directional shifts versus statistical noise.

For example, an operational fragility score of 72 at a sovereign wealth fund may imply a risk different from the same score at a $500 million endowment. Normalization protocols enable consistent governance interpretation across sleeves.

B.4 Assumptions and Limitations

Area	Assumption or Limitation
Backtestability	ARMOR-CAP assumes partial historical reconstruction of scores using narrative or proxy data.
Subjectivity	While anchored in structured criteria, scoring remains subject to institutional interpretation.
Non-predictive	Scores indicate fragility, not return forecasts or financial impairment.
Governance dependency	Effective use requires pre-defined escalation pathways and board familiarity with diagnostics.

All illustrative uses of ARMOR-CAP in this book are fictional and proposed; no real-world entity has adopted this methodology.

B.5 Implementation Modalities

Institutions may use ARMOR-CAP via:

- Excel-based templates,
- API integrations with internal dashboards,
- governance overlays linked to IPS documents,
- manual scoring embedded in investment review workflows.

The book showcases fictionalized prototypes. Actual implementation would require governance approval, data access, and scoring calibration.

Appendix C

ARMOR-CAP Domain Definitions and Scoring Rubric

This appendix provides detailed definitions of each fragility domain used in the ARMOR-CAP framework, along with illustrative scoring criteria. These rubrics are meant as guides for constructing institution-specific scoring protocols and training governance users. All domain descriptions, examples, and scoring ranges are fictionalized and illustrative only.

C.1 Domain: Legal Fragility

Definition: Measures the risk that an asset, strategy, or entity faces from legal enforceability issues, litigation exposure, regulatory ambiguity, or jurisdictional inconsistency in legal protections.

Score Range	Illustrative Criteria
0–40	Robust contracts, aligned with jurisdictional law; recent legal audit confirms enforceability.
41–64	Minor inconsistencies in contracts or potential enforcement challenges; legal risks disclosed but not material.
65–84 (Yellow)	Ambiguous contract language, pending legal actions, or use of lightly regulated entities.
85–100 (Red)	Active litigation risk, unenforceable provisions, or legal structure flagged by regulators.

C.2 Domain: Operational Fragility

Definition: Captures internal vulnerabilities related to business continuity, staffing, systems, vendor reliance, or process controls.

Score Range	Illustrative Criteria
0–40	Well-documented controls; continuity plans tested annually; key person dependencies mitigated.
41–64	Some reliance on third parties; minor audit flags; aging IT systems with upgrade plans.
65–84 (Yellow)	Key vendor concentration; high staff turnover; control breaches not escalated.
85–100 (Red)	Multiple audit failures; missing policies; untested or obsolete business continuity plan.

C.3 Domain: Jurisdictional Fragility

Definition: Assesses risk arising from the location of operations, investments, or counterparties, focusing on political instability, property rights, and regulatory reliability.

Score Range	Illustrative Criteria
0–40	Investment in OECD or treaty-bound jurisdiction; strong property rights.
41–64	Non-OECD market but with stable governance and bilateral legal protections.
65–84 (Yellow)	Exposure to countries with volatile regimes, rule-of-law gaps, or sanctions watchlists.
85–100 (Red)	Investments domiciled in conflict zones, recent expropriation history, or sanctioned regimes.

C.4 Domain: Sovereign Compatibility Fragility

Definition: Evaluates alignment of investment activity with national interest, home-country regulatory expectations, or reputational risk related to geopolitical alignment.

Score Range	Illustrative Criteria
0–40	Investment strategy consistent with national ESG policies and international agreements.
41–64	Some mismatch with climate or national development priorities but low reputational risk.
65–84 (Yellow)	Counterparties or markets with misaligned transparency norms, ESG standards, or values.
85–100 (Red)	Engagement with entities under political scrutiny; domestic backlash risk; breach of soft-law principles.

C.5 Notes on Score Interpretation

- *Directional movement matters*: A shift from 42 to 64 may be more important than a static score of 70.
- *Composite ≠ complete*: Domain-level readings offer more diagnostic power than a single composite score.
- *Escalation triggers*: Scores above 85 should be reviewed within the governance structure outlined in Chapter 9.

These domain definitions are designed for educational and illustrative purposes. Institutions adopting ARMOR-CAP should calibrate scoring protocols based on internal risk policies and available data.

Appendix D

Methodological Foundations of the ARMOR-CAP Framework

This appendix outlines the methodological principles used in designing the ARMOR-CAP (Allocation for Resilient Markets and Operational Readiness-Capital Allocation Protection) framework. It clarifies how diagnostic modules were developed, the rationale for domain inclusion, and the analytical boundaries of the model. While ARMOR-CAP is presented as a prototype framework in this book, its architecture reflects interdisciplinary inputs from finance, operational resilience, geopolitical risk, and institutional governance.

D.1 Conceptual Origins

The ARMOR-CAP framework was developed to address a recurring limitation in traditional risk models: their inability to preempt non-financial fragility that manifests through operational, legal, or jurisdictional channels. This framework blends insights from:

- organizational risk theory (Power, 2007; Weick & Sutcliffe, 2001),
- resilience engineering in critical infrastructure (Hollnagel, Woods, & Leveson, 2006),
- geopolitical investment risk modeling (Bremmer, 2010),
- governance escalation systems in public pension and endowment oversight (Fung, Graham, & Weil, 2014).

Each of the four fragility domains—legal, operational, jurisdictional, and sovereign compatibility—was selected to capture systemic vulnerabilities that are often omitted in market-based risk models.

D.2 Scoring Structure and Banding Logic

ARMOR-CAP scores range from 0 (no fragility) to 100 (maximum fragility) in each domain. These scores are interpreted through escalating bands:

- 0–64: Acceptable or managed fragility range.
- 65–84 (Yellow Band): Heightened fragility requiring monitoring.
- 85–100 (Red Band): Critical fragility triggering review or override consideration.

This structure was informed by stress-testing frameworks (e.g., CCAR), safety alert bands used in aerospace operations, and compliance thresholding logic in regulated financial entities.

D.3 Use of Fictionalized Illustrations

As of this writing, no real institution has adopted ARMOR-CAP. All case illustrations, scorecards, and override templates are fictionalized composites designed to highlight how institutions could use the framework. They draw from observed governance patterns, escalation mechanisms, and oversight committee behaviors but are not based on actual data or institutions.

This approach is used intentionally to:

- encourage adaptation rather than replication,
- prevent misrepresentation of usage,
- protect confidentiality while maximizing realism.

D.4 Design Constraints and Transparency

While ARMOR-CAP aspires to transparency and adaptability, its current iteration is a conceptual prototype. Key design constraints include the following:

- *Data availability*: Many institutions lack standardized inputs for scoring certain domains.
- *Governance heterogeneity*: Scoring thresholds and override pathways must be customized to each institutional setting.
- *Non-predictive logic*: ARMOR-CAP does not attempt to forecast market returns or macro shocks. It highlights underlying structural vulnerabilities such as misaligned legal frameworks, jurisdictional frictions, or fragile operational dependencies that may compromise an institution's ability to maintain resilience during periods of stress.

D.5 Future Adaptation

ARMOR-CAP is intended as a living framework, capable of being refined, extended, and stress-tested in academic, policy, and institutional environments. Areas of potential development include:

- enhanced data ingestion models (e.g., NLP for legal filings),
- integration with ESG and systemic risk tools,
- empirical validation through backtesting and governance event studies.

This appendix is intended to provide methodological context, not a model specification or validation guide. All proposed methods remain subject to institutional customization and future testing.

Bibliography

Aaronson, S. A. (2024). *The Age of AI Nationalism and Its Effects* (CIGI Papers No. 306). Centre for International Governance Innovation.

Alicke, K., Barriball, E., & Trautwein, V. (2021). *How COVID-19 Is Reshaping Supply Chains*. McKinsey & Company.

Amel-Zadeh, A. & Serafeim, G. (2018). Why and how investors use ESG information: Evidence from a global survey. *Financial Analysts Journal*, *74*(3), 87–103. https://doi.org/10.2469/faj.v74.n3.2.

Atilgan, Y., Demirtaş, K., & Şanlı, A. (2020). ESG investing and asset pricing: An emerging market perspective. *Borsa Istanbul Review*, *20*(2), 135–143. https://doi.org/10.1016/j.bir.2019.12.001.

Barberis, N., Shleifer, A., & Wurgler, J. (2005). Comovement. *Journal of Financial Economics*, *75*(2), 283–317. https://doi.org/10.1016/j.jfineco.2004.04.003.

Bénabou, R. & Tirole, J. (2010). Individual and corporate social responsibility. *Economica*, *77*(305), 1–19. https://doi.org/10.1111/j.1468-0335.2009.00843.x.

Berg, F., Kölbel, J. F., & Rigobon, R. (2022). Aggregate confusion: The divergence of ESG ratings. *Review of Finance*, *26*(6), 1315–1344. https://doi.org/10.1093/rof/rfac033.

Bernanke, B. S. (2022). *21st Century Monetary Policy: The Federal Reserve From the Great Inflation to COVID-19*. W. W. Norton.

Bholat, D. (2015). Big data and central banks. *Central Banking*, *25*(4), 54–58.

Bradford, A. (2020). *The Brussels Effect: How the European Union Rules the World*. Oxford University Press.

Bremmer, I. (2010). *The End of the Free Market: Who Wins the War Between States and Corporations?* Portfolio.

Brunnermeier, M. K. & Sannikov, Y. (2014). A macroeconomic model with a financial sector. *American Economic Review*, *104*(2), 379–421.

Chander, A. & Lê, U. P. (2015). Data nationalism. *Emory Law Journal*, *64*(3), 677–739.

Claessens, S. & Kodres, L. (2014). *The Regulatory Responses to the Global Financial Crisis: Some Uncomfortable Questions* (IMF Working Paper No. WP/14/46). International Monetary Fund.

Clements, R. D. (2020). Clean energy ETF performance in a low carbon world. *Journal of Investing*, *29*(1), 91–106. https://doi.org/10.3905/joi.2020.1.122.

Cochrane, J. H. (2005). *Asset Pricing* (Rev. ed.). Princeton University Press.

Cochrane, J. H. (2014). Challenges for cost-benefit analysis of financial regulation. *Journal of Legal Studies*, *43*(S2), S63–S105. https://doi.org/10.1086/675357.

Cochrane, J. H. (2017). Macro-finance. *Review of Finance*, *21*(3), 945–985. https://doi.org/10.1093/rof/rfx010.

Cochrane, J. H. (2021). The fiscal theory of the price level: An introduction. *Journal of Economic Perspectives*, *35*(3), 129–156. https://doi.org/10.1257/jep.35.3.129.

Cochrane, J. H. (2023). *The Fiscal Theory of the Price Level*. Princeton University Press.

Cohen, L., Gurun, U. G., & Malloy, C. J. (2017). Resident networks and firm value. *Journal of Finance*, *72*(1), 435–463. https://doi.org/10.1111/jofi.12474.

Collier, P. (2007). *The Bottom Billion: Why the Poorest Countries Are Failing and What Can Be Done About It*. Oxford University Press.

Council on Foreign Relations. (2021). *Reshoring and Economic Security*. https://www.cfr.org/.

Creal, D. (2012). A survey of stochastic volatility models and inference. *Journal of Econometrics*, *173*(1), 1–2. https://doi.org/10.1016/j.jeconom.2012.12.001

Daskal, J. (2016). Law enforcement access to data across borders: The evolving security and rights issue. *Journal of National Security Law and Policy*, *8*, 473–501.

de Fontnouvelle, P., Rosengren, E. S., & Jordan, J. S. (2005). Implications of alternative operational risk modeling techniques. *Brookings–Wharton Papers on Financial Services*, *2005*(1), 139–160. https://doi.org/10.1353/pfs.2006.0003.

Derman, E. (2001). *My Life as a Quant: Reflections on Physics and Finance*. Wiley.

DesRosiers, J. (2023). Fiduciary duty and strategic fragility: An argument for resilience indexing. *Journal of Portfolio Management*, *49*(5), 55–72. https://doi.org/10.3905/jpm.2023.1.481.

Dorfman, M. (Ed.). (2011). *The Handbook of International Insurance: Between Global Dynamics and Local Contingencies*. Springer.

Duffie, D. (2010). The failure mechanics of dealer banks. *Journal of Economic Perspectives*, *24*(1), 51–72. https://doi.org/10.1257/jep.24.1.51.

Duffie, D. & Singleton, K. J. (2003). *Credit Risk: Pricing, Measurement, and Management*. Princeton University Press.

Dunbar, N. (2000). *Inventing Money: The Story of Long-Term Capital Management and the Legends Behind It.* Wiley.

Dyck, A., Lins, K. V., Roth, L., & Wagner, H. F. (2019). Do institutional investors drive corporate social responsibility? International evidence. *Journal of Financial Economics, 131*(3), 693–714. https://doi.org/10.1016/j.jfineco.2018.08.013.

Easley, D. & O'Hara, M. (2010). Microstructure and ambiguity. *Journal of Finance, 65*(5), 1817–1846. https://doi.org/10.1111/j.1540-6261.2010.01595.x.

Easterly, W. (2006). *The White Man's Burden: Why the West's Efforts to Aid the Rest Have Done So Much Ill and So Little Good.* Penguin Books.

El Karoui, N., Jeanblanc, M., & Shreve, S. E. (1998). Robustness of the Black and Scholes formula. *Mathematical Finance, 8*(2), 93–126. https://doi.org/10.1111/1467-9965.00047.

Engle, R. (2002). Dynamic conditional correlation: A simple class of multivariate generalized autoregressive conditional heteroskedasticity models. *Journal of Business & Economic Statistics, 20*(3), 339–350. https://doi.org/10.1198/073500102288618487.

Engle, R. F., Ghysels, E., & Sohn, B. (2013). Stock market volatility and macroeconomic fundamentals. *Review of Economics and Statistics, 95*(3), 776–797. https://doi.org/10.1162/REST_a_00300.

Erb, C. B., Harvey, C. R., & Viskanta, T. E. (1996). Political risk, economic risk, and financial risk. *Financial Analysts Journal, 52*(6), 28–46. https://doi.org/10.2469/faj.v52.n6.2038.

Esty, D. C. & Cort, T. (2020). Corporate sustainability metrics: What investors need and don't get. *Journal of Environmental Investing, 10*(1), 120–145.

Fabozzi, F. J. (2025a). From financial efficiency to strategic resilience: A corporate case for ARMOR-CAP. *Journal of Applied Corporate Finance*, 1–9. https://doi.org/10.1111/jacf.70006.

Fabozzi, F. J. (2025b). ARMOR-CAP investing: Building resilient portfolios for a geopolitical era. *Journal of Portfolio Management, 51*(10), 152–167. https://www.pm-research.com/content/iijpormgmt/51/10/153

Fabozzi, F. J. (2025c). ESG isn't enough: Why portfolio resilience needs its own framework. *Journal of Investing, 34*(6), 6–10. https://www.pm-research.com/content/iijinvest/34/6/6

Fabozzi, F. J., & Stenholm, C. C. (2025). Strategic discipline: How asset management mirrors military operations. *Journal of Portfolio Management, 52*(1), 202–221.

Fama, E. F. & French, K. R. (1993). Common risk factors in the returns on stocks and bonds. *Journal of Financial Economics, 33*(1), 3–56. https://doi.org/10.1016/0304-405X(93)90023-5.

Farhi, E. & Werning, I. (2012). Dealing with the trilemma: Optimal capital controls with fixed exchange rates. *IMF Economic Review*, *60*(4), 429–461. https://doi.org/10.1057/imfer.2012.19.

Farrell, G. (2003). *Crash of the Titans: Greed, Hubris, the Fall of Merrill Lynch, and the Near-Collapse of Bank of America*. Crown Business.

Farrell, H. & Newman, A. (2019). Weaponized interdependence: How global economic networks shape state coercion. *International Security*, *44*(1), 42–79. https://doi.org/10.1162/isec_a_00351.

Fenichel, E. P. & Abbott, J. K. (2014). Natural capital: From metaphor to measurement. *Journal of the Association of Environmental and Resource Economists*, *1*(1–2), 1–27. https://doi.org/10.1086/676034.

Fernández, A., Klein, M. W., Rebucci, A., Schindler, M., & Uribe, M. (2016). Capital control measures: A new dataset. *IMF Economic Review*, *64*(3), 548–574. https://doi.org/10.1057/imfer.2016.11.

Financial Stability Board. (2021). *Enhancing the Resilience of Non-Bank Financial Intermediation*. https://www.fsb.org/.

Friedman, M. & Schwartz, A. J. (1963). *A Monetary History of the United States, 1867–1960*. Princeton University Press.

Fung, A., Graham, M., & Weil, D. (2014). *Funding Discipline for U.S. Public Pension Plans: An Empirical Analysis of Institutional Design*. SSRN. https://doi.org/10.2139/ssrn.2151556.

Funke, M., Schularick, M., & Trebesch, C. (2016). Going to extremes: Politics after financial crises, 1870–2014. *European Economic Review*, *88*, 227–260. https://doi.org/10.1016/j.euroecorev.2016.03.006.

Giese, G., Nagy, Z., & Lee, L.-E. (2020). Deconstructing ESG ratings performance: Risk and return for E, S, and G by time horizon, sector, and weight. MSCI Research Insight.

Gennaioli, N., Shleifer, A., & Vishny, R. (2015). Money doctors. *Journal of Finance*, *70*(1), 91–114. https://doi.org/10.1111/jofi.12188

Gereffi, G. (2020). What does the COVID-19 pandemic teach us about global value chains? The case of medical supplies. *Journal of International Business Policy*, *3*(3), 287–301. https://doi.org/10.1057/s42214-020-00062-w.

Gorton, G. & Metrick, A. (2012). Securitized banking and the run on repo. *Journal of Financial Economics*, *104*(3), 425–451. https://doi.org/10.1016/j.jfineco.2011.03.016.

Greenwood, R. & Hanson, S. G. (2015). Waves in ship prices and investment. *Quarterly Journal of Economics*, *130*(1), 55–109. https://doi.org/10.1093/qje/qju035.

Grinblatt, M. & Titman, S. (2002). *Financial Markets and Corporate Strategy* (2nd ed.). McGraw-Hill.

Grossman, G. M. & Helpman, E. (1994). Protection for sale. *American Economic Review*, *84*(4), 833–850.

Gu, S., Kelly, B., & Xiu, D. (2020). Empirical asset pricing via machine learning. *Review of Financial Studies*, *33*(5), 2223–2273. https://doi.org/10.1093/rfs/hhaa009.

Guiso, L., Sapienza, P., & Zingales, L. (2006). Does culture affect economic outcomes? *Journal of Economic Perspectives*, *20*(2), 23–48. https://doi.org/10.1257/jep.20.2.23.

Harvey, C. R., Liu, Y., & Zhu, H. (2016). … and the cross-section of expected returns. *Review of Financial Studies*, *29*(1), 5–68. https://doi.org/10.1093/rfs/hhv059.

Hausmann, R. & Rigobon, R. (2003). An alternative interpretation of the 'resource curse': Theory and policy implications. In D. Lederman & W. F. Maloney (Eds.), *Natural Resources: Neither Curse nor Destiny* (pp. 78–122). Stanford University Press.

He, Z. & Krishnamurthy, A. (2013). Intermediary asset pricing. *American Economic Review*, *103*(2), 732–770. https://doi.org/10.1257/aer.103.2.732.

Hofstede, G. (2001). *Culture's Consequences: Comparing Values, Behaviors, Institutions, and Organizations Across Nations* (2nd ed.). Sage Publications.

Hollnagel, E., Woods, D. D., & Leveson, N. (Eds.). (2006). *Resilience Engineering: Concepts and Precepts*. CRC Press.

Hong, H. & Kacperczyk, M. (2009). The price of sin: The effects of social norms on markets. *Journal of Financial Economics*, *93*(1), 15–36. https://doi.org/10.1016/j.jfineco.2008.09.001.

Ilhan, E., Sautner, Z., & Vilkov, G. (2021). Carbon tail risk. *The Review of Financial Studies*, *34*(3), 1540–1571.

Ilmanen, A. (2011). *Expected Returns: An Investor's Guide To Harvesting Market Rewards*. Hoboken, NJ: Wiley.

Ilzetzki, E., Mendoza, E. G., & Végh, C. A. (2013). How big (small?) are fiscal multipliers? *Journal of Monetary Economics*, *60*(2), 239–254. https://doi.org/10.1016/j.jmoneco.2012.10.011.

International Monetary Fund. (2021). *Global Financial Stability Report: Managing Divergent Recoveries*. https://www.imf.org/.

Jensen, M. C. & Meckling, W. H. (1976). Theory of the firm: Managerial behavior, agency costs and ownership structure. *Journal of Financial Economics*, *3*(4), 305–360. https://doi.org/10.1016/0304-405X(76)90026-X.

Johnson, S. & Kwak, J. (2010). *13 Bankers: The Wall Street Takeover and the Next Financial Meltdown*. Pantheon Books.

Kahneman, D. & Tversky, A. (1979). Prospect theory: An analysis of decision under risk. *Econometrica*, *47*(2), 263–291. https://doi.org/10.2307/1914185.

Kaminsky, G. L. & Reinhart, C. M. (1999). The twin crises: The causes of banking and balance-of-payments problems. *American Economic Review*, *89*(3), 473–500. https://doi.org/10.1257/aer.89.3.473.

Kaplan, R. S. & Mikes, A. (2016). Risk management—the revealing hand. *Journal of Applied Corporate Finance*, *28*(1), 8–18.

Kaufmann, D., Kraay, A., & Mastruzzi, M. (2009). *Governance Matters VIII: Aggregate and Individual Governance Indicators, 1996–2008* (World Bank Policy Research Working Paper No. 4978). World Bank.

Kiyotaki, N. & Moore, J. (1997). Credit cycles. *Journal of Political Economy*, *105*(2), 211–248. https://doi.org/10.1086/262072.

Kose, M. A., Prasad, E., Rogoff, K., & Wei, S. J. (2009). Financial globalization: A reappraisal. *IMF Staff Papers*, *56*(1), 8–62. https://doi.org/10.1057/imfsp.2008.36.

KPMG. (2020). *Global CEO Outlook: COVID-19 Special Edition*. https://kpmg.com/.

Krippner, L. (2013). Measuring the stance of monetary policy in zero lower bound environments. *Economics Letters*, *118*(1), 135–138. https://doi.org/10.1016/j.econlet.2012.10.011.

Krugman, P. (1998). *What Happened to Asia?* (MIT Working Paper). Massachusetts Institute of Technology. https://web.mit.edu/krugman/www/DISINTER.html.

La Porta, R., Lopez-de-Silanes, F., Shleifer, A., & Vishny, R. W. (1998). Law and finance. *Journal of Political Economy*, *106*(6), 1113–1155. https://doi.org/10.1086/250042.

Laeven, L. & Valencia, F. (2013). Systemic banking crises database. *IMF Economic Review*, *61*(2), 225–270. https://doi.org/10.1057/imfer.2013.12.

Lambrecht, B. M. & Myers, S. C. (2007). A theory of takeovers and disinvestment. *Journal of Finance*, *62*(2), 809–845. https://doi.org/10.1111/j.1540-6261.2007.01227.x.

Larsen, G. (2019). ESG ratings and the real economy. *Journal of Investment Management*, *17*(2), 23–40.

Laudicina, P. A. & Peterson, E. R. (2020). *The Volatility Imperative: How Capital Markets Fuel Geopolitical Fragmentation—and What Companies Can Do About It*. A.T. Kearney.

Levine, R. (2005). Finance and growth: Theory and evidence. In P. Aghion & S. Durlauf (Eds.), *Handbook of Economic Growth* (Vol. 1, pp. 865–934). Elsevier.

Lo, A. W. (2017). *Adaptive Markets: Financial Evolution at the Speed of Thought*. Princeton University Press.

Lo, A. W. & Mueller, M. (2010). Warning: Physics envy may be hazardous to your wealth! *Journal of Investment Management*, *8*(2), 13–63.

López de Prado, M. (2018). *Advances in Financial Machine Learning*. Hoboken, NJ: Wiley.

Mandelbrot, B. & Hudson, R. L. (2004). *The (Mis)behavior of Markets: A Fractal View of Risk, Ruin, and Reward*. Basic Books.

Markowitz, H. (1952). Portfolio selection. *Journal of Finance*, *7*(1), 77–91. https://doi.org/10.1111/j.1540-6261.1952.tb01525.x.

Matsakis, L. (2021). The cloud under nation-state siege. *Wired*. https://www.wired.com/.

Merton, R. C. (1973). Theory of rational option pricing. *Bell Journal of Economics and Management Science*, *4*(1), 141–183. https://doi.org/10.2307/3003143.

Merton, R. C. (1995). Financial innovation and the management and regulation of financial institutions. *Journal of Banking & Finance*, *19*(3–4), 461–481. https://doi.org/10.1016/0378-4266(94)00133-N.

Mikes, A. (2009). Risk management and calculative cultures. *Management Accounting Research*, *20*(1), 18–40.

Minsky, H. P. (1977). The financial instability hypothesis: An interpretation of Keynes and an alternative to standard theory. *Challenge*, *20*(1), 20–27. https://doi.org/10.1080/05775132.1977.11470296.

Minsky, H. P. (1986). *Stabilizing an Unstable Economy*. Yale University Press.

North, D. C. (1990). *Institutions, Institutional Change and Economic Performance*. Cambridge University Press.

Obstfeld, M. & Taylor, A. M. (2004). *Global Capital Markets: Integration, Crisis, and Growth*. Cambridge University Press.

OECD. (2021). *Geopolitical Risk and Foreign Direct Investment*. Organisation for Economic Co-operation and Development.

Pagano, M. & Volpin, P. F. (2006). Shareholder protection, stock market development, and politics. *Journal of the European Economic Association*, *4*(2–3), 315–341. https://doi.org/10.1162/jeea.2006.4.2-3.315.

Perrow, C. (1984). *Normal Accidents: Living With High-Risk Technologies*. Basic Books.

Pistor, K. (2019). *The Code of Capital: How the Law Creates Wealth and Inequality*. Princeton University Press.

Posner, E. (2009). *The Perils of Global Legalism*. University of Chicago Press.

Power, M. (2007). *Organized Uncertainty: Designing a World of Risk Management*. Oxford University Press.

Rajan, R. G. & Zingales, L. (2003). The great reversals: The politics of financial development in the twentieth century. *Journal of Financial Economics*, *69*(1), 5–50. https://doi.org/10.1016/S0304-405X(03)00125-9.

Reinhart, C. M. & Rogoff, K. S. (2009). *This Time Is Different: Eight Centuries of Financial Folly*. Princeton University Press.

Rodrik, D. (2011). *The Globalization Paradox: Democracy and the Future of the World Economy*. W. W. Norton & Company.

Rosenberg, B. (1985). Prediction of beta from investment fundamentals. *Financial Analysts Journal*, *41*(1), 61–65. https://doi.org/10.2469/faj.v41.n1.61.

Sachs, J. D. (2001). The strategic significance of global inequality. *The Washington Quarterly*, *24*(3), 187–198. https://doi.org/10.1162/01636600152102160.

Scharfstein, D. S. & Stein, J. C. (2000). The dark side of internal capital markets: Divisional rent-seeking and inefficient investment. *Journal of Finance*, *55*(6), 2537–2564. https://doi.org/10.1111/0022-1082.00299.

Schularick, M. & Taylor, A. M. (2012). Credit booms gone bust: Monetary policy, leverage cycles, and financial crises, 1870–2008. *American Economic Review*, *102*(2), 1029–1061. https://doi.org/10.1257/aer.102.2.1029.

Sheffi, Y. (2007). *The Resilient Enterprise: Overcoming Vulnerability for Competitive Advantage*. Cambridge, MA: MIT Press.

Shiller, R. J. (2000). *Irrational Exuberance*. Princeton University Press.

Shleifer, A. & Vishny, R. W. (1997). A survey of corporate governance. *Journal of Finance*, *52*(2), 737–783. https://doi.org/10.1111/j.1540-6261.1997.tb04820.x.

Shleifer, A. & Vishny, R. W. (1998). *The Grabbing Hand: Government Pathologies and Their Cures*. Harvard University Press.

Sorkin, A. R. (2009). *Too Big to Fail: The Inside Story of How Wall Street and Washington Fought to Save the Financial System—and Themselves*. Viking.

Stern, G. H. & Feldman, R. J. (2004). *Too Big to Fail: The Hazards of Bank Bailouts*. Brookings Institution Press.

Stulz, R. M. (2019). Risk management failures during the financial crisis. *Journal of Financial Economics*, *104*(3), 392–412. https://doi.org/10.1016/j.jfineco.2008.12.002.

Taleb, N. N. (2007). *The Black Swan: The Impact of the Highly Improbable*. New York, NY: Random House.

Tufano, P. (2011). Financial innovations and consumer behavior. *Journal of Financial Economics*, *99*(2), 227–247. https://doi.org/10.1016/j.jfineco.2010.08.005.

Tversky, A. & Kahneman, D. (1974). Judgment under uncertainty: Heuristics and biases. *Science*, *185*(4157), 1124–1131. https://doi.org/10.1126/science.185.4157.1124.

UNCTAD. (2021). *World Investment Report 2021: Investing in Sustainable Recovery*. United Nations Conference on Trade and Development.

Wagner, W. (2010). Diversification at financial institutions and systemic crises. *Journal of Financial Intermediation*, *19*(3), 373–386. https://doi.org/10.1016/j.jfi.2009.07.002.

Weick, K. E. & Sutcliffe, K. M. (2001). *Managing the Unexpected: Assuring High Performance in an Age of Complexity*. Jossey-Bass.

Wójcik, D. & Camilleri, J. (2015). 'Capitalist tools in socialist hands?' China mobile's acquisition of Millicom's Cambodian operations. *Economic Geography*, *91*(2), 149–170. https://doi.org/10.1111/ecge.12081.

Zingales, L. (2000). In search of new foundations. *Journal of Finance*, *55*(4), 1623–1653. https://doi.org/10.1111/0022-1082.00262.

Author Index

N

P

S

T

V

W

Subject Index

Q

R

S

www.ingramcontent.com/pod-product-compliance
Lightning Source LLC
LaVergne TN
LVHW011811200926
848484LV00005B/1146